LIVING ABROAD IN
Belize

FIRST EDITION

Lan Sluder

© Lan Sluder

AVALON
TRAVEL

CONTENTS

Introduction   1

Prime Living Locations   57

Daily Life 173

Resources 321

Preface

I discovered Belize, at least in my imagination, more than two decades ago. Backwaters appeal to me, and I was attracted by Aldous Huxley's oft-quoted comment: "If the world had any ends, British Honduras would surely be one of them."

Living then in New Orleans, once the gateway to Latin America, I first visited Central America in 1982, but I didn't get to Belize until 1991. I've been banging around the country ever since, poking my nose into all its obscure corners and a few of its secrets, making friends and, here and there, an enemy.

Fascinated by Belize, I started a little newsletter about the country, and that grew into a little magazine, *Belize First*. From there, I jumped to books, writing four guidebooks to Belize. I've also contributed articles about Belize to magazines and newspapers around the globe.

In this book, I've tried to share with you my understanding of the country, which I admit is as incomplete as anyone else's. Belize is a small country, but it is incredibly complicated. The more time I spend in Belize, the less I realize I know about it.

I've found that even many Belizeans know only a little about their country—or they know a lot, but only about a little part of it. Living in, say, Belize City, they know all the crannies and grannies of that port town, but Punta Gorda in Belize's far south or Sarteneja in northeastern Belize is as foreign to them as Peoria is to a New Yorker, or Sardinia to most Londoners.

My goal is to provide you with information that will help you decide if Belize is for you, and if so, what options you will have in the country. This is not a guide to every aspect of daily living in Belize, because that would take many thousands of pages, but a guide to making your first decisions about living in Belize as a retiree, part-time resident, full-time businessperson, employee, or student, or simply someone who has an abiding fascination for Belize.

You'll learn about the history of the country's culture and people, how to get good health care and find affordable housing, how to travel around the country and where to find more information about it, and how to move to Belize. You'll find specific information on the areas of Belize that are likely to be the most attractive for retirement, relocation, investment, or just visiting awhile for school or fun—including the Northern Cayes, Corozal and the rest of Northern Belize, Cayo in Western Belize, and Hopkins, Placencia, and Punta Gorda in Southern Belize. Throughout, I've been as candid as I can, sharing with you the bad aspects of Belize as well as the beautiful.

If you have specific questions that aren't answered in this book, drop me an email at the address below, and I'll try to respond to your questions as soon as possible. Through the years, I've answered about 10,000 questions about Belize.

After you finish this book and begin your Belize adventure, whatever that means to you, you can do something for me: Tell me what you discover. If you find a great bargain or a bad egg, or if you come across a better way of doing things than I've described here, drop me a note in the mail care of the publisher, or email me at bzefirst@aol.com or llsluder@bellsouth.net.

Belize is changing rapidly, and only one thing is certain: Before the ink is dry on these pages, costs will have changed, people will have moved on, and places will be a little different from when I was last there. Let me hear from you.

—Lan Sluder

Introduction

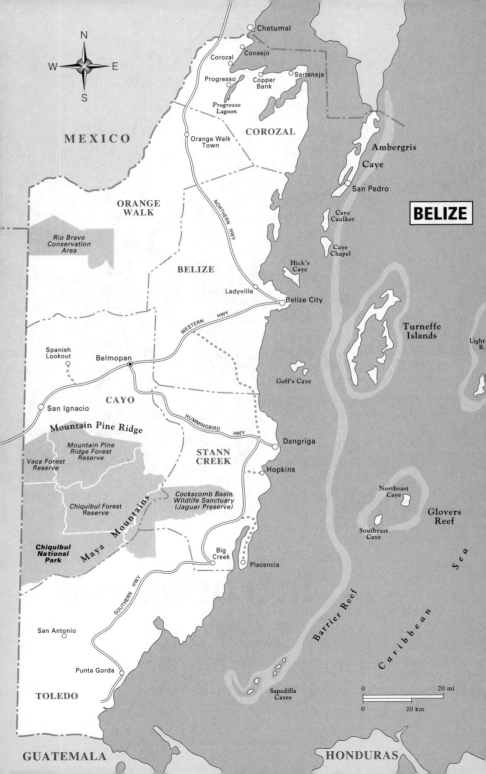

Welcome to Belize

Hold on! You're about to experience Belize, and I guarantee it will be one of the most surprising, exasperating, fascinating, and frustrating experiences of your entire life. Whether you're coming to Belize to live, retire, buy property, build a vacation home, attend college or medical school, or just to experience a different culture, you're in for an adventure you'll never forget.

To start with, Belize is simply beautiful. It is a place of incredible natural beauty, mint green or turquoise seas and emerald green forests, and the longest barrier reef in the Western and Northern Hemispheres, with more kinds of birds, butterflies, flowers, and trees than in all of the United States and Canada combined. Massive ceiba trees and exotic cohune palms stand guard in rainforests where jaguars still roam free and toucans and parrots fly overhead. Rivers, bays, and lagoons are rich with hundreds of different kinds of fish. Belize is one of the world's wild frontiers, a kind of pint-sized, subtropical Alaska.

Belize also has an interesting mix of cultures, ethnicities, and heritages. It's a dilemma, an enigma, and an exception to most of the rules of its region: an English-speaking country in a Spanish-speaking world, a British colony in Latin America, and a Caribbean culture in a Latino society.

With a stable, democratic government, Belizeans treasure their freedom, but politics is intensely personal and often cutthroat. Belize is usually safe and friendly, but it can be dangerous; there are sharks on land, as well as in the sea. Theft is endemic. Belize is a little country with big problems to overcome. It has both corrupt politicians and proud bureaucrats who expect respect, not bribes. It's a poor, developing country, but even so, it seems to pay more attention to the environment than do its richer neighbors to the north. Belize is a nation in the making, but also a land with a 4,000-year history of achievement. While Europe huddled in ignorance during the Dark Ages, Belize was the center of an empire of wealth and sophistication and a land of a million people, four times the population of the country today. The Maya were mathematicians, architects, and theologians of great skill, who erected buildings that still remain the tallest in the region.

Belize is probably not like any other place you've ever been. Despite the palm trees, frost-free climate, and slow pace of daily life, it's not a land where the living is always easy. It's cheap or expensive, depending on how you choose to live. You can't just move to Belize and vegetate in comfortable retirement or hide behind the gated walls of a housing

© Lan Sluder

an afternoon well spent

development for expatriates. It's not a place in which to make easy money, and it's all too easy here to lose the money you have.

Take a little bit of Africa, a little of Europe, a little of the Caribbean, a little of Mexico and Guatemala, and a little of the United States, and you almost have Belize. Yet Belize is more than that.

You've probably heard someone say about a certain part of the world, "I like it, but it is not for everyone." Of course not. Not everyone likes New York City, not everyone likes London or Montana or New Zealand or any other dot on the map. No place is for everyone. But Belize is *really* not for everyone.

Some years ago, I was a business newspaper editor in New Orleans. A real estate agent I interviewed one time told me he could tell within minutes of meeting a prospective new resident at the airport whether that person would like New Orleans. He said that people either got off the plane complaining about the heat and humidity, swatting bugs, and yelling at workers to hurry up with their bags, in which case they immediately hated New Orleans; or else they were enchanted by this most storied and eccentric of American cities and fell in love with it from the moment they stepped off the plane.

Coming to Belize for the first time is a little like that. You arrive at a little airport at the edge of nowhere. The hot, humid air hits you like a steaming blanket. Inside the airport is a confusing mélange of people of every color and station in life, speaking many different languages, and everywhere you look is a mix of anxious tourists and laid-back locals.

En route to wherever you're going, you soon pass a wide, dark river that looks like something out of a Joseph Conrad novel. You see run-down, pastel-colored shacks like those in Jamaica, unfinished concrete houses such as those in Mexico, and new homes with chain-link fences and signs in Chinese. You pass by bars and brothels that would have attracted the famous novelist and jammed streets with rickety wood-frame buildings. Just when you think you're ready to turn around and go back to where you came from, you catch a glimpse of an unbelievably blue sea, a group of friendly schoolchildren in khaki uniforms who wave and shout, or, perhaps, the mysterious Maya Mountains in the far distance.

Belize may not be for you. But then, maybe you are that one person in 10 who will fall in love with Belize, with all its failings and frustrations. You won't find it paradise. You won't find it perfect. But you'll wish you'd found it sooner.

IS BELIZE RIGHT FOR YOU?

Through the years, I've talked with hundreds of people who have moved to Belize or who are considering doing so. Here's what they say they like about the country:

Life on a human scale: Belize operates at 98.6 degrees. It's about people. Belize is a culture of relationships—it is still a country of villages and small towns where people know each other. The only city, Belize City, is hardly more than an overgrown town. The most American of places, the suburbs, with big houses separated by automobiles, barely exist at all in Belize.

Belizeans are usually remarkably friendly and open. Money is often secondary to respect in relationships, and disrespect can get you in serious trouble with Belizeans. They take people one at a time, and you'll often be amazed at how welcoming they are to foreigners, but that doesn't mean they won't grumble about wealthy foreigners buying up their country.

Reasonable cost of living: Living as some do in America or Canada, with a big SUV in the driveway, the air conditioner turned to frigid, and three fingers of Jack Daniel's in the glass, will cost more here than back home. But if you live like a local, eating the same foods Belizeans do, drinking Belizean rum, using public transport, and living in a Belize-style home with ceiling fans and cooling breezes, you can get by on a few hundred U.S. dollars a month, certainly less than a thousand. In between, combining some elements of Belizean life and some from your former way of doing things, you can live well for less than you would pay in the United States, Canada, or Europe.

Health care, the cost of renting, buying, or building a home in most areas, personal and auto insurance, property taxes, the cost of heating (who needs a furnace in Belize?), household labor, and most anything produced in Belize are less expensive than what you're used to paying. Real estate and rental costs in popular areas such as Ambergris Caye are near those you'd pay in Florida, but in rural areas and low-cost towns such as Corozal, you can find nice rentals for US$250 or less a month, build for US$30 to US$90 a square foot, or buy an attractive modern home for US$75,000–200,000. Land in large tracts is available for US$200 an acre or less and farmland with good access is US$500–1,500 an acre.

The greenback is still king: The U.S. dollar has taken its lumps in Europe and elsewhere, but in Belize, it's still king. Although Belize has

Checklist: Is Belize for You?

Belize may be for you if you want to...

[ ] Live on or near the Caribbean Sea, where you can enjoy world-class diving, snorkeling, fishing, beachcombing, and boating year-round.

[ ] Live where English is the official language.

[ ] Stay warm in a subtropical, frost-free climate similar to South Florida's, ideal for those who wish to garden and enjoy an active outdoors lifestyle.

[ ] Escape pollution, turnpikes, and large cities and return to a simpler way of life.

[ ] Live better on a small to moderate income from investments, Social Security, a pension, or other sources than you can in the United States, Canada, or Western Europe.

[ ] Live where a seaside house still rents for as little as US$250 a month, land (in larger tracts) sells for US$500 or less an acre, a seaview building lot costs US$10,000, and full-time household help costs US$10–15 a day.

[ ] Become a part of a fascinating multicultural society combining ancient Maya, African, Latino, Caribbean, and European influences.

[ ] Live in a stable, democratic country that's a member of the British Commonwealth, with a familiar English common-law tradition.

[ ] Enjoy wide-open spaces in the large parts of the country devoted to national parks and reserves.

[ ] Experience a warm welcome for new residents and retirees (students and vacation homeowners, too), with reasonable residency programs and a retired persons incentive program offering tax-free advantages and easy residency for those age 45 and over who qualify.

[ ] Relax into a friendly, laid-back lifestyle.

[ ] Live in a country where non-citizens can own real estate, including seafront land, with few restrictions.

[ ] Have modern conveniences—such as fiber-optic telecommunications, Internet connections, air-conditioning, and North American–style houses—but without franchised fast-food restaurants, chain stores, or frenetic consumer culture.

[ ] Take advantage of being just two hours by air from gateway cities in the Southern United States.

Belize may *not* be for you if...

[ ] You aren't comfortable sharing life with people of every color, background, and heritage. Belize is not for bigots or those who think the world is run by white Anglo-Saxon Protestants.

[ ] You love opera, the theater, bookstores, and art and must be a part of a vibrant cultural scene. Belize is a long, long way from the Upper West Side.

[ ] You're a shop-till-you-drop kind of person. Belize doesn't even have a Wal-Mart.

[ ] You like things done in a certain way: fast, efficiently, and just to your liking. "Belize time" is different.

(continued on next page)

Checklist: Is Belize for You? (cont'd)

[ ] You're on the financial edge and looking for a budget place to live—Belize is definitely not the cheapest spot in the world.

[ ] You're a hard-driving entrepreneur looking for a way to make big bucks fast—the good old USA can't be beat for that. As the old saying goes, the easiest way to end up with a small fortune in Belize is to start with a large one.

[ ] You have a serious chronic illness and need state-of-the-art medical care. You can get caring and inexpensive medical services in Belize and neighboring Guatemala and Mexico, but the latest health-care technology and power pills may be not be available.

[ ] You're a political animal who thinks your voice is as important as the next person's. Unless you're willing to become a citizen, your impact on Belizean politics will be slim to none. Politicians will listen politely, then totally ignore what you say. Even as a citizen, you'll probably never be fully plugged into Belizean political life.

its own central bank and currency, the American greenback is accepted everywhere, and for decades, the Belize dollar has been pegged to the U.S. dollar at exactly 2 to 1. (Because of that simple and easy-to-figure peg, prices in this book generally are shown in U.S. dollars.)

Unspoiled nature and wildlife: Most of Belize remains lightly populated by humans and untouched by developers, so it is a paradise for wild critters and birds. More than 500 species of birds have been spotted in Belize. The country has as many as 700 species of butterflies. Animals rare elsewhere still thrive in Belize's bush.

Fun on the water: Regardless of your level of ability or physical condition, you can enjoy activities on Belize's Caribbean Sea, rivers, and lagoons. Diving around the atolls is world-class, excellent on the reef off Stann Creek and Toledo Districts, and not bad even around the more visited parts of the Belize Barrier Reef. Snorkeling, fishing, boating, kayaking, canoeing, and other water activities are all excellent. And, for most people, the best part is that property on or near the water is affordable—not cheap, but compared with prices for beachfront land in the United States, reasonable.

Fascinating history: Belize was the heart of the Maya world, and today, you can visit dozens of ruins without the hordes of tourists common in Mexico and elsewhere in the region. Among the most interesting ruins in Belize for the nonarchaeologist are Lamanai, Caracol, Xunantunich, Altun Ha, El Pilar, and Lubaantun. In nearly every pasture or backyard are signs and relics of the Maya past, just waiting to be discovered.

Exciting adventures: Belize is a great place for adventure, soft or otherwise. Enjoy hiking, canoeing, kayaking, sailboarding, and caving. Indeed, Belize offers some of the best caving anywhere, with huge cave systems, some yet unexplored, in the Maya Mountains and elsewhere. Actun Tunichil Muknal cave in Cayo District is one of the highlights of any visit to Belize.

Diverse and rich culture: Belize offers a laboratory of human culture, all in a small and accessible space. Belize is a truly multiracial, multicultural, and multilingual society. Though far from perfect, Belize is a continuing education. The country does not have many museums or art galleries, and only a few bookstores and theaters. But something is always going on, and there's always something new to discover about the people and the world.

> Most of Belize remains lightly populated by humans and untouched by developers, so it is a paradise for wild critters and birds.

Frost-free climate: If you tire of cold northern winters, Belize is for you. It never snows in Belize, and the temperatures never drop even close to freezing. The weather is a bit like you find in South Florida—humid and warm to hot, but tempered on the coast and cayes by prevailing sea breezes. Subtropical fruits and vegetables such as mangoes, papaya, bananas, and citrus grow almost like weeds.

English spoken: Let's face it: If you didn't learn a language as a child, you're going to have a tough time becoming fluent later in life. In Belize, you don't have to go to school for years to learn a new language. Because English is the official language of Belize and is used in all official documents, adapting to the new culture is a lot easier for English-speakers than needing to come to terms with Spanish in Costa Rica or Mexico. In fact, Belize is one of the few countries in the world where English is the official language. (English is not the official language of the United States—the United States has no official language.) Spanish, Creole, a mixture of English and other vocabulary and West African grammar and syntax, Garifuna, and several Maya languages are also spoken in Belize. Many Belizeans are trilingual—usually in English, Spanish, and Creole. Beyond the language, Belize (formerly known as British Honduras) has other heritages from England, including English Common Law, which the United States also shares.

Lay of the Land

The most important thing to understand about Belize is this: Belize is like a little kid trying to survive in a grown-up world where almost all the adults are bigger, more powerful, and richer.

Imagine a country about the size of the state of Massachusetts. But instead of having the population of Massachusetts, about six million, this country has only 280,000 people, or about the population of Savannah, Georgia. Instead of having the resources of Savannah, this country has the resources of a small community of 40,000 people. With a per capita income of just US$5,600, about one-ninth that of the United States, Belize has the financial, educational, and structural resources of a small town.

Now imagine trying to run an entire country with the resources of a small town: establish and maintain the national government; raise an army; staff embassies around the world; participate in the United Nations; have your political leaders travel globally and meet with the president of the United States, with the heads of other countries, and with the pope in

Golf carts are a common form of transportation on Ambergris Caye.

© Lan Sluder

No Bright Lights, No Big Cities

Populated areas in Belize are officially designated as a city, town, or village. Belize City is the only real city, with an official population of 44,067, according to the 2000 Belize Census, and a metropolitan population of around 70,000. Belmopan, the capital, has been designated as a city, but with a population of barely 8,000, it's hardly more than a small town. Orange Walk and San Ignacio are the country's two largest towns, each with fewer than 14,000 residents.

The country's "metropolitan areas," in order of population from largest to smallest as of the latest census in 2000, are:

Belize City	44,067
Orange Walk Town	13,483
San Ignacio	13,260
Dangriga	8,814
Belmopan City	8,130
Corozal Town	7,888
Benque Viejo	5,088
San Pedro	4,490
Punta Gorda	4,329

Rome; provide health care, police, and all the other services of a modern state; build a road system; educate the two-thirds of the population under age 20; and do it all with the economic base of a small town.

Whenever you have a problem in Belize, chances are it can be traced back to the fact that Belize is just a little guy struggling to make it in a big, big world.

WHERE IS BELIZE?

Belize is that little spot on the map just to the right of Guatemala and just below Mexico. The Rio Hondo separates Mexico, a country with 100 million people and an area of about three-quarters of a million square miles, from Belize, with its area of 8,866 square miles. Its neighbor to the west, Guatemala, the most populated country in Central America, long claimed Belice (as it's known in Spanish) as a province. Belize and its allies, Britain and the United States and most of the rest of the world, have successfully denied this claim, and Guatemala has reluctantly all but given up on making Belize a province.

By air, Belize is a little over two hours from Miami or Houston. Driving to Belize through Mexico from Texas takes about four days.

THREE TOPOGRAPHIES

Mainland Belize has three distinct topographies. A low-lying coastal plain, much of it covered by mangrove swamp, stretches 190 miles along the sea. As you go inland from the coastal plain, the land gradually rises, though not to the towering heights of its Central American compatriots Guatemala, Honduras, and Costa Rica. The Maya Mountains and the Cockscomb Range form the backbone of the southern interior of the country, the highest point being Doyle's Delight in the Cockscomb Range, 3,700 feet above sea level. The Cayo District in the west includes the Mountain Pine Ridge, ranging from around 1,000 to 3,000 feet. Northern Belize is flatter, with many rivers.

The inner coastal waters are shallow, protected by a line of coral reef called the Belize Barrier Reef, the fifth-longest in the world and the longest in the Western and Northern Hemispheres. Belize's Caribbean is dotted with small islands called cayes and pronounced "keys." Of the 400 or so islands, Ambergris Caye is the largest, followed by Caye Caulker. These two islands are the most populated of Belize's cayes, with around 8,000 people combined, and these also are the primary destinations for island tourism.

Belize is divided into six districts, similar to American counties: Belize, Corozal, Orange Walk, Cayo, Stann Creek, and Toledo. Population density is only about 27 people per square mile, one of the lowest figures in the Western Hemisphere. It's even lower than the statistics suggest, since population is mostly concentrated in Belize City (metro area population about 70,000) and a few district towns, including Corozal, Orange Walk, San Ignacio, Dangriga, and Punta Gorda, none with a population of more than 20,000. About 40 percent of the country's land is devoted to parks and reserves.

WEATHER

The climate of Belize is subtropical, similar to that of South Florida. Daytime temperatures are generally in the 80s or 90s for most of the year, with nighttime temperatures in the 60s in the winter and 70s in the summer. In higher-altitude areas, such as the Pine Ridge and Maya Mountains, winter temperatures may occasionally fall into the 40s or low 50s. Humidity is high year-round, often 90 percent or higher, tempered on the coast and cayes by prevailing breezes from the sea. Rainfall varies from 150 to 200 inches a year in the far south, feeding lush rainforests and jungle, to 50 inches in the north, as in most of the southeastern United States. The so-called rainy season—late June through early November for most of the country—means not monsoons, but a couple of hours of rain daily, often at night,

Weather in Belize

The following are average temperature and rainfall statistics for Belize.

Corozal Town/Consejo Area
Average Daily Temperature
January 73°F
July 83°F
Average Monthly Rainfall
January 3.7 inches
July 5.9 inches

Belize City
Average Daily Temperature
January 75°F
July 84°F
Average Monthly Rainfall
January 5.5 inches
July 9.3 inches

San Ignacio Area
Average Daily Temperature
January 74°F
July 82°F
Average Monthly Rainfall
January 4.7 inches
July 8.9 inches

Placencia/Hopkins Area
Average Daily Temperature
January 76°F
July 83°F
Average Monthly Rainfall
January 6.5 inches
July 10.5 inches

Punta Gorda Area
Average Daily Temperature
January 75°F
July 82°F
Average Monthly Rainfall
January 5.0 inches
July 29.5 inches

Source: Belize National Meteorological Service

followed by hours or days of sunshine. Inland, the "dry season" in the late spring is hot (temperatures may reach 100°F), and forest fires are common.

Hurricanes and Other Calamities

The Western Caribbean does not get as many hurricanes as the southeastern U.S. Atlantic Coast or the Gulf Coast of Texas, but, yes, Belize is in the hurricane belt. On average, Belize is visited by a hurricane or serious tropical storm about once every four or five years. Tropical storm and hurricane season in Belize is June through November, with most storms coming late in the season, particularly September through early November.

Only five storms in the past 100 years have done significant damage: An unnamed hurricane in 1931 killed 2,500; Hurricane Janet did massive damage in Northern Belize in 1955, but loss of life was limited; and Hurricane Hattie in 1961 killed about 300 and badly damaged much of Belize City.

In late September and early October 2000, Hurricane Keith slammed Ambergris Caye and Caye Caulker with 125-mile-per-hour winds, destroying hundreds of houses and killing three people on Ambergris. Post-hurricane flooding on the mainland and other effects of Keith resulted in some US$275 million in

A Century of Hurricanes

Eighteen hurricanes have hit Belize in the past 100 years—that's an average of one hurricane every 5.5 years. As you can see, September has been the unluckiest month.

Hurricane	Cat.:	Date
Unnamed	Cat. 1	Sept. 9, 1916
Unnamed	Cat. 2	Oct. 15, 1916
Unnamed	Cat. 3	Sept. 10, 1931
Unnamed	Cat. 1	Sept. 12, 1933
Unnamed	Cat. 1	Sept. 22, 1941
Unnamed	Cat. 2	Oct. 10, 1942
Unnamed	Cat. 1	Oct. 4, 1945
Janet	Cat. 5	Sept. 28, 1955
Abby	Cat. 1	July 15, 1960
Anna	Cat. 1	July 24, 1961
Hattie	Cat. 4	Oct. 31, 1961
Francelia	Cat. 2	Sept. 3, 1969
Carmen	Cat. 3	Sept. 9, 1974
Fifi	Cat. 2	Sept. 19, 1974
Greta	Cat. 2	Sept. 19, 1978
Mitch	Cat. 5	Oct. 27, 1998
Keith	Cat. 3	Oct. 1, 2000
Iris	Cat. 4	Oct. 9, 2001

Saffir-Simpson Hurricane Scale
Category 1: 74–95 mph
Category 2: 96–110 mph
Category 3: 111–130 mph
Category 4: 131–155 mph
Category 5: 155 mph or faster

Source:
Belize National
Meteorological Service

damages. However, by early 2001, things were back to normal in Belize, and visitors, except for noting a lot of downed trees and palms stripped by the storm, might not even have known a big hurricane had blown through the country.

Then in October 2001, Hurricane Iris hit Southern Belize. From Placencia to near Punta Gorda, the storm took a terrific toll on property and human life. On the back side of the Placencia Peninsula, near Big Creek, a live-aboard dive boat trying to weather the storm capsized and 21 people perished. About nine out of 10 homes and buildings on the Placencia Peninsula were damaged, and in Toledo District, entire Maya villages were flattened and many tropical hardwood trees were blown down. Today, however, if you visit Placencia or Toledo, you may not even realize a devastating storm came through, as homes have been rebuilt and forests are regenerating. No hurricanes have hit Belize since Iris. Keep your fingers crossed.

Even without hurricanes, flooding does frequently occur in low-lying areas, especially at the beginning of the rainy season, typically in June or July. Heavy rains from June through September in Southern Belize can also cause flooding at any time during this period.

Happily, Belize is rarely subject to that other scourge of Central America—earthquakes. While earthquakes have occurred in Belize,

Belize's Wild Side

Belize has more than 500 species of birds, 700 species of butterflies, 700 species of trees, 4,000 species of native flowering plants, and hundreds of species of fish, mammals, and reptiles. The Belize Zoo, on the Western Highway about 30 miles from Belize City, is the easiest place to see many of Belize's wildest creatures. If you're wondering just what these beasts are and how to spot them, consider the following:

American crocodiles are called alligators in Belize.

© Brooks Lambert-Sluder

Crocodiles
What: Belize's two species of crocs, Morelet's and the larger American crocodiles, are called alligators in Belize
Where: New River Lagoon, Orange Walk District, but present on Ambergris, Caulker, and other cayes, and all over the mainland

Gentle Nurse Sharks and Stingrays
Where: Shark-Ray Alley, Hol Chan Marine Reserve, near Ambergris Caye, and elsewhere in the Caribbean sea

Howler Monkeys:
What: Often called baboons in Belize
Where: Baboon Sanctuary, near Bermudian Landing, Belize District; at Lamanai ruins, Orange Walk District; along the Belize River Valley, Cayo District; and near Monkey River, Stann Creek District

Jabiru Storks
What: The largest bird in the Western Hemisphere, standing five feet tall, with a wingspan of up to 10 feet
Where: Crooked Tree Preserve and Northern Lagoon, Belize District
When: January to April

Jaguars
Where: Cockscomb Preserve, Stann Creek District; Chan Chich Lodge, Orange Walk District; and rural areas of Toledo District

Scarlet Macaws
Where: Red Bank Village area, Stann Creek District

West Indian Manatees
Where: Lagoons and shallow seas all along the coast, especially in Southern Lagoon near Gales Point, Belize District, and in Placencia Lagoon, Stann Creek District, but they can show up anywhere

Whale Sharks
What: The world's largest fish
Where: Gladden Spit off Placencia, Stann Creek District
When: April–June

notably in Southern Belize, no severe quakes have hit Belize in modern times. Likewise, there are no active volcanoes in the country. Forest fires are a risk at the end of the dry season, typically April and May.

Tsunamis are possible in the Western Caribbean—in the past two centuries, two tsunamis have occurred on the Atlantic/Caribbean side of Central America, according to papers presented to the Tsunami Society at a 1999 meeting. However, they are thought to be very unlikely in Belize, and none has been recorded. The barrier reef all along the coast acts as an obstacle to wave energy.

FAUNA

The jaguar *(Panthera onca)* is Belize's most famous denizen of the wild. Often called "tiger" by Belizeans, the jaguar is the largest cat in the Western Hemisphere. The spotted jaguar and the black jaguar are the same species. There may be several hundred jaguars in Belize, but you need extraordinary luck to see one of these beautiful nocturnal animals, except at the Belize Zoo, which has both spotted and black jaguars. Belize has four other species of wild cats: puma, margay, jaguarundi, and ocelot.

Baird's tapir *(Tapirus bairdii)*, locally called "mountain cow," is the national animal of Belize. It eats only veggies and is shy and nonaggressive.

Black howler monkeys *(Alouatta pigra)*, sometimes called "baboons" in Belize, are found only in parts of Belize, Guatemala, and Mexico. Almost wiped out by disease in the 1950s, they are making a comeback in Belize, thanks to efforts at protection, such as at Community Baboon Sanctuary, and through reintroduction elsewhere.

Several species of iguanas make their home in Belize. An effort is under way to promote the raising of green iguanas *(Iguana iguana)*, locally prized as a chickenlike dish.

Among other animals you may see in Belize is the quash, or white-nose coatimundi *(Nasua narica)*. This relative of the raccoon is sometimes kept as a pet in Belize. The kinkajou *(Potos flavus)* looks a little like a monkey, but it also is a relative of the raccoon. The bush dog or tayra *(Eira barbara)* is a weasel-like animal that often visits Belize gardens.

Belize has more than 500 species of birds. For serious birders, the sighting of an obscure finch brings joy to one's life list; most of the rest of us are easily impressed by big, colorful, splashy birds such as these:

The keel-billed toucan *(Ramphastos sulfuratus)* is the national bird of Belize. It frequents lowland forests under 2,000 feet and is found in many parts of Belize, including, commonly, on T-shirts in resort areas. The Jabiru stork *(Jabiru mycteria)* is a white-bodied stork, standing four to five feet tall with a wingspan of 10 feet or more. It gives Big Bird a run for his money in the size department. The Jabiru is the largest wild bird in the Americas. It loves marshes and lagoons—Crooked Tree Lagoon and Mexico Lagoon are good places to see one, especially December to March.

The scarlet macaw *(Ara macao)*, with its wings of scarlet, yellow, and blue and its brilliant scarlet head, breast, and tail, is unmistakable. Flocks can be seen in the Cockscomb Preserve and near Red Bank village. Belize has eight species of parrots and parakeets—parakeets have pointed tails, parrots have square tails. Yellow-headed parrots *(Amazona ochrocephala)*, unfortunately often trapped and caged, can be seen in rural areas of Belize, including in Cayo and Northern Belize.

Oscellated turkeys *(Agriocharis ocellata)* can be seen on the ground in several parts of Belize, including commonly around Gallon Jug and at Caracol. The great curassow *(Crax rubra)* is a turkey-sized bird with a wacky hairdo. "Quam" is its local name.

The king vulture *(Sarcoramphus papa)* is a warty old fellow with a naked head who may remind you of one of your uncles. It's fairly common in the Cockscomb Preserve. Belize does not have the resplendent quetzal—to see the avian Liberace, you'll have to go to Guatemala—but

Butterfly Farms

There are more than half a dozen butterfly ranches in Belize. Some sell pupae to museums and butterfly farms overseas, while others are set up as tourist attractions. They provide an easy way to see some of Belize's 700 species of butterflies, including the strikingly beautiful Blue Morpho.

Blue Morpho Butterfly Centre, at the Lodge at Chaa Creek, Cayo District

Community Butterfly Farm, Maya Centre, Southern Highway in Stann Creek District

Fallen Stones Butterfly Ranch, near Lubaantun in Toledo District

Green Hills Butterfly Farm, Mile 8, Pine Ridge Road, Cayo District

Shipstern Butterfly Center, Shipstern Nature Preserve, near Sarteneja in Corozal District

Tropical Wings Butterfly Center, near Xunantunich, Cayo District

Xochil Ku Community Butterfly Center, near Lamanai and Indian Church, Orange Walk District

the colorful slatey-tailed trogon *(Trogon massena)* is in the same family, as are the collared, violaceous, and black-headed trogons.

Belize has some 700 species of butterflies, but the Blue Morpho *(Morpho peleides)*, with its electric color, is the most striking.

Three species of sea turtles—the loggerhead, the green, and the hawks-bill—nest in Belize, usually in the months of June through August.

Underwater, you'll find a whole new world of living creatures in Belize. The West Indian manatee *(Trichechus manatus)*, a distant relative of the elephant, is a gentle herbivore and an endangered species. There have been reports of the slaughter of families of manatees in Toledo District by Guatemalan fishermen. Manatees can be seen in the Southern Lagoon, along the coast, the lagoons near Placencia, Hopkins, and Punta Gorda, and even in the Belize City harbor.

The whale shark *(Rhincodon typus)* is the biggest fish in the world. This gentle giant can be seen in Belize waters April through June. There are many species of true sharks in Belize waters, from the terrifying hammerhead *(Sphyrna zygaena)* to the nearly harmless nurse shark *(Ginglymostoma cirratum)*. You can cavort with placid nurse sharks at Shark-Ray Alley near San Pedro.

Bottlenose dolphins *(Tursiops truncatus)*, smart, social, and aware of humans, are common around the cayes and off the coast of Belize. In late 2004, against the recommendation of Belizean and international conservation organizations, the Belize government approved a captive dolphin park near Spanish Lookout Caye, 10 miles east of Belize City. Visitors will pay a big sum to swim with dolphins kept in prison. Manta rays *(Manta hamiltoni)* are huge and mean-looking fellers, but they are harmless to humans (though hell on plankton). The spiny lobster *(Panulirus argus)*, which lacks the big claws of its cold-water cousins, is very tasty, but only in season—mid-June to mid-February.

FLORA

More than 4,000 flowering plants and 700 species of trees are native to Belize. The cohune palm *(Orbignya cohune)*—locally pronounced koh-HOON—grows over much of mainland Belize. It's a beautiful and highly useful tree. Its fronds are used as cheap roof thatch, its fruits provide oil, and its husks and nuts can be burned for fuel. Considered a symbol of fertility by the ancient Maya, today it is often a flag for hidden Maya ruins. Mangroves—the dominant red *(Rhizophora mangle)*, plus black

Colorful heliconia grow like weeds in Belize.

and white varieties—cover most of the coast and many of the cayes of Belize. Greedy developers would love to get rid of them so that their lots have a better view of the water, but mangroves are invaluable as protection against erosion and hurricane damage and as a nursery for sea life.

The big-leafed Honduran mahogany *(Swietenia macrophylla)* is the national tree of Belize and appears on the country's flag. Logging has eliminated much of Belize's natural supply of these beautiful trees. Though not native to Belize, the coconut palm *(Cocos nucifera)*, tall and stately, is the defining tree on many beaches. It is now being threatened by a disease called Lethal Yellowing, although injections of antibiotics or other treatment can save individual trees.

The ceiba *(Ceiba pentandra)*, also known as the kapok or cotton tree, is one of the tallest and loveliest of all the trees in the jungle. You can spot it by its gray trunk and towering stature.

NATIONAL PARKS AND PRESERVES

About two-thirds of Belize's land area is still forested, and almost two-fifths of the country's land is protected in reserves and national parks. The following are the major parks and preserves in Belize.

Cockscomb Basin Wildlife Preserve, Stann Creek District, is the world's first jaguar preserve. This lush jungle reserve of more than 100,000 acres is a must for anyone interested in natural Belize. With a guide, you can hike to Victoria Peak National Monument, one of the highest points in Belize. The Belize Audubon Society manages it.

National Parks in Belize

Almost 40 percent of Belize's land is protected in national parks and reserves such as:

Bacalar Chico National Park and Marine Reserve, Ambergris Caye

Blue Hole National Park, Hummingbird Highway

Cockscomb Basin Wildlife Preserve, Stann Creek District

Community Baboon Sanctuary, Bermudian Landing

Crooked Tree Wildlife Sanctuary, Crooked Tree

Eligio Panti National Park, Cayo District

Five Blues Lakes National Park, Hummingbird Highway

Guanacaste National Park, Belmopan

Half Moon Caye Natural Monument, Lighthouse Reef

Hol Chan Marine Reserve, Ambergris Caye

Laughing Bird Caye National Park, off Placencia

Manatee Preserve, Belize District

Mountain Pine Ridge Forest Reserve, Cayo District

Port Honduras Marine Reserve, off Southern Belize

Rio Bravo Conservation and Management Area, Orange Walk District

Sapodilla Cayes Marine Reserve, off Southern Belize

Shipstern Nature Reserve, Corozal District

Slate Creek Preserve, Cayo District

Tapir Mountain Nature Reserve, Belmopan area

Half Moon Caye Natural Monument at Lighthouse atoll was Belize's first marine preserve. Half Moon Caye is a beautiful island with 10,000 acres of surrounding reef, also managed by the Belize Audubon Society.

Mountain Pine Ridge Reserve, Cayo District, has more than 300 square miles of nearly unpopulated land in Western Belize. Controlled logging is allowed.

Rio Bravo Conservation and Management Area in Orange Walk District comprises some 200,000 acres of jungle, including mahogany forest, managed by Programme for Belize.

BARRIER REEF

You'll frequently hear that the Belize Barrier Reef is the second-longest in the world, after the one in Australia. Strictly speaking, that's not true. It ranks only number five in the world. But, stretching along virtually the entire 190-mile coastline of Belize, it *is* the longest barrier reef in both the Western and Northern Hemispheres, in itself a pretty impressive statistic.

The barrier reef is one of the things that differentiates Belize from many of the other countries in Central America or the Caribbean. The reef is like an underwater rainforest, a rich and lushly productive home for a variety of sea life, from conchs to lobsters to sharks. It is a protective necklace of coral that slows the sweep of tropical storms and even tsunamis. It is a godsend for divers and anglers. It is also a fragile national treasure, always at risk from hurricanes, rising sea temperatures, diseases that strike the living coral, and the impact of human use.

> The reef is like an underwater rainforest, a rich and lushly productive home for a variety of sea life, from conchs to lobsters to sharks. It is a protective necklace of coral that slows the sweep of tropical storms and even tsunamis.

In addition, the reef is the reason that the beaches of Belize, while beautiful to see, are not always the best for swimming or snorkeling from shore. Inside the reef, the wave energy is very low—there is really no surf on the coast or at most of the cayes. The water is shallow, and there is usually a good deal of sea grass on the sea floor. The sea grass is an integral part of the barrier reef ecology, a living nursery for young sea creatures. Removing sea grass, like removing mangroves, while possibly aesthetically appealing, is a crime against Mother Nature.

Social Climate

Belize is a multiethnic and multicultural society. Almost 5 in 10 Belizeans are Mestizos, people of mixed Indian and European heritage, most originally from neighboring Latin American countries, and most living in Northern and Western Belize; fewer than three in 10 are Creoles, of mixed African and European descent, concentrated in and around Belize City; one in 10 is Maya; and one in 10 is Garifuna, of mixed African and Carib Indian heritage. The Garifuna live mainly in Southern Belize along the coast. Kekchi and Yucatec Maya are in Southern, Western, and Northern Belize. The rest are Chinese, East Indians, Americans, Europeans, and other white folks.

With a mix of so many cultures, Belize cannot be understood through generalities. What may be the case in Mestizo culture in Northern Belize may not apply at all among the Garifuna at the other end of the country.

The exact number of foreign expats from the United States, Canada, Asia, and Europe in Belize is unknown. Estimates range from around a thousand to several thousand. Some have established permanent residency in Belize. According to the Belize Tourist Board, which administers the retirement program, about 200 foreign expats, mostly Americans, have registered under the Qualified Retired Persons program. Many foreigners living in Belize are not in the country as official residents. Either they are in the country illegally, as in the case of many Guatemalan and Honduran refugees, or they are in Belize for only part of the year, as in the case of American and Canadian snowbirds. At any rate, the number is as yet small, although interest in Belize as a second home, retirement, or relocation destination has been growing by leaps and bounds in recent years. Expect a huge increase in the number of Americans, Europeans, and others buying property, living, retiring, or going to school in Belize.

ATTITUDE TOWARD FOREIGNERS

Most people who have spent any time in Belize realize that, by and large, Belizeans deal with non-Belizeans the same way they deal with other Belizeans—on a case-by-case basis.

From time to time, Belizeans do voice concern when they see land being bought by foreign investors, or worry that one group or another is taking over. But Belizeans soon revert to their live-and-let-live philosophy.

As one Ambergris Caye expat, Diane Campbell, put it: "This is the friendliest place I have ever been, and I have traveled a lot. Belizeans take people one at a time—foreign or local is not the issue. How you behave and how you are in your heart is what makes the difference. If you are nice, kind, and honest, you will be well-loved and respected here. The resident foreigners who live here long term are basically good people. They show the respect and decency... and therefore they, too, take people one at a time. If you get used to living here, you won't be able to imagine living elsewhere."

The happiest expat residents and retirees in Belize seem to be those who get actively involved in their local communities, especially as volunteers with hospitals, medical clinics, schools, churches, and in civic clubs. Some even establish familylike relationships with Belizeans they've come to know well. You'll hear references to "my Belizean family" to distinguish those close local relationships from blood ties back home.

History, Government, and Economy

At the height of the Maya Classic period (c. A.D. 250-900) Belize's population was several times the population of the country today. As such a large part of the Maya empire, the prominent cities of the Caracol, Tikal, and Chetumal regions rivaled the classic Greek city states as centers of commerce, religion, and learning. Later, the Spanish conquistadores and British buccaneers tussled over control of the land, and eventually the British won and went about cutting and exporting the mahogany forests of what they called British Honduras; Belize finally became an independent nation in 1981, though it remains a member of the British Commonwealth.

With so many different cultures in present-day Belize—urbanized Creoles, rural Maya, Mestizos in small villages and towns—the interests of each group are bound to collide at times. With tensions between conservationists and developers, tourism operators and fisherman or farmers, city dwellers and country folk, it can be a boiling political cauldron. However, perhaps more so than in any other country in the region, democracy thrives in Belize. People take their politics seriously—understandably so, as many of the best jobs in Belize are political patronage positions. It is rare when less than 80 percent of registered voters turn out at the polls. Turn on any radio talk show in Belize and you'll get an earful of strong political opinions.

Belize's democracy was tested in 2005, when Belizeans took to the streets to protest tax increases imposed by the fiscally strained government of the People's United Party and alleged corruption at high levels of the government. So far, Belizean democracy has passed the test with flying colors. Strikes and protests soon gave way to negotiations between the government and various interest groups, and many observers think the country will emerge stronger than ever.

Compared with Mexico or the United States, or even with its Lilliputian Central American neighbors, Belize is an economic gnat, with a home market too small to provide economies of scale for either manufacturing or retailing. Its best hope is in tourism and agriculture, the two largest industries in the nation. Tourism is especially thriving, with an increase in the number of visitors every month since 2002. Unfortunately, the political and fiscal crises of late 2004 and 2005 also have taken a toll on Belize's economy.

Belize's National Symbols

National Animal: Tapir or Mountain Cow *(Tapirello bairdii)*
National Flower: Black Orchid *(Encyclia cochleatum)*
National Bird: Keel-Billed Toucan *(Ramphastos solfurantus)*
National Tree: Mahogany Tree *(Swietenia macrophylla)*
National Motto: *Sub Umbra Florero*—"Under the shade [of the mahogany], I flourish"
National Flag: Royal blue, with a horizontal red stripe at the top and bottom and Belize's coat of arms in the center

© Brooks Lamber-Sluder

Baird's tapir is the national animal of Belize.

History

Belize may be a small country, but its history has the long, dramatic sweep and color of a grand epic tale. It starts with one of the world's great civilizations—the magnificent cities and ceremonial centers of the Maya empire in Belize were built as much on complex intellectual and spiritual foundations as on the riches of gold and jade. Then came the Spanish conquerors and swashbuckling English pirates, who fought to the death on the Caribbean Sea. Add wars, raging storms, and the long shadows of slavery and colonialism, then cap it all with the struggle to forge an independent modern nation out of many cultures and languages.

WORLD OF THE MAYA

Much of the history of Belize is the history of the Maya. Hunter-gatherers from Asia, the ancestors of the indigenous peoples of the Americas, first came to what is now Belize and the rest of Mesoamerica around 25,000 years ago. Maya Indians began farming in Belize 3,000-4,000 years ago, or possibly earlier. By 2,500–1,000 B.C., the Maya were building sophisticated structures at Santa Rita, Cuello, and elsewhere in Northern Belize.

Belize today has about two dozen major Maya sites in various stages of excavation and restoration, and hundreds of other sites remain to be excavated.

During the Classic period (ca. A.D. 250–950), there were perhaps a million Maya in what is now Belize—four times today's population. Maya achievements in architecture, engineering, mathematics, and astronomy during their Golden Age far exceeded that of Europeans during the same period. They undertook extensive road-building projects and created elaborate cities in the jungle, quarrying and moving huge blocks of stone. Two temples in Western Belize, one at Caracol and another at Xunantunich, remain the tallest man-made structures in Belize, rising 15 stories from the jungle floor.

The Maya understood the mathematical concept of zero, unknown even to the wise philosophers of ancient Greece and Rome. Their number system was based on 20, rather than 10, and through complex calculations, they were able to predict eclipses and other astronomical events with astonishing accuracy. The "long count" calendar invented

Key Dates in Belizean History

2,500 B.C.: The first important Maya centers in Belize are established at Santa Rita and elsewhere.

A.D. 250–900: Classic Maya period, when what is now Belize was the heart of the Maya empire, with a population of one million.

1500s: The first Europeans—Spaniards—arrive in Belize; the Maya resist.

1600s: English buccaneers use the Belize coast as a base to attack Spanish ships, then later settle in Belize River Valley and begin logging.

1798: Baymen defeat the Spanish at the Battle of St. George's Caye on September 10, Belize's national day.

1823: Garifuna from Honduras settle in southern Belize.

1838: Slaves are emancipated.

1848: Caste Wars begin in Yucatán, driving Mexican Mestizos into Northern Belize.

1862: Britain declares British Honduras a colony and a member of the British Commonwealth.

1931: The worst hurricane in Belize history strikes on September 10, killing 2,500.

1949: Protests against devaluation of the British Honduran dollar lead to the formation of the People's United Party (PUP) headed by George Price, sowing seeds of independence.

1954: All literate Belizean adults get the right to vote.

1958: As many as 5,000 Mennonites from Canada and Mexico begin settling and farming in Northern and Central Belize; some later relocate to South America.

1961: Hurricane Hattie nearly levels Belize City on the night before Halloween, killing 300.

by the Maya allowed them to conceive of enormous spans of time and make predictions for thousands of years in the future.

During the Maya reign, Altun Ha, Lamanai, Cerros, Lubaantun, and Nim Il Punit were among the important trading centers or sizable cities in the region. In its heyday, the city-state of Caracol alone probably had a population of about 200,000, nearly as many people as live in all of Belize now. In the 6th century A.D., Lord Water, ruler of Caracol, conquered the warlords of mighty Tikal in present-day Guatemala.

By A.D. 1,000, for reasons still under debate, the Maya empire went into decline. Some archaeologists think that rather than a single factor, a combination of several factors—possibly including climatic changes, social disruptions, and declining agricultural output due

1964: Constitutional self-government begins January 1; Price and his PUP dominate politics in Belize for much of the rest of the century.

1973: The country's name is officially changed to Belize, and the capital moved to Belmopan from Belize City.

1981: On September 21, Belize becomes a fully independent member of the British Commonwealth.

1984: The Opposition United Democratic Party (UDP), under Manuel Esquivel, wins election and comes to national power for first time. UDP and PUP, both centrist, alternate winning elections for most of the rest of the century.

1985: Tourism development begins in earnest on the cayes and mainland.

1998: PUP, riding wave of dissatisfaction with economy and taxes, sweeps national elections; Said Musa becomes prime minister.

2000: Hurricane Keith slams Ambergris Caye, Caye Caulker, and the central coast; damage is estimated at US$275 million, but there are few deaths and the country recovers quickly.

2001: Hurricane Iris hits Placencia and Southern Belize, killing 21 and devastating much of Toledo District, but the region has now recovered.

2003: PUP wins national elections again.

2004: The government faces a big budget deficit and other financial problems; belt-tightening and tax increases are set.

2005: Beginning in late January, a series of protests and strikes called by union leaders, teachers, and the UDP disrupts some businesses and schools.

to deforestation—contributed to the decline, which took place at different times in different areas. Some sites, such as Lamanai, were occupied into colonial times. Belize today has about two dozen major Maya sites in various stages of excavation and restoration, and hundreds of other sites remain to be excavated.

EUROPEANS ARRIVE

The first Europeans arrived via shipwreck in 1511. In 1525, the conquistador Hernán Cortés passed through the southwest corner of present-day Belize. The Spanish established missions in Northern Belize beginning in the late 1500s.

During the next century, conflicts developed between British settlers, the Baymen (a small group of former pirates), and the Spanish, culminating in the Battle of St. George's Caye in 1798. About 350 British pirates and their slaves, with one sailing sloop, a few fishing boats, and seven rafts, defeated a Spanish force of 500 men in a fleet of 30 vessels. St. George's Caye Day is now a major national holiday in Belize, celebrated throughout the country each year on September 10.

BRITISH ERA

Thus began the British era in Belize, which lasted until the mid-20th century. British Honduras, as it was then known, officially became a British colony in 1862, at the time of the U.S. Civil War. After the Civil War, about 1,500 Confederate supporters came to British Honduras. Many settled in Toledo in Southern Belize.

Much of the British period was marked by the traditional colonial approach of exploiting the natural resources of the colony. Though slavery was abolished in Belize in 1838, two decades before the abolishment of slavery in the United States, English and Scottish companies continued to employ hardworking Belizean black people to log the native forests and then exported the timber back to Europe.

During this time, Belize began to become a mix of races and ethnic backgrounds. The old Baymen families, with names such as Usher and Fairweather, married former slaves, creating a kind of provincial Creole aristocracy in Belize City. The Maya, fleeing the Caste Wars of mid-19th-century Mexico, intermarried with the Spanish and were then called Mestizos. Hundreds of Garifuna from Honduras, with African and Caribbean Indian heritage, settled in Southern Belize.

In the colonial period, land ownership in Belize became highly concentrated in a few hands, mostly those of English and Scottish investors. Indeed, one company, the British Honduras Company, later known as Belize Estate and Produce Company, was a London firm that owned one-half of all the private land in Belize. Belize Estate and Produce dominated the Belize economy and politics for more than 100 years, well into the 20th century.

Guatemalan Claims

A debate between Britain and Guatemala over ownership of Belize began early in the 19th century and continued until recent times. Officially, Guatemala has renounced its territorial claims to Belize. Britain pulled most of its troops out of Belize in 1994, but the English still do jungle training in Belize, and their Harrier jump jets remain on call in case Guatemala decides—an unlikely event—to reassert its claim over what jingoist Guatemalan politicians refer to as their 13th province.

In 2003, negotiators for Belize and Guatemala reached an agreement whereby Guatemala is to recognize Belize's existing land boundaries. In exchange, a slight border realignment would be established to give Guatemala about three square miles of land. Guatemala also would gain important new maritime rights off Southern Belize, including a share in a 2,000-nautical-mile economic zone in the Caribbean. The deal still languishes, however, as it has not been ratified by voters in both countries, as required by the agreement.

MODERN TIMES

As the 20th century dawned, British Honduras was a sleepy backwater of the British Empire. But underneath the sleepiness, things were stirring. Jamaican-born Marcus Garvey helped raised black consciousness in Belize, as he did elsewhere in the Caribbean. The worldwide Great Depression, followed by a terrible hurricane in 1931 that killed almost 2,000 people in and around Belize City, both had a great impact on Belize.

In modern times, the history of Belize has been dominated by several key themes. One is the struggle to escape from colonialism and build, with very limited resources, a new nation. Another is the effort to maintain an English-speaking culture in a predominantly Latino region. Still another is the effort to meet the needs of citizens of many different races and backgrounds.

Americans far outnumber the British in Belize, and American influence, from television shows to NBA basketball, is paramount.

Over the last two to three decades, waves of immigrants from neighboring Latin American countries—combined with the migration of tens of thousands of Belizeans, mostly Creoles, to the United States—have changed the nature of Belize's population and politics, giving more importance to

© Lan Sluder

Hand-pulled ferries are becoming a thing of the past in Belize, as ferries like this one near Belmopan are gradually being replaced by modern bridges.

Spanish as a language and Mestizos as a political force. After Hurricane Hattie in 1961, Belize's capital was moved away from the coast in Belize City inland 50 miles to the new town of Belmopan.

Unlike some other former British colonies, Belize never had a large European settler community. Visitors to Belize today often are surprised that the country has so few British residents, numbering at most a few hundred. Americans far outnumber the British in Belize, and American influence, from television shows to NBA basketball, is paramount. The United States has provided all types of aid to Belize, from hurricane relief to a large cadre of Peace Corps volunteers. In the 1980s, the Peace Corps had more than 200 volunteers in Belize, the organization's highest volunteer-to-country-population ratio in the world; the number of volunteers in Belize has since declined.

Government

You don't have to worry about a coup in Belize. Politics in Belize is highly personal and can be rough-and-tumble, even dirty, but Belizeans take their democracy seriously. The voter turnout in the last national election was almost 80 percent, much higher than in any election in the United States. Along with Costa Rica, Belize has the most stable political system in the region.

POLITICS

The modern political history of Belize dates back about two generations. The end of World War II sparked anticolonial feelings in most of Britain's overseas colonies, and the first political movements favoring independence from Britain arose in Belize. Of these, the People's United Party (PUP) under George Price, the "George Washington of Belize," was the most important.

In 1954, a new constitution for the colony was introduced, for the first time giving all literate adults the right to vote. Up until then, only about three in 100 Belizeans were allowed to vote. In 1964, George Price negotiated a new constitution that granted British Honduras full internal self-government, although it remained a British colony.

In 1973, the country's name was changed officially to Belize. On September 21, 1981, Belize became an independent nation, with Price as prime minister. The Hon. George Price is now retired.

Leaders of Modern Belize

Since independence in 1981, Belize has had only three prime ministers. The following are brief biographical sketches of the political leaders of modern Belize.

George Cadle Price, born in Belize City on January 15, 1919, is the eldest of 10 children. Price was a good student at St. John's College, a Jesuit "sixth form" school in Belize City. Price, who was of mixed Creole and Mestizo heritage, studied for a while in Guatemala to be a priest but returned to Belize and entered municipal politics in Belize City, serving on the town board starting in 1947. By 1956, he had become mayor of Belize City and had helped found the People's United Party. In 1961, Price became "First Minister" of what was then British Honduras. The title changed to Premier in 1964 when Britain granted Belize internal self-government. With independence, Price became the first prime minister of independent Belize. However, the PUP lost the 1984 election to the United Democratic Party and Price was replaced as prime minister by Manuel Esquivel. The PUP under Price won back power in 1989 and then lost it again in 1993. Known for living an ascetic, simple lifestyle, and known for never taking advantage of political office for personal gain, Price never married and has no children. He now has the title of Senior Minister in the current PUP government and is widely honored in Belize as the father of the country.

Manuel Esquivel, U.S.-educated and more in the mold of a techno-crat than the rough-and-tumble world of Belizean politics, was born May 2, 1940, in Belize City. Like Price, he came from a mixed Creole and Mestizo family background, which made it possible for him to bridge the worlds of Belize's two most important ethnic groups. He attended local schools and then earned a bachelor's degree in physics from Loyola University in New Orleans, and he did postgraduate study in physics at the University of Bristol in England. Returning to Belize, he made his way into the United Democratic Party and became mayor of Belize City. In 1984, the UDP turned out the long-standing PUP, and Esquivel served as prime minister until 1989, when George Price and the PUP were returned to power in a narrow victory. In 1993, the UDP won again and the self-assured Esquivel resumed his role as prime minister. Esquivel promoted a pro-United States, business-oriented governmental policy and encouraged the development of tourism, which had languished under the PUP. However, slow economic growth, a scandal involving the sale of Belizean citizenships, and the introduction of a highly unpopular 15 percent Value Added Tax did his party in, and in 1998 the PUP under Said Musa swept to a huge victory, winning virtually every contested seat. In the face of the defeat, Esquivel turned the party leadership over to Dean Barrow, a Creole Belize City lawyer. Today, Esquivel lives quietly in Belize. Some think he may be biding his time, hoping to return to power should the PUP fall from

(continued on next page)

Leaders of Modern Belize (cont'd)

political grace and the present UDP leadership fail to take advantage of the situation.

Said Musa, born March 19, 1944, in San Ignacio, was one of eight children. His father was from Palestine and his mother from Cayo District. He was an able student and after his family moved to Belize City, he distinguished himself at Belize's St. Michael's and St. John's colleges. Musa then studied law at Manchester University in England, where he took a degree in law. Returning to Belize in 1967, he took legal posts and established a law firm in Belize City. He became active in People's United Party pol-

itics, serving as attorney general and in other posts. In 1996, he took over the leadership of the PUP and became prime minister after his party's sweeping victory in the elections of 1998. Reelected in 2003, Musa, quick on his feet and a savvy politician, attended his first inauguration in jeans and T-shirt. At first Musa enjoyed great popularity, but charges of PUP cronyism, fiscal mismanagement, and corruption became more vocal. In 2005, he faced the crisis of his career. Students and labor unions called for his resignation, his own political party divided into at least two factions, and the government mired in a swamp of debt and deficits.

Democracy found fertile roots in Belize, and today the little country has a dynamic two-party system. The United Democratic Party (UDP), under former schoolteacher Manuel Esquivel, who was educated in the United States, first defeated the PUP in the 1984 national elections and again in 1993. The People's United Party regained power in 1998 and has held it ever since, winning another national election in 2003. Both parties are centrist, with fairly moderate economic agendas. On economic issues, the PUP usually leans a little to the left, more like the Democratic Party in the United States, and the UDP is more like the U.S. Republican Party.

WESTMINSTER-STYLE DEMOCRACY

Belize is a member of the British Commonwealth, with a Westminster-style government system similar to that in England, and the titular head of state is the British monarch. The prime minister, officially appointed by the British governor general, is always the head of the party that wins national elections, which, according to the constitution, must be held at least every five years. The prime minister chooses the cabinet ministers, who need not be elected members of the house. The last election was held in March 2003, and the next is scheduled for 2008, but it may happen earlier. The legislature is bicameral, with a house of representatives of 29 members elected for five-year terms and an appointed 12-person senate. Six senators are appointed by the prime minister, three by the head of the opposition, and the remaining three by several business, civic, and religious groups. The supreme court is headed by a chief justice appointed by the governor general on advice of the prime minister.

The current PUP prime minister is Said Musa, a lawyer of mixed Belizean and Palestinian heritage, educated in England. His party currently controls 21 of the 29 seats in the house. The UDP loyal opposition is headed by Dean Barrow, another lawyer. Barrow is a Creole from Belize City.

Economy

Small by international standards, unpopulated and undeveloped, modern Belize has struggled to create a viable economy and infrastructure.

In the 20th century, agriculture, especially citrus, bananas, and sugar, replaced logging as the country's main industry. More recently, tourism has joined agriculture as a primary industry, and aquaculture, especially shrimp farming, has generated significant export earnings.

Belize's economy, always subject to cyclical booms and busts, has had its ups and downs in recent years. With a current gross domestic product of only about US$1.78 billion, a small domestic market, a limited ability to raise money from internal taxation, and shrinking global demand for key products such as sugar and bananas, Belize's governments have borrowed heavily from the World Bank and other international lenders, including the government of Taiwan. They have also depended on regressive import duties and consumption taxes to raise funds. Many of Belize's most skilled workers have moved to the United States, yet unemployment in Belize remains high, averaging 9 to 12 percent in recent years.

The current People's United Party government, which swept back to office in 1998, defeating the United Democratic Party, eliminated the unpopular 15 percent Value Added Tax instituted by the previous UDP government, cut income taxes, and introduced a series of economic reforms designed to get the economy growing again. It privatized or sold off a number of industries, including telecommunications, the

Average Costs for Belize Basics

Here's a sampler of costs for common items in Belize. All prices are given in U.S. dollars. As in the United States, prices for many items vary depending on where and when you buy them.

Transportation
Gallon of unleaded gas: $4.25
Gallon of diesel fuel: $3
Bus fare from Belize City to San Ignacio: $3 regular, $4 express
Ferry from Belize City to San Pedro, Ambergris Caye: $15
One-way airfare from Belize City Municipal Airport to Placencia: $68
One-way airfare from Corozal Town to San Pedro: $37

Utilities/Communications
One kilowatt-hour of electricity: $.21
Installation of residential telephone: $50
Monthly residential telephone service: $10
10-minute daytime call from Corozal to Belize City: $2
10-minute daytime call to United States: $8
DSL Internet access: $50–200 a month
Water and sewer service: $10–40 or more (varies by area and usage)
Dirt (trash) pickup: Free to $8 (varies by area)
Cable TV: $20 a month
Tank of butane (100 pounds), delivered: $35

Groceries
Potatoes: $.50 per pound
Red beans: $.50 per pound
Coffee (Belizean): $6.50 per pound
Milk: $2.25 per half gallon
Ground steak (lean ground beef): $1.50 per pound
Pork chops: $2 per pound
Chicken: $1 per pound
Loaf of white bread: $.65 (whole wheat $1.35)
Corn tortillas, freshly made: $.02 each
Bananas: 20 for $1
Avocados (called "pears" in Belize): 6 for $1
Flour, bulk: $1.50 per pound
Onions: $.40 per pound
Soft drink: $.50–.75 per 12-oz. can/bottle
Local rum: $5–9 per liter
Sugar: $.20 per pound
Crackers (Saltines): $3.32
Cigarettes, Independence (local brand): $2.25 per pack
Cigarettes, Winston (vending machine): $3.50 per pack
Cereal (Raisin Bran): $5
Cooking oil (1-2-3 brand from Mexico): $1.75 per half liter

ports, and the international airport. It even considered privatizing the Belize postal service.

The Belize economy, which grew rapidly in the late 1980s and early 1990s, but slowed dramatically in the late 1990s, resumed more rapid growth under PUP leadership. In the late 1990s and the early part of the new century, it expanded at rates of 4 percent to more than 10 percent a year.

ECONOMIC PROBLEMS

Unfortunately, the latest PUP government also borrowed heavily and spent money like a drunken sailor. By 2004, the Belize government faced a series of unprecedented financial problems: a current annual budget deficit nearing 6 percent of the GDP (about the same as the U.S. deficit under George W. Bush); the probable liquidation of the Development Finance Corporation, an entity that provides money for housing construction; the reorganization of the country's largest transportation company, Novelo's bus line, which the government had supported with a large loan; and fiscal scandals within the Social Security system. With a large trade deficit and debt payments equal to about 60 percent of government revenues, the Belize dollar was put under pressure, and rumors rose anew about dropping the peg to the U.S. dollar. "Many errors were made," said PUP Prime Minister Musa.

In late 2004, the International Monetary Fund was called in, government programs were cut back, a freeze was instituted on government hiring, foreign embassies and consulates were closed, some government ministers and employees took a salary cut, and a variety of new or increased taxes and fees, especially in tourism, were proposed.

Events in 2005

In early 2005, the PUP government announced a series of new taxes and tax increases. Among these was an increase in part of the sales tax, making the total tax 11 percent on most items sold in Belize except for food staples and medicine. Increases in property taxes, business taxes, fees paid by tourists, work permit fees, and other areas were announced. In reaction, a two-day countrywide strike, supported both by labor and some businesses, was held in January 2005. Water and other public utilities were shut down, and many schools and businesses were closed.

© Ian Sluder

tourist shops on Barrier Reef Drive, locally known as Front Street

About 500 protesters clashed with police in Belmopan, as lawmakers voted to approve tax hikes opposed by a majority of the country's population. Citing economic necessity, the government went ahead with most of the tax increases, though it rolled back a few of the most onerous and said it would review others periodically. Throughout the winter and early spring of 2005, work stoppages and protests continued, but eventually these were replaced by negotiations between the government and various interest groups, including unions, business groups, and government workers. At press time, many Belizeans seem optimistic that the political process in Belize was working and that the economic problems would also eventually be worked out. However, in April 2005, Standard & Poor's lowered Belize's long-term foreign currency sovereign credit rating to CCC and warned that the credit rating could fall further if the Belize government does not solve its debt problems and increase the international currency reserve.

© Lan Sluder

People and Culture

Belize is a multicultural society, where people of many different races and backgrounds live and work side by side. People of color are in the majority and control most political and social resources, along with a good deal of the economy. Four major groups—Mestizo, Creole, Maya, and Garifuna—make up more than 90 percent of the population, but Belizean life is rich with residents of many other ethnic, geographic, and racial backgrounds, including East Indians, Chinese, Lebanese, Palestinians, and white people from the United States, Canada, South Africa, and Britain.

Regardless of background or language, Belize's population is young. Almost two-thirds of Belizeans are age 20 or younger, and two-fifths are 14 or younger. The median average age of Belizeans is 19. Compare this to the average age of 35 in the United States and 38 in the United Kingdom. This demographic fact is one reason why crime is on the rise in Belize, since teenagers and young adults nearly everywhere have higher rates of crime than older groups. It also affects Belize's economy, since young people who don't work don't pay taxes and contribute little to the society at large.

Ethnicity

Mestizos are people of mixed European and Maya heritage, typically speaking Spanish as a first language and having social values more closely associated with Latin America than with the Caribbean. Mestizos, who make up about 49 percent of the population, are concentrated in Northern and Western Belize, with sizable populations on Ambergris Caye and Caye Caulker. There is often a distinction made between Mestizos who came to Belize from Mexico's Yucatán during the Caste Wars of the mid-19th century, and who are now well-integrated into Belizean life, and more recent immigrants from Central America. In many cases, members of the latter group live on the margins, taking transient jobs in agriculture and living in shanty villages. Mestizos are the fastest-growing segment of the population. Most can speak English, but many speak Spanish among friends or at home.

> Garifuna, also known as Garinagu or Black Caribs, comprise about 6 percent of Belize's population and are of mixed African and Carib Indian heritage.

Creoles are usually, but not always, people of African heritage. Their ancestors came as slaves to then-British Honduras, generally by way of English settlements in the Caribbean. Once they were the majority in Belize. Today, they make up about 25 percent of the country's population. Typically, they speak Creole and English and often have a set of social values derived from England and the Caribbean. Creoles are concentrated in Belize City and Belize District, although there are predominantly Creole villages elsewhere, including Monkey River and Placencia villages in Stann Creek District.

At one time, Belize was home to more than a million Maya Indians. Today, about 25,000, or approximately 11 percent of the population, live in Belize. The Maya mostly belong to one of three different groups: Yucatec Maya in Corozal and Orange Walk districts, Mopan Maya in Toledo and Cayo Districts, and Kekchi Maya in about 30 villages in Toledo District.

Garifuna, also known as Garinagu or Black Caribs, comprise about 6 percent of Belize's population and are of mixed African and Carib Indian heritage. The Garifuna (pronounced gah-RIFF-ooh-na) people have a fascinating history. Before the time of Columbus, Indians from the South American mainland came by boat to the island of St. Vincent in the southeast Caribbean. They conquered, and then intermarried with, Arawak Indians, adopting much of the Indian language. The resulting group went by the name Kwaib, from which the names Carib and Garifuna, meaning "cassava-eaters," probably evolved. Then, in the 17th century, slaves from Nigeria were shipwrecked off St. Vincent. They, too, mixed with the Caribs or Garifuna. Europeans called them Black Caribs.

For years, Britain tried to subdue these free people of color, but the Garifuna, with the support of the French, fought back until the late 1700s, when the French and Garifuna finally surrendered to the British. In 1797, several thousand surviving Garifuna were taken by ship to Roatán in Honduras. Many Garifuna moved from Roatán up the coast of Central America to Belize, where they worked in logging. Some settled in what is now Dangriga. Punta Gorda, Hopkins, Seine Bight, and Barranco also have sizable Garifuna populations. The

Rice and Beans

The national dish of Belize is Rice and Beans, also called Stewed Rice and Beans. Some say the other national dish is Beans and Rice, which usually means that the beans and rice are served separately rather than stewed together. There are many variations of the basic Rice and Beans recipe, but here is a common one.

Rice and Beans
1/2 lb. red kidney beans
1/2 tsp. black pepper
1/2 tsp. thyme
1 tsp. salt
2 plugs garlic, crushed
1 medium onion, sliced
1 cup coconut milk (dehydrated coconut milk, sold in Belizean groceries, can also be used instead of regular coconut milk)
1 lb. uncooked rice
1 small pig tail or salted beef (or other salted meat for seasoning,

such as a slice of bacon or fatback)
6 to 8 cups of water

Preparation:
Soak beans in 6 cups of water for 4 to 6 hours
Bring beans and water to boil, then add garlic, onion, and meat seasoning and cook over low heat until tender.
Season beans with black pepper, thyme, and salt.
Add coconut milk. Stir and taste. Bring to a boil.
Add rice to seasoned beans. (Note: One cup of uncooked rice usually absorbs two cups of water, but this varies with the type of rice kernels.) Stir, then cover.
Cook on low about 30 minutes or until water is absorbed and rice is tender. If necessary, add more water gradually. Serve with stewed chicken, pork, or fish.

largest migration to Belize took place in 1823, and today that event is commemorated every November 19 as Garifuna Settlement Day.

The Garifuna settlements you may see in Belize appear poor, but below the poverty lies a rich culture. The Garifuna in Belize are working hard to continue their language and culture. They have a complex system of religious beliefs, combining African and South American elements, as well as Catholicism. Dugu, or "Feasting of the Dead," is one of the ancestral rites practiced by Garifuna. Garifuna are known as good linguists. Many have become teachers, and quite a number have traveled the world in the merchant marine or on cruise ships.

Another group, representing around 9 percent of the population, includes several thousand Mennonites, who came to Belize from Canada and Mexico in the 1950s. Divided into conservative and progressive groups, they farm large acreages in Belize. Conservatives, who live mostly in Shipyard, Barton Creek, and Little Belize, avoid the use of modern farm equipment and speak a German dialect among themselves. Progressives, who own tractors and drive brawny pickup trucks, live mostly in Blue Creek, Progresso, and Spanish Lookout.

Lebanese and Palestinians, most of whom emigrated to Belize in the early 20th century, are a small but important segment, running stores and businesses. Belize also has sizable communities of East Indians, who live mainly around Belize City and in Toledo, and Chinese, mostly from Taiwan, living in Belize City and in towns throughout the country. The Taiwanese government, fighting its own turf battles with mainland China in the United Nations, has befriended Belize, offering loans and cash grants. Taiwanese businesspeople have invested in Belize real estate and own many of the stores in Belize City, San Ignacio, and elsewhere.

White people in Belize, or "gringos," as we are sometimes called without any intended slur, are mostly expatriate retirees, farmers, ranchers, or tourism operators from the United States, the United Kingdom, and Canada. By one estimate, 80 percent of Belize's hotels are owned by foreigners. Expat communities are concentrated in San Pedro, Placencia, Cayo, Belize City, and Corozal Town.

MIXED-RACE POPULATION

The Belizean cultural and racial mix is even more complex than it sounds, because Belizeans have mixed and intermarried thorugh the years. Walk down a street in Belize City, and you may run into a light-skinned Creole with straight black hair and blue eyes who is speaking in a blur of Spanish, English, and Creole to a young girl who looks British, except that her skin is a deep bronze and her hair is done up in Jamaican-style braids. Even within the same family, you often see considerable variations in physical characteristics and skin color.

The prime minister of Belize and head of the currently dominant People's United Party, Said Musa, is of mixed Palestinian and Belizean, mostly Mestizo, heritage. The United Democratic Party opposition leader, Dean Barrow, is a dark-skinned Creole. Other political leaders come from nearly every ethnic and racial segment of Belizean society.

Race Relations

Race relations are not perfect in Belize, and Belizeans are as quick to stereotype their neighbors as anyone else. Mestizos claim that Creoles are lazy. Creoles worry that "the Spanish"—by which they mean Mestizos or Latinos from other countries—are taking over the country and turning it into a miniature Guatemala or Mexico. Or they rail at Chinese merchants, who they say dominate commerce in much of the country. Expat gringos slam the "port city crowd," saying that the country is run by a small minority of Belize City Creole bureaucrats and politicians. Maya and Garifuna intellectuals argue that their cultures are being destroyed by the actions of larger groups in Belizean society.

However, at the end of the day, Belizeans simply aren't as hung up as Americans or the British on racial and ethnic definitions. Overt racism or racial tension is rare. Belize does not suffer from the deep fear and distrust between and among races that, at times, seems to overwhelm America. "Belize is multiethnic. People who don't feel comfortable with different appearances or customs won't feel comfortable here," said John Lankford, a New Orleanian who lived in San Pedro for many years before his death in Alabama in 2003. "People who can't abide the occasional categorical snub won't feel comfortable here either. Belizeans give and take a considerable degree of ethnic reference, even slur and badinage, without resorting to litigation or combat."

As a Creole saying goes, *"Al a we mek Belize"*—"All of us make Belize."

Creole Influence

Despite the growing influence of the Spanish language and Latino culture, Creole culture and the Creole language continue to play a

For much of the 20th century, the Creole culture was dominant in Belize, and political power rested with the elite, usually Jesuit-educated Creoles of Belize City.

vital role in modern Belize. For much of the 20th century, the Creole culture was dominant in Belize, and political power rested with the elite, usually Jesuit-educated Creoles of Belize City. These self-mockingly named "royal Creoles"—usually lighter-skinned Creoles with generations of history in Belize—still are a powerful force in politics and the professions. "Roots Belizeans" generally are Creoles from the lower or middle strata of society. Tens of thousands of Creoles have emigrated to the United States, and Los Angeles, Chicago, New York, and New Orleans now all have sizable Belizean communities.

Social Hierarchy

As in all societies, there is a social and political pecking order in Belize. Creoles, especially old-family Creoles trained in the country's elite Catholic schools and in England, are at the top, and this group, while not as powerful as in the past, still dominates politics and professions in Belize City and Belmopan. The Maya generally are at the bottom of the ladder, with the Garifuna about on the same rung. Mestizos are becoming a potent political and economic force, especially in the far north and west. A number of Belizeans of British or American descent, but whose roots go back several generations in Belize, have large landholdings and extensive business interests in Belize. The Roe, Bowen, and Bowman families are among these.

Gringos, including expat retirees, part-time residents, and others, are not so much at the bottom or top as off to the side, as they do not vote or have good political connections (with rare exceptions). This can be a rude shock for white North Americans, who are used to running things "back home." Belize politicians usually listen politely to complaints or suggestions from gringos, but somehow no action is ever taken.

Generally tolerant, with a live-and-let-live attitude, Belizeans have generally welcomed expats from Europe, the United States, and Canada. Immigrants, often illegal, from El Salvador, Honduras, Nicaragua, Guatemala, and China, have been less well-received.

As in many countries, there is an undercurrent of resentment of "wealthy" foreigners who buy up prime beachfront and farm land.

The old and the new sit side by side in Belize: thatch and concrete.

This has been exacerbated by recent economic problems in Belize. Several expat residents of Corozal Town, for example, say that just walking around town now, they see more resentment of gringos. "I have a couple of friends leaving," says Rick Zahniser, an American who has become a permanent resident of Belize. "[One] has been here five winters, skipped last winter, and is dismayed by the change in attitude on the part of the locals. Lots of dirty looks. He was robbed of US$200 and all of his travelers checks, and he's disgusted with immigration's policies."

Family Relationships and Gender Roles

Especially in Creole and Garifuna families, women traditionally play important roles, economically and otherwise. Belizean women routinely work outside the home and run a number of successful family businesses. Many women are active in politics and social and civic organizations. However, complete equal rights for women is far from a reality in Belize, and many women's rights taken for granted in Europe or the United States may not be present under Belize law or common practice.

"In my opinion, women in Belize are still second-class citizens," says Karen Cochran, a South Dakota native who owns a house in Independence village in Stann Creek District. "I caution women coming to Belize to make sure, if property purchases or car or boat registrations are involved, that the husband makes it very clear that he wants the name of his wife to be on the title of anything of value. If not, the woman will find herself automatically excluded. To most Belizeans, women have no rights to the property, and in case of the husband's death, it bypasses the wife and goes to the kids."

On the flip side, Belize doesn't have the same machismo tradition of its Latino neighbors—although a man who pays too much attention to a married or "spoken for" woman may find himself in serious trouble with her husband or boyfriend.

Though they often hate to admit it, Belizeans frequently have dysfunctional family relationships. Many children are born out of wedlock, and kids in a single family may come from several different parents.

GAY AND LESBIAN CULTURE

Under one interpretation of Belize legal statutes, sexual acts between two men is illegal—but no one has been prosecuted in recent times, and the statute does not specifically mention homosexuality.

While there are likely as many gays and lesbians in Belize as anywhere else, the general attitude toward homosexuality in Belize is similar to that in the United States a generation or two ago. Public displays of affection between same-sex couples are not socially acceptable. The U.S. military's "Don't ask, don't tell" policy could well serve as Belize's motto on the subject also.

Openly gay or lesbian bars or clubs don't exist, and the country's only openly gay resort, on Ambergris Caye, closed (the cause of the closing apparently had nothing to do with sexual orientation). That said, gay and lesbian visitors to Belize report no problems, to my knowledge.

SEX AND ALCOHOL

Brothels are legal in Belize—there are several in Belize City, and some in Orange Walk Town, San Ignacio, and elsewhere. Marital infidelity is hardly uncommon, and bed-hopping is sometimes called Belize's national sport. But by and large, Belizeans have a conservative public attitude toward sex. Blame it on the British influence. Don't look for nude beaches in Belize, because there aren't any, and only the occasional Italian and French tourist goes topless at beach resorts.

Belizeans do like to party, though. Thursday, not Friday, is often considered the beginning of the weekend. Drinking—favorites are rum and the local beer, Belikin—is a national pastime. It's all part of the more laid-back, easygoing lifestyle in Belize. Puritans will hate it, but many North Americans come to love the "don't worry, be happy" attitude.

Religion

British Anglican heritage notwithstanding, about one-half of Belizeans are at least nominally Roman Catholic. About one-fourth are Protestants of various flavors. Protestant evangelical groups, including the Mormons, Seventh-Day Adventists, Jehovah's Witnesses, and some fundamentalist sects have made inroads in Belize in recent years. Missionaries are active in the country as well. It is said that some hotels in Punta Gorda and Corozal Town, already suffering low occupancies, would go broke if it weren't for the business of missionaries, who often arrange for long group stays at local hotels.

Customs and Etiquette

Rules of etiquette and social interaction in Belize are at least superficially the same as in the United States or Canada, and the influence of stateside television via cable or satellite has, if anything increased the similarity. However, behind the surface likeness are some important cultural differences. Family connections in Belize are very important, and Belizeans often have a complex web of family relationships—cousins, in-laws, and other relatives.

Belizeans of most backgrounds tend to be open and outgoing, and this is something any visitor to Belize will notice immediately. People will come up to you on the street or sit next to you on the bus and immediately start a friendly, even intimate, conversation. They're usually not trying to sell you something or hustle you in any way; they just want to get to know you. You'll be invited to visit people's homes, and before long, you will be considered a friend of the family. However, regardless of your income, be aware that some Belizeans

sign at Five Blues Lakes National Park

may assume you're a "rich" foreigner. They may begin to expect you to buy Fantas or Belikins all around, provide rides to the doctor, or make small loans.

Showing respect and maintaining personal dignity are very important to Belizeans. It is not wise to run down an employee in front of others. This is such a loss of face that the employee may wait and find an opportunity to get back at you, possibly even with a physical attack. In general, however, Belizeans tend not to be confrontational.

In the same vein, don't run down one Belizean to other Belizeans. You never know who is related to whom. Also, because politics is so intensely personal in Belize, and almost every Belizean is either blue (the colors of PUP) or red (UDP), it's wise for the expatriate resident to avoid taking sides or expressing a political opinion.

Even longtime residents who have become Belizean citizens may have to watch what they say and to whom. One rancher who has been in Belize for more than two decades told me in a whispered tone, "You know, we have to be careful what we say over there," pointing toward Belmopan, the capital.

In my own case, Belizeans have brought up uncomplimentary things I wrote about a specific hotel or restaurant in books or articles 10 years ago. Recently, I received a letter from the Belize Tourist Industry Association complaining about archived materials on my website, dating from the mid-1990s, that negatively reviewed several hotels. I had long forgotten the comments, but these Belizeans still remembered and took me to task.

Sometimes envious or resentful neighbors or business competitors aren't reluctant to rat on you to the Belizean tax or police authorities. Cases in point: An American married to a Belizean and running a remote jungle lodge was turned in to authorities for possessing an unlicensed gun for protection, which is illegal (though very common in bush areas). The hotelier was able to escape jail, but he paid many thousands of dollars in fines and attorney's fees. In Belize City, an area where there are frequent drive-by shootings and robberies with guns, an American businessman who says he has never owned a gun in his life was awakened at his home at four in the morning by a large group of police officers. They searched his house and finally found a single bullet cartridge. He faces a sizable fine and reportedly is selling his business and leaving the country. Another woman, an American in San Pedro in the hotel business, was brutally attacked and beaten on a deserted beach by a former Belizean employee who apparently held a grudge about something that had happened on the job.

Such incidents are rare, but they do happen. The best way to avoid confrontation with authorities or locals is to stay quiet, calm, and respectful of all the country's rules and regulations. Take time to learn what is and is not permitted by Belizean law.

National Holidays

The following are legal public holidays in Belize:

New Year's Day: January 1
Baron Bliss Day: March 9
Good Friday
Holy Saturday
Easter Sunday: March or April, dates vary yearly
Easter Monday: March or April, dates vary yearly
Labour Day: May 1
Commonwealth Day: May 24
St. George's Caye Day: September 10
Independence Day: September 21
Columbus Day: October 12
Garifuna Settlement Day: November 19
Christmas Day: December 25
Boxing Day: December 26

BUSINESS AND SOCIAL ETIQUETTE

Dress in Belize is informal. Men rarely wear coats and ties. Even the prime minister and other top government officials conduct the business of office wearing just slacks and a guayabera shirt or long-sleeved white shirt. Women in business wear cotton dresses or simple skirts and blouses. On the cayes, T-shirts and shorts rule for both sexes.

The firm handshake so popular with Type-A American businessmen is rarely used in Belize. In this respect, Belizeans are more like their Latino neighbors. A Belizean-style handshake involves a gentle meeting of the hands and a soft shake.

The attitude of Belizeans toward time is more like that of Mexicans than of Americans or Canadians. Shop clerks may open an hour later than the sign on the door claims, and lunch hours are flexible. The farther you get from Belize City, the less time-consciousness you find. According to Emory King, an American who was shipwrecked in Belize in the 1950s and never left, there are three time zones in Belize: In Belize City, if you are within an hour of your appointment, you are on time; in Belmopan, if you are within two hours of your appointment, you are on time; elsewhere in the country, if you get there the same day, you are on time. In remote villages, many Belizeans have never held a full-time job and may never have worked for pay. They may not own a watch or clock. These good folks simply aren't used to the strict and punctual routines we in industrialized countries have had drilled into us all of our lives.

One way in which Belizeans do differ greatly from their Latino neighbors is in their attitude toward bribes. The system of petty bribes common in many Latin American countries is absent in Belize. Most customs officials and low-level government workers in Belize want respect, not *mordida* (literally, "bite," meaning a bribe). Corruption is hardly unknown in Belize, but it exists at higher levels than in Mexico or Honduras.

The system in Belize is more like the old-boy network, whereby those who get government or other contracts are expected to share a bit with family and business associates. Doing so is not considered unethical, and, in fact, not doing so would be a breach of ethics. Painless loans and fat contracts to well-connected political chums are a routine part of Belizean party politics, just as they traditionally have been in Louisiana. It's a share-the-wealth system, and everyone, at least at a certain level of society, gets a turn eventually.

The Arts

If traditional fine arts—opera, dance, symphony, theater, galleries, and the like—are a priority, Belize may not be for you. There's only one movie theater in the entire country, at the Princess Hotel and Casino in Belize City, and you may have to wait a long time before seeing a Broadway-type performance in Belize City.

The Belize National Dance Theater is an innovative dance group and the Bliss Center for the Performing Arts in Belize City, which underwent a renovation in 2004, is the main venue for dance, music, and other arts performances in the country.

LITERATURE

Cubola Productions, a small publishing house in Benque Viejo del Carmen in Western Belize, has published a number of modern Belize writers. Among them is Zoila Ellis, the Garifuna author of *On Heroes, Lizards, and Passion,* a collection of short fiction. *On Words,* one in a series of texts put out by Cubola in the 1990s directed to the student market, collected the works of 35 Belizean poets, including Raymond Barrow, Ronald Clark, Leo Bradley, Corinth Lewis, Richard Bradley, and Yasser Musa.

Zee Edgell's noteworthy novel, *Beka Lamb,* published in England, is about Belize in the 1950s. The late Byron Foster, an English-born academic, wrote a number of books on Belize history and archaeology, including *Warlords and Maizemen,* a survey of Maya archaeological sites in Belize, and *Heart Drum,* a study of Garifuna traditions.

Several of the most celebrated books about Belize and the region are by authors who only visited Belize, including John L. Stephens, whose two-volume *Incidents of Travel in Central America, Chiapas, and Yucatán* is a 19th-century classic. Ronald Wright's *Time Among the Maya: Travels in Belize, Guatemala, and Mexico* is also a classic.

More recently, Richard Timothy Conroy wrote a fascinating memoir of his life as a U.S. diplomat in British Honduras in the 1950s and early 1960s, *Our Man in Belize,* with infamous Hurricane Hattie playing a central role. Although the book is now out of print, copies sell for more than US$100 on eBay.

Belize, The Novel is a Michener-style saga of Belize by former resident Carlos Ledson Miller. The redoubtable Emory King, who was shipwrecked

Belize's National Anthem

Until 1981, Belize's national anthem was "God Save the Queen," Great Britain's anthem. With independence in 1981, "Land of the Free" was adopted as the new country's anthem. The national anthem was written in 1963, with lyrics by Samuel Alfred Haynes (1898–1971), a Creole nationalist who had helped lead demonstrations against the British rule of Belize in 1919. The music was written by another Belizean, Selwyn Walford Young (1899–1977). The Belizean anthem is played at official functions and, often, in schools at the beginning of the school day. You can listen to Belize's national anthem at www.belize.gov.bz/belize.mid.

Land of the Free
O, land of the free by the Carib Sea,
Our manhood we pledge to thy liberty!
No tyrants here linger, despots must flee
This tranquil haven of democracy.

The blood of our sires which hallows the sod,
Brought freedom from slavery oppression's rod,
By the might of truth and the grace of God.
No longer shall we be hewers of wood.
Arise! Ye sons of the Baymen's clan,
Put on your armor, clear the land!
Drive back the tyrants, let despots flee.

Land of the free by the Carib Sea!
Nature has blessed thee with wealth untold,
O'er mountains and valleys where prairies roll;
Our fathers, the Baymen, valiant and bold
Drove back the invader; this heritage hold
From proud Rio Hondo to old Sarstoon
Through coral isle, over blue lagoon;
Keep watch with the angels, the stars and moon;
For freedom comes tomorrow's noon.

in Belize in 1954 and never left, has written a number of self-published guides and entertaining histories of Belize. The *Great Story of Belize* is a four-volume history. (For more about books on Belize and by Belizeans, see *Suggested Reading* in the *Resources* section.)

GRAPHIC ARTS

Established artists such as Walter Castillo (originally from Nicaragua and now living on Caye Caulker) and Benjamin Nicholas (a Garifuna with a studio in Dangriga) command high prices for original work, but Belize also has a growing number of young, highly creative artists working in various media. Yasser Musa (son of Belize's current prime minister) is a poet, painter, and teacher who has been involved with The Image Factory, a gallery in Belize City. The gallery is a good place to see the work of talented Belizean artists, and sometimes to meet the artists themselves. Musa is also the director of the Museum of Belize in Belize City. Other noted artists include Leo Cal, a Mestizo from Orange Walk; Betty Cooper from Dangriga; Pamela Braun, an American who lives near Belize City; Sergio Hoare; Brad Steadman; and many others.

Pen Cayetano, a Garifuna born in Dangriga in 1954, is a painter and musician who now lives in Germany. His vividly colored paintings depict daily Garifuna life in Belize. In the early 1980s, he helped create punta rock, a combination of traditional Garifuna music and rock.

An American expatriate, Carolyn Carr, who, along with her husband, John, runs Banana Bank lodge near Belmopan, is one of Belize's most popular painters. Her realistic paintings of Belize street scenes and wild creatures (sometimes both at once) have been widely exhibited, and she has a studio at the lodge. One of her best-known works, titled *Jimmy Hines*, shows the old market in Belize City where fishermen clean lobster, snapper, and "jimmy hines," the local name for a type of sea bass or grouper. A few years back, one of her paintings appeared on the cover of the Belize telephone directory.

MUSIC

Music in Belize is very eclectic, from Creole brukdown and cunga to Garifuna punta rock and Mestizo marimba—not to mention Caribbean-style ska, reggae, calypso, and, of course, hip-hop. Classic Belize artists include world-famous punta masters Andy Palacio (Barranco-born), Creole kings Mr. Peter's Boom and Chime, and Bredda David, but young hipsters will quickly find out the best new talents. Belize's most popular band, Santino's Messengers, disbanded in 2004, but some of its members are now in New Sensation Band. Cubola Productions's Stonetree Records is a top Belize record studio. A practical musical tip: Avoid buying pirated tapes.

Artist-musician Pen Cayetano's punta group, the Turtle Shell Band, played all over Central America and the United States. Today, punta rock is the best-known type of music that originated in Belize.

CRAFTS

Belize has a number of talented carvers who turn out well-made kitchen bowls and sea and wildlife art from *zericote* and other local woods. One of the best places to buy authentic Belizean crafts at fair prices is the National Handicraft Center in Belize City. Other good craft markets include Maya Centre at the Cockscomb preserve, where a local Maya cooperative sells its handmade items; and Caesar's Place, a commercial gift shop on the Western Highway near San Ignacio, which has a huge selection of items at some of the best prices in the country.

BELIZE ON-SCREEN

For movie buffs, two movies with extensive footage of Belize are *The Dogs of War* (1981) and *Mosquito Coast* (1986). In *The Dogs of War,* starring Christopher Walken and Tom Berenger, Belize stands in for a fictitious African country in the throes of political change. *Mosquito Coast* is based on the Paul Theroux novel about a would-be escape from modern society. Its star, Harrison Ford, got to know Belize well during the filming.

A brooding TV version of Joseph Conrad's novella *The Heart of Darkness* was shot in Belize in 1994 and starred John Malkovich. The movie *After the Storm,* based on a Hemingway short story, was shot in San Pedro, Placencia, and Belize City in 2000. An early "reality-based" TV show, *Temptation Island,* was shot on Ambergris Caye in the fall of 2000. The show's production crew were caught by Hurricane Keith but escaped without injury. An episode of the *Wildboyz* MTV series was also shot in Belize in 2003.

Emory King, the American-turned-Belizean author described above, is Belize's official commissioner of film. In 2003, he helped establish the Belize International Film Festival, which is held annually in January or February at the Bliss Center for the Performing Arts. It screens short films and nature documentaries made in Belize, along with other films by Caribbean filmmakers.

Prime Living Locations

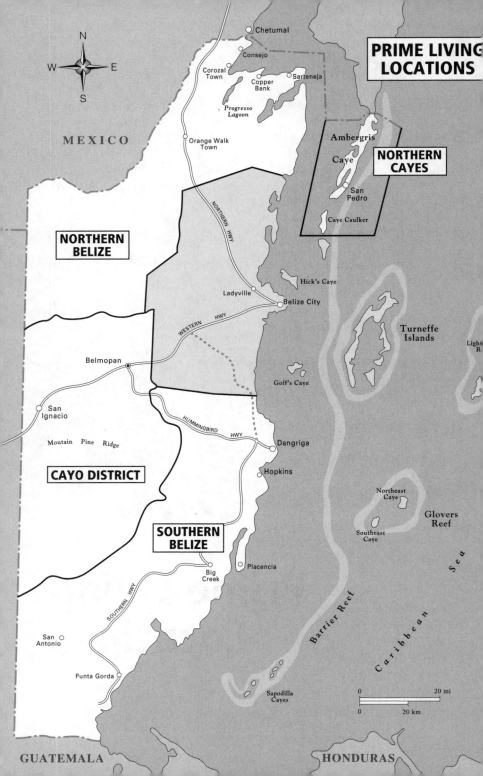

© Ian Sluder

Overview

P rime living locations—Northern Cayes, Northern Belize, Cayo District in Western Belize, and Southern Belize—are the best choices for living, retiring, and spending time in Belize. The following chapters explore the options in each of these regions of the country, including a closer look at what each area offers, the cost of living, price and availability of homes and land, and other practical matters.

Northern Cayes

Belize has scores of named cayes (pronounced "keys") in the Caribbean Sea. In addition, there are many other small spits of sand and mangrove that dot the sea off Belize's 190-mile-long coast. The vast majority of these islands are undeveloped and unoccupied. The two largest and most populated cayes are in the north—Ambergris Caye (pronounced "am-BUR-griss") and Caye Caulker, sometimes known as Caye Corker.

Ambergris Caye

Ambergris Caye is the top tourist destination in Belize. It also is the most popular place for retirees and other expats to live in Belize. It offers the beauty of the Caribbean in a fairly compact, accessible package. You can dive, snorkel, swim, and fish to your heart's content. San Pedro, Ambergris Caye's only town, has Belize's biggest selection of restaurants and nightlife.

> Ambergris Caye is the top tourist destination in Belize. It also is the most popular place for retirees and other expats to live in Belize.

The island's population, officially less than 4,500 in the 2000 Belize census, has since grown to 7,000 or more. No one knows for certain how many people live on the island. In addition, the caye's population fluctuates seasonally, with snowbirds coming south for the winter from Canada and the United States. Belizeans also come and go, looking for construction or other work. Estimates of expats on the island vary, but the number is probably in the range of about 1,000. Most are here for only part of the year.

The real-estate market here is white-hot. While beachfront house and lot prices are no longer the bargain they once were, with high-quality beach lots going for US$2,000–3,500 per front foot, they are still reasonable in comparison with most U.S. coastal areas. You can buy a buildable beach lot for US$50,000–100,000 and up, or build a pleasant seaside home for US$100,000–200,000. Condos start at around US$25,000, but can cost up to US$400,000 or more. A few inexpensive rental apartments and houses are available, but generally rents are similar to those in the United States.

Most of the island's economy is focused on tourism. If you aren't busy selling real estate or running a hotel, the island offers some volunteer opportunities. Some expats help out at the local library or do church work (the island has one Catholic church and several Protestant denominations). The San Pedro chapter of the Lions Club is the island's most active civic organization. Its weekly barbecue on Saturday nights is delicious and cheap, as well as a fund-raiser for the group's good works.

Caye Caulker

Caye Caulker is Ambergris Caye's "little sister" island—smaller and less developed. Caulker, whose name derives from the Spanish word for coco plum, *hicaco,* has the kind of laid-back, sandy-street, tropical-color, low-key Caribbean charm that travelers pay thousands to experience—but here, they can have it for peanuts. A small number of foreigners also now call Caye Caulker home. However, residents here have managed to maintain close ownership of land on the island. Lots and homes are only occasionally available for public sale, but the good news is they cost less than on Ambergris Caye. A few apartments are for rent, starting at around US$300 a month.

Private Islands

The days of buying your own private island for a song are long gone, but if you have money to burn and the willingness to rebuild after the next hurricane, one of Belize's remote islands could be yours, beginning at about US$75,000 and going up to several million dollars. Developers also are selling lots, starting at US$15,000, on a few small cayes. The difficulties of building on a remote island are many, and the environmental issues are complex. *Caveat emptor.*

Northern Belize

Northern Belize is the "Sugar Coast" of Belize, land of sugar cane and sweet places to live. Corozal and Orange Walk Districts are the two northernmost districts in Belize, and Corozal abuts Mexico. Corozal District is one of the undiscovered jewels of Belize. There's not a lot to do, but it's a great place to do it. The Sugar Coast—sugar cane is a main agricultural crop here, as it is in Orange Walk District just to the south—is a place to slow down, relax, and enjoy life. The climate is appealing, with less rain than almost anywhere else in Belize, and the fishing is excellent. The sunny disposition of residents—Mestizos, Creoles, Maya, Chinese, East Indians, and some North Americans—is infectious.

Corozal Town

Many visitors to Belize either never get to Corozal Town or pass through quickly en route to somewhere else. But Corozal Town and the nearby Consejo area offer a lot for those staying awhile: low prices, friendly people, a generally low-crime environment (although 2004–2005 saw a spate of high-profile violent crimes, and a majority of expats here say they've experienced thefts or burglaries), the beautiful blue water

Rainy Days

Here are the average number of days per year with at least some rain in Belize. There can be considerable variation within a district and also from year to year. Much of the rain comes in the early morning and is called "night rain" by Belizeans.

Northern Cayes	110
Corozal District	90
Belize City	171
Cayo District	150
Stann Creek District	183
Toledo District	200

of Corozal Bay, and the extra plus of having Mexico next door for shopping. There are large department stores, hypermarkets, and even a couple of McDonald's restaurants in Chetumal.

Real estate and living costs in Corozal are among the lowest in Belize. Modern North American–style homes with three or four bedrooms in Corozal Town or Consejo Shores go for US$75,000 to around US$200,000, but Belizean-style homes start at less than US$50,000. Waterfront lots are available for US$50,000 or less, and big lots with water views are US$10,000–25,000. Rentals are relatively inexpensive—US$100–300 for a nice Belizean-style house, or US$300–800 for a modern, American-style house.

Sarteneja Peninsula

On the peninsula just east of Corozal Town, the villages of Progresso, Copper Bank, and Sarteneja beckon the intrepid expat looking for low prices and a slow pace of life. But this is still the old Belize, and you're hard put even to find a grocery store.

Orange Walk District

Orange Walk Town—the name comes from the orange groves in the area—could be any number of towns in Mexico. There's a formal plaza, and the town hall is called the Palacio Municipal. The businesses and houses along the main drag—Queen Victoria Avenue, or the Belize-Corozal Road—have barred windows, and some of the hotels and bars are in fact brothels. However, Orange Walk Town is a gateway to a magical area of Belize: the wide sky, fertile rural land, and unpopulated forests of Belize's northwest shoulder, pressed against the Guatemalan border.

Cayo District

Cayo District is the "Wild West" of Belize, but these days, it's attracting adventuresome retirees, ex-hippie farmers, old Belize hands who prefer hills to beaches, and students who want to try out college in Belize. Cayo District has a lot going for it: wide-open spaces, cheap land, few bugs, and friendly people. This might be the place to buy a few acres and grow oranges.

San Ignacio

The major towns in Cayo District are San Ignacio and its twin Santa Elena, with a combined population of about 15,000, about 10 miles from the Guatemalan border. San Ignacio sits close to the edge of Guatemala, a little more than an hour-and-a-half's drive from the marvelous ruins of Tikal. Around San Ignacio is a group of villages on the Western Highway, Bullet Tree Falls, and the Mennonite area of Spanish Lookout. Any of these could be your little piece of paradise.

Agriculture, ranching, and, increasingly, tourism are the major industries here. In the early 1980s, the first small jungle lodges began operation around San Ignacio. Now there is a flourishing mix of hotels, cottages, and jungle lodges near San Ignacio and in the Mountain Pine Ridge, along with many natural attractions and outdoor activities—canoeing, caving, hiking, and horseback riding, to name a few. The country's most accessible Maya ruins are here, as is Caracol, in its heyday a larger city-state than Tikal.

Mountain Pine Ridge

To the south of San Ignacio are the hills of the Mountain Pine Ridge, little populated but ideal for those who want to really get away from civilization. The Pine Ridge is the largest forest reserve in Belize, full of wild caves and beautiful waterfalls.

Belmopan

Situated between Belize City and San Ignacio, Belmopan is the downsized, sleepy capital of Belize, with a population of about 8,000. A campus of the University of Belize is here, along with an offshore medical school, but most of the attractions are in the surrounding countryside. The Belize Zoo is nearby, as are several excellent lodges set in wild jungles. Along the scenic Hummingbird Highway south of Belmopan are barely explored caves, rivers, and national park areas. Small farms are available for US$20,000–50,000.

Southern Belize

In Southern Belize the climate is truly tropical, with temperatures rarely falling below 60°, even in the winter. The rain often falls in buckets during the summer and fall, and that abundance of moisture breeds true rainforests, especially in the far south, with lush carpets of deep green. This is the only part of Belize where rice can be easily grown in the flooded fields.

Lovers of the sea will enjoy the great sailing, kayaking, diving, and snorkeling all along the southern coast. Anglers will find one of the world's best permit fisheries—and fishing for tarpon, snook, and bonefish is excellent here, too.

Southern Belize comprises two districts, Stann Creek and Toledo. Three areas of particular interest are the Hopkins village area, the Placencia Peninsula, and Punta Gorda. These areas comprise the most rural part of Belize, with long stretches of citrus groves or unimproved land broken only by a few small villages.

Placencia

You'll love Placencia if you're looking for a little bit of the South Pacific in Central America. Placencia boasts the finest beaches on the mainland, and it's an appealing seaside alternative to the bustle of Ambergris Caye. This peninsula in Southern Belize has about 16 miles of beachfront along the Caribbean; a total population of fewer than 3,000, mostly in two small villages; a backside lagoon where manatees are frequently seen; a few dozen hotels and restaurants; and an increasing number of expatriates and foreign-owned homes.

> Placencia boasts the finest beaches on the mainland, and it's an appealing seaside alternative to the bustle of Ambergris Caye.

In recent years, the Placencia Peninsula has undergone a boom that slowed only briefly after Hurricane Iris in 2001. Building lots have been sold by the score to foreigners who think they'd someday like to live by the sea. Seafront real-estate costs are higher in Placencia than anywhere else in Belize except Ambergris Caye. Beachfront lots cost US$1,600–2,000 per front foot, pricing a seaside lot at around US$80,000. Lots on the lagoon or canal are less expensive. There is little North American–style housing available for sale or rent, so most expatriates build their own homes, with construction costs ranging US$45–85 or more per square foot, depending on the type of residence.

Hopkins

On the southern coast of Belize in Stann Creek District, between Dangriga and Placencia, Hopkins has become what neighboring Placencia was like just a decade or so ago. Expatriates are moving to Hopkins, a friendly Garifuna village that got telephones only in the mid-1990s, and to real-estate developments nearby. New small seaside hotels are going up in Hopkins and Sittee Point. Although at times the sandflies can eat you alive here, you can also find some excellent fishing and beach time, with day trips to the nearby Cockscomb jaguar reserve and boat trips to the reef. You'll love Hopkins if Placencia is too developed for you.

Punta Gorda

Rainy, beautiful, and remote, Punta Gorda in far Southern Belize is the jumping-off point for unspoiled Maya villages and onward travel to Guatemala and Honduras. Through the next several years, as the final few miles of the Southern Highway to Punta Gorda are paved and the road is extended into Guatemala, this area is expected to take off, both in terms of tourism and as a place for expatriate living. "PG," as it's known, is Toledo District's only population center, with about 4,500 people, mostly Garifuna, local Maya, and immigrants from Guatemala. Maya villages, hardly changed for centuries, are situated around PG. Cayes and the south end of the barrier reef offer good snorkeling and fishing. Lumbering and fishing are about the only industries.

Undeveloped land is inexpensive here, with property beginning at a couple of hundred dollars an acre. Few North American–style homes are for sale. Quality rentals are expensive because of demand from missionaries and lack of supply.

Planning Your Fact-Finding Trip

O nly one thing will tell you for sure whether Belize is right for you, and that is an initial visit. If you've never been to the country before, I recommend an initial scouting trip to learn firsthand about how Belize feels and to gauge your personal reaction to it. Then, as time and budget allow, return to Belize at least once or twice more before making any final decisions about living or investing here. Ideally, one of these follow-up trips should be an extended stay of at least a few weeks, preferably in a rented apartment, condo, or house, so you can get a feel for the nitty-gritty of daily life—as opposed to a vacation trip, where bumpy reality is smoothed over by solicitous hotel and tour operators.

Preparing to Leave

INDEPENDENT TRAVEL OR GROUP TOUR?
It makes sense to plan to travel on your own in Belize rather than going on a group tour. If you feel uncomfortable traveling solo on a brief

exploratory trip, you may have real problems living long-term in Belize. After all, the pioneering spirit is alive and well in Belize, where the ability to fix a flat tire on a deserted road or deal with a scorpion in your shoe are handy skills to have. Those who usually prefer to have a tour director help them explore a new place may have trouble adapting to daily life in a developing country. If dealing with people with different cultural values from yours is difficult for you, living permanently in the diverse cultural quilt of modern Belize may not be for you.

It's easy to travel independently in Belize. Since English is widely spoken, you won't have a language problem. Most of Belize is wired, so you can quickly make hotel and other reservations via the Internet or by fax. You'll probably also save money by traveling on your own. Package tours to Belize are rarely a real bargain—although sometimes they offer the easiest option for those with special travel interests, such as diving or caving. But even if you save a few bucks, you're locked into a fixed itinerary or into staying at one of the larger resorts. As most hotels in Belize are family-run places with only a few rooms, owners generally prefer that you book directly with them, if possible via the Internet, saving them 15 percent to 40 percent in travel agent and wholesaler commissions, plus expensive long-distance telephone charges. Usually some of the savings are passed on to you in the form of lower direct-booking rates.

The exception to independent travel may be if you want to take a retirement or real-estate tour to Belize, such as those offered occasionally by *International Living* newsletter. While usually more expensive than independent travel, these tours do provide a lot of relocation information in a short period. Typically, you visit three or four areas in a week's time—usually Ambergris Caye, Cayo, Placencia, and either Corozal or Punta Gorda—and hear speakers in each area who represent real-estate companies, law firms, and Belize government agencies. The disadvantages are that it's a whirlwind visit, and some of the speakers you hear may have a vested interest in getting you to buy something.

WHEN TO GO

There is really no single best time to visit Belize, but there are a few timing factors you might consider. The country gets the most visitors from Thanksgiving to Easter, when tourists come south to escape cold weather. But this isn't necessarily the ideal time for a scouting trip to Belize, because prices are higher and hotels are busier.

Late spring is a good time to come, since hotel prices drop after Easter and there's usually little rain, though it can be hot inland. Water visibility is excellent, and many flowers and trees are in full bloom. Summer and fall are a part of the "rainy season," but unless you're very un-lucky, this doesn't mean that it rains all the time. You may get rain for an hour or two each day, often at night or in the early morning, and other-wise there's plenty of sun. The landscape is green and lush. However, it can be very humid and hot. September and October are prime tropical storm months, but the chances of a hurricane are low. These are the slowest months of the year for tourism, and some hotels offer steep discounts or free nights, although a few hotels and restaurants are closed during this time.

> In recent years, weather patterns in Belize, perhaps reflecting changes in global patterns, have been less predictable than in the past. It has been dry in the rainy season and rainy during the win-ter and early spring.

In recent years, weather patterns in Belize, perhaps reflecting changes in global patterns, have been less predictable than in the past. It has been dry in the rainy season and rainy during the winter and early spring.

PACKING

Belize is a very casual country. You don't need evening clothes or even a coat and tie or other U.S.-style business dress. You'll live in T-shirts, shorts, and loose-fitting slacks, skirts, and shirts. A really dressy occa-sion for men might require a guayabera or long-sleeved shirt and long pants, for women, a simple skirt or dress.

Leave all your fancy jewelry and Rolex watches at home. They will impress only a thief. Also leave your rain gear behind. It will probably rain, but raincoats will just make you sweat. Here are some other ideas for your packing list:

- U.S. currency in smaller bills, your ATM card, a credit card or two, and travelers checks.
- Lightweight cotton clothes or quick-drying cotton/synthetic blends.
- Comfortable walking shoes. Consider light boots for hiking and sandals for the beach.
- Extra swimsuits.
- Maps, guidebooks, and reading material. If available at all in Belize, these will cost more than back home and may be old editions.

• Cap or hat—be sure it's one that won't blow off in windy conditions on the water.

• Sunglasses—the darker, the better.

• Small flashlight with extra batteries, baggies in various sizes, a roll of duct tape, a large garbage bag, a pen and writing pad, and a Swiss Army–style knife. With these, you can go anywhere and do anything.

• Your favorite snacks—some American and international brands are available in Belize, but they are expensive.

• Extra film and a camera battery, or the digital equivalent—you'll shoot many more photos in Belize than you think you will. Film is readily available in Belize, but it's expensive.

• Health kit consisting of your prescription medicines, plus aspirin, insect spray with 30 percent DEET, Cactus Juice Eco-Safe insect repellent for sandflies, sunscreen, Pepto-Bismol or other tummy medicine, bandages, sunburn lotion, toilet tissue, moist wipes, seasickness pills, and other over-the-counter medicines you think you'll need.

Optional:

• Battery-operated radio, if coming during tropical storm/hurricane season (June–November).

• Snorkel mask—you can rent snorkel and diving gear in Belize, but rental masks often don't fit well.

• Fishing gear.

• Head lamp, if you are going caving or river cave tubing.

• A cotton sweater or light jacket may be needed in the winter, especially on the water or in the higher elevations of the Mountain Pine Ridge.

MONEY

Bring a combination of credit cards, your ATM card, cash in U.S. currency (mostly $20 bills and smaller), and travelers checks. Visa and MasterCard are accepted at most hotels and some restaurants, shops, and tour operations. American Express is also accepted at some establishments, but Discover is rarely accepted. Some places levy a surcharge, usually 3 percent to 5 percent, if you pay with a credit card instead of cash. In addition, many credit card issuers add a currency conversion fee when you use your credit card outside your home country, typically 2 percent to 3 percent.

About a dozen Belize Bank ATMs around the country accept foreign-issued ATM cards on the PLUS and CIRRUS networks. Banks in Belize and your home country will charge a few dollars in fees for each withdrawal, so it's best to withdraw larger amounts, rather than make a series of small withdrawals. You'll get cash in Belize dollars. First Caribbean Bank (formerly Barclay's), which has branches in Belize City, Belmopan, and Dangriga, also accepts ATM cards issued outside Belize. Note that there are no ATMs that accept foreign cards in either Placencia or Caye Caulker. Most banks will also provide a cash advance on your Visa or MasterCard for a fee of US$5–15, plus any fees or interest charged by your bank.

Now that you've got the facts, remember: You don't need to exchange money in Belize. U.S. dollars are accepted everywhere at the rate of two Belize dollars to one U.S. dollar. When paying in U.S. dollars, you often will get change in a combination of U.S. and Belize

Advice Fit for a King

Emory King is Belize's best-known expat. An American shipwrecked in Belize in 1954, Emory decided to make the country his permanent home. He became a Belizean citizen, a successful businessman, and the author of 14 books on Belize. Here are a few words of his wisdom for those contemplating retirement or relocation in his adopted homeland.

King advises the following for a potential retiree or other expat in Belize:

1. If you qualify, consider Belize's Qualified Retired Persons program.

2. Come down first and spend at least a month here visiting each district, talking to people, and getting a feel for the place.

3. You will soon find out that Belize is not a cheap place to live. We have plenty of poor people here. We don't need any more. People trying to stretch their Social Security or other meager income should try Mexico or somewhere

else. You can't enjoy life on a shoe-string in Belize.

4. Understand that there are no laws governing real-estate agents. No licenses, no examinations, no bonds. Any jerk who says, "I am a real-estate agent," is one. So, be very careful about buying land.

5. Avoid anyone who tells you he is friendly with someone in the government who can get you permits, licenses, etc. for the payment of graft.

These last few years, the level of dishonesty has risen alarmingly in this country. And, worse, the idea seems to have acceptance in the society. Some say it's perfectly OK to lie, cheat, and steal from tourists, foreigners, investors—because they are rich and they only come here to swindle us out of our heritage, anyway. So, as they say, "When thief thief from thief, God laugh."

Otherwise, Belize is still the delightful place it always was.

currencies. When quoted a price, be sure it's clear whether it's U.S. or Belize dollars by asking politely, "Is that 20 *Belize* dollars?" Most hotels, car rental companies, and tour operators post rates in U.S. dollars. Restaurants and shops almost always price in Belize dollars. If you decide to exchange money, a *casa de cambio* (currency exchange) will usually give you a slightly better exchange rate than a bank. The rate can be 2.05 to 2.15 to one or higher, but this rate varies with demand for U.S. dollars. Canadian dollars, Euros, and other foreign currencies are rarely accepted in Belize, although banks in Belize City may exchange them. In mid-2005, the government was considering eliminating or restricting private currency exchange offices.

Travelers checks are accepted at most hotels and at businesses frequented by tourists. You sometimes get a slightly lower rate on travelers checks than cash, around BZ$1.98 to US$1.

INFORM YOURSELF

Before you come, it's a good idea to read about Belize in everything from magazines to guidebooks, such as the newly updated *Moon Handbooks Belize* (see *Suggested Reading* in the *Resources* chapter for recommendations on guidebooks). Get the ITMB *Belize Traveller's Map* and familiarize yourself with the country's geography. If you are driving, get the latest edition of Emory King's *Driver's Guide to Belize*.

Arriving in Belize

ENTRY REQUIREMENTS

To enter Belize, you *must* have a valid passport with at least six months left before expiration. Visas are not required for citizens of the United States, Canada, the United Kingdom, the European Union, Australia, New Zealand, Norway, Hong Kong, Mexico, Venezuela, and Caricom (Caribbean community) countries. Citizens of these countries enter on a tourist card issued upon arrival.

Visas are required of citizens of most other countries. In countries where there is no Belize embassy or consulate, the British High Commission (embassy) usually handles Belize affairs. The visa application fee is BZ$200 (US$100), except for citizens of the People's Republic of China, Pakistan, Bangladesh, and Sri Lanka, who must pay a whopping US$2,000 for a visa. Note that citizens of the following countries currently require not only a visa, but clearance from the Belize director of immigration to enter the country: Bolivia, the People's Republic of China, Colombia, Cuba, Ecuador, Egypt, India, Iran, Iraq, Israel, Jordan, Lebanon, Libya, Nigeria, Pakistan, Palestine, Peru, Sri Lanka, Syria, and United Arab Emirates.

You should also have an onward or return ticket (air or bus). Belize officials rarely require this, but some airlines do. In theory, you also need to demonstrate that you have the means to support yourself while in the country—either US$60 a day in cash or a credit card. But again, unless you look completely disreputable, Belize immigration officials won't ask you about this.

If you are traveling with your children but without their other parent, you should also have a notarized statement from that parent allowing the children to be taken outside their home country. You may never be asked to show this document, but it's important to have it—just in case.

Entry to Belize is granted for up to 30 days. Extensions can be obtained at government offices in Belize City, Belmopan, Corozal Town, Dangriga, and elsewhere for US$25 monthly for the first three months and then US$50 per month for up to a total of 12 months.

When leaving Belize by air, if you have been in Belize for more than 24 hours, there is a US$35 exit tax that must be paid in cash in either Belize or U.S. dollars if it was not included in your airline ticket price. Most airlines flying to Belize now include the exit tax in your ticket price. Leaving by land, you pay US$18.75 exit tax. Save your receipt, as the conservation fee part (US$3.75) of the total border fee can be used to reduce your air exit tax. If you're leaving by boat, the only exit charge is US$3.75.

TRANSPORTATION

Five international airlines fly to Belize from the United States: American, Continental, Delta, TACA, and US Air. All international flights arrive at Philip S. W. Goldson International Airport in Ladyville, about nine miles north of Belize City, perhaps the only airport in the world with a mahogany ceiling. The airport is small but fairly modern, having opened in 1990. A new domestic terminal area opened in late 1998. This airport also has domestic flights to all parts of the country, but you'll save up to 50 percent on domestic fares by flying from the old Municipal Airport in Belize City. Taxi fare from the International Airport to

© Lan Sluder

Cessna Caravans and other small planes are used to get around quickly in Belize.

any point in Belize City, including the Municipal Airport, is US$20 for up to four people. Ride only in official taxis with green license plates. There is no bus service from the International Airport to Belize City, though you can hike about two miles to the Northern Highway and flag down a bus there.

In Belize, your visit will probably involve a combination of several types of transportation. You'll fly or take water taxis to island destinations. For your mainland destinations, bus travel is the cheapest option, but having your own rental car is the best way to see the most in the least time. Taxis are available in Belize City and in towns around the country. Shuttle vans serve some visitor destinations, such as San Ignacio. The four main highways in Belize—Northern Highway, Western Highway, Southern Highway, and Hummingbird Highway—are paved and fairly well-signed.

The two domestic air carriers in Belize are Tropic Air and Maya Island Air. From their hubs in Belize City, both serve most of the major visitor destinations, including San Pedro, Placencia, Corozal Town, and Punta Gorda, along with Flores in Guatemala.

Bus travel is a bargain in Belize, with frequent and inexpensive service on main routes. Because of consolidation, Novelo's and its subsidiaries offer the only national bus service. As of press time, the company was being reorganized beacuse of financial problems. (For detailed information on all your travel options, see the *Travel and Transportation* chapter.)

CUSTOMS AND IMMIGRATION

After your airplane taxis to the Goldson International Airport terminal building, you disembark the old-fashioned way down a set of stairs. You cross the tarmac and enter the immigration and customs area. Most days, you feel the humidity right away.

The immigration officer will look at your passport and usually ask the purpose of your visit and how long you are staying. You can be granted a visitor's entry permit (tourist card) of up to 30 days, but that's not automatic. If you say you are staying 10 days, the officer may grant only that period or two weeks at most. If you think there's any chance you may want to stay a little longer than your current reservations, be generous about estimating the time you'll stay. The officer will then stamp your passport and enter the arrival date. From here, you move to a small baggage claim area and then go through customs. Belize now has a Green/Red customs system. If you have nothing to declare, you can go through the Green line, although an officer may still ask to see inside your bags.

Customs and immigration officers are generally courteous and efficient, but like government officials in most countries, they are not known for being overly friendly. Treat them with respect, and you'll be treated similarly. Do not even think of offering a bribe. That is not how things work in Belize. The entire immigration and customs process usually takes from 15 minutes to half an hour.

After your bags pass customs, you can go into the main airport lobby or out to the taxi or rental car area. Porters are available to assist with bags, if necessary. If you are continuing on a domestic flight, move quickly to the Maya or Tropic domestic check-in area, as the carriers use small airplanes and they fill up quickly.

The rectangular passenger lobby, which usually bustles with people, has a Belize Bank office (but no ATM), a few tourist shops, and some airline ticket counters. Upstairs to your left are bathrooms (fairly clean) and a restaurant. There is another restaurant in the new terminal section. No luggage storage lockers are available at the airport. The Embassy Hotel, just across the airport parking lot, will keep left luggage for a small charge.

Taxis are available right outside the airport passenger lobby. Rental car kiosks are beyond the taxi line in the airport parking lot. Next to the line of rental car kiosks is a Belize Telecommunications Ltd. office, where you can rent cell phones for US$5 a day.

SAFETY PRECAUTIONS

Most visitors to Belize feel quite safe. Unlike in some other countries in the region, the police in Belize, though not always well-trained, make an effort to control crime and bring criminals to justice. Thanks to their British heritage, most Belizeans expect police to solve crimes and are outraged when they don't.

Nonetheless, Belize City has a reputation—probably worse than the reality—as a crime center. While street crime, gangs, and drugs are real problems for the city, visitors are rarely affected. The Belize government works hard to stop crime against tourists. More than 50 tourist police are on patrol, mostly in Belize City. Thanks to a rapid justice program, anyone caught committing a crime against a tourist can expect to be tried, sentenced, and, if convicted, sent to jail in the same day. Even so, in Belize City, with the exception of the Fort George section where tourist police regularly patrol, you should take cabs at night and avoid walking around alone or even in small groups.

> While street crime, gangs, and drugs are real problems for the city, visitors are rarely affected.

Petty thefts do occasionally occur, especially in resort areas, where "rich" tourists are magnets for thieves. Use standard travel precautions, such as putting your valuables in the hotel safe and keeping your cash and passport in a hidden pocket.

Many Belizeans smoke "Belize breeze"—marijuana—and some use other drugs, including crack cocaine, but visitors are advised not to partake. Belize's drug laws are strict, and the Hattieville Ramada, the national jail, has been called one of the worst prisons in the world.

In 2004, the head of the Belize police department announced that police would no longer arrest or prosecute individuals for possession of a small amount of marijuana. Technically, however, possession is still illegal.

TAXES AND TIPPING

Belize has a national sales tax of 9 percent, plus a 2 percent environmental tax, on most purchases, except some medicine and food items. The tax applies to restaurant meals, car rentals, dive and tour trips, and most other purchases you'll make in Belize. There is a hotel tax of 9 percent of the room rate.

Belizeans rarely tip, but they usually expect visitors to do so. At better restaurants, 10 percent to 15 percent is usually sufficient; at small local restaurants, you can leave loose change. Many hotels add a service charge of 5 percent to 15 percent, in which case there's no need to tip anything extra. Tip tour guides 5 percent to 10 percent of the tour amount. Don't tip taxi drivers or gas station attendants.

RESERVATIONS

If you're traveling in the high season (roughly Thanksgiving through Easter), it's a good idea to book ahead. This is especially wise for travel during the peak Christmas–New Year period, Easter week, and late January through March. But even during the busiest times of year, you can almost always find *some* place to stay in Belize without reservations, but the best—and best-value—places will often be fully booked. You don't want to spend all your time hunting for a room. Sleeping on the beach may sound romantic, but remember that the sandflies got there first.

In the off-season, you usually don't need reservations. Indeed, walk-in rates in resort areas such as Ambergris Caye are sometimes lower than even direct-booked Internet rates. Beachfront rooms that go for US$150 a night in season and US$100 off-season may cost you just US$75 as a walk-in. Of course, you run the risk that rooms may be in tight supply on a given night.

Sample Itineraries

How long should you plan to stay on your initial scouting trip? A week is not really long enough to see the highlights of the country; I recommend 10–14 days minimum. Belize is a small country, but getting from one place to another almost always takes longer than you think it will, thanks to bad roads, transportation delays, and, in many cases, the Belizean "go slow" attitude. Figure that a trip of 100 miles in Belize will take at least as long as a trip of 200 miles in the United States.

Where you go in Belize and how long you stay in each area depends in part on your preferences for a place to live. If, for example, you're dead set on living on or near the sea, you'll want to spend more of your time on the coast or cayes. On the other hand, if you're looking for a sizable tract of land, you'll want to allocate more time for inland areas, such as Cayo and Toledo Districts.

BASIC 10-DAY ITINERARY

Day 1: Fly into Belize City and spend the night. Most visitors think Belize City is the least appealing part of Belize. If you can put up with Belize City, you'll probably love the rest of Belize.

Day 2: Fly (20 minutes) or take a water taxi (1.25 hours) to Ambergris Caye. Relax and get on Belize time.

Day 3: Continue exploring San Pedro and the rest of the island.

Day 4: Return to Belize City and pick up a rental car. Drive to Corozal Town (two hours minimum).

Day 5: Continue exploring Corozal and Northern Belize.

Day 6: Drive to San Ignacio (about 3.5 hours from Corozal Town via the Barrel Boom shortcut).

Day 7: Continue exploring Cayo District.

Day 8: Drive to Placencia via Hummingbird Highway, Belize's most scenic route (about 3.5 hours).

Day 9: Continue exploring Placencia.

Day 10: Drive back to Belize City, stopping en route at Hopkins. Turn in rental car and fly home from the International Airport.

Optional Extensions:

1–2 Days: Hopkins/Sittee Point (can be added between Cayo and Placencia stops).

2–3 Days: Punta Gorda and Toledo District.

2–4 Days: Visit Caye Caulker; a remote caye, such as South Water; or an atoll, such as Glovers or Lighthouse.

IN-DEPTH 21-DAY ITINERARY

Day 1: Fly into Belize City and spend the night.

Day 2: Fly (20 minutes) or take a water taxi (1.25 hours) to Ambergris Caye. Relax and get on Belize time.

Days 3–4: Continue exploring San Pedro and the rest of the island.

Day 5: Water taxi to Caye Caulker and explore the island.

Day 6: Return to Belize City and pick up a rental car. Drive to Corozal Town (two hours minimum).

Days 7–9: Continue exploring Corozal and Northern Belize.

Say Hello to a Jaguar

You turn a corner on the trail. Suddenly, you're face to face with the biggest wildcat in the hemisphere. *Panthera onca. El Tigre.* Jaguar. You're two feet from 250 pounds of rippling muscle and raw power. Up close, the big cat's teeth look as big as Shaq's shoes. The jaguar growls, a deep, rumbling cough. Involuntarily, you jump back, thankful a strong but inconspicuous fence separates you and the jaguar. You're at the Belize Zoo, one of the smallest zoos in the world at just 29 acres, but arguably one of the best. It's been called "the finest zoo in the Americas south of the U.S."

Here, less than half an hour from Belize's unprepossessing capital of Belmopan, you can see more than 125 species of wild things native to Belize, including jaguars. The zoo has both the spotted and the rarer black versions; they look very different, but they are the same species. The spotted jaguar, a male, has been nicknamed C. T. Katun; the black jaguar is called Ellen.

Jaguars once roamed much of Central and South America, but today, they are endangered. Belize is one of the few remaining places where the jaguar still exists in sizable numbers. Estimates say that as many as 600 to 1,000 jaguars are in Belize's jungles, primarily the Maya Mountains and the Cockscomb Jaguar Preserve in Southern Belize, and in Orange Walk District in Northwest Belize.

At the Belize Zoo, you'll also see the four other wildcats of Belize: the puma, the margay, the ocelot, and the jaguarundi. Most of the animals are behind wire barriers under a canopy of subtropical trees. The zoo does not capture wild animals but instead provides a home for animals that have been orphaned, injured, born at the zoo, or sent there from other zoological institutions. The black jaguar, for example, came from a zoo in Texas, and the spotted one from Guatemala.

© Brooks Lambert-Sluder

black jaguar at the Belize Zoo

Day 10: Drive to San Ignacio (about 3.5 hours from Corozal Town via the Barrel Boom shortcut).

Days 11–12: Continue exploring Cayo District, including the Mountain Pine Ridge.

Day 13: Drive to Placencia via Hummingbird Highway, Belize's most scenic route (about 3.5 hours).

Days 14–15: Continue exploring Placencia.

Day 16: Drive south on Southern Highway to Punta Gorda.

Days 17–18: Continue exploring Punta Gorda and Toledo.

Day 19: Drive back up Southern Highway to Hopkins and explore.

Day 20: Drive the coastal road, exploring Gales Point and areas in rural Belize District.

Day 21: Drive back to Belize City, turn in rental car, and fly home from the International Airport.

Optional Extensions:

2–3 Days: Visit Tikal (after San Ignacio).

2–3 Days: Visit Chetumal and southern Mexico (after Corozal).

2–7 Days: Visit a remote caye, such as South Water or Glover's; or Turneffe or Lighthouse atoll.

Practicalities

ACCOMMODATIONS

Belize has more than 450 hotels, with about 5,000 total rooms. Most of these hotels are small, owner-operated places; about 70 percent have 10 or fewer rooms. Only two hotels have more than 100 rooms: the Princess Hotel and Casino and the Radisson Fort George, both in Belize City.

You can expect to find a variety of accommodations to fit almost any budget and preference. Among the uniquely Belizean accommodations are the so-called jungle lodges. These are mostly in remote areas, but despite the remote locations, you don't have to forgo life's little luxuries, such as cold beer, hot showers, and comfortable mattresses. The best of these places, including Chaa Creek and Ek' Tun in Cayo, Blancaneaux in the Mountain Pine Ridge, and Chan Chich and Lamanai Outpost in rural Orange Walk, are as good as any bush lodge in the world. Birding and wildlife-spotting around the lodges are usually excellent, and jungle lodges offer all the amenities you may want to enjoy after the day's adventures are done. Most, though not all, have bay thatch *cabañas* built with a nod to Maya-style construction but done up in much more luxury and style than traditional Maya cottages. While the top places are first class in every way, with rates to match—often US$150–300 or more a night in season—you don't have to pay much to get an authentic lodge experience. Places such as Clarissa Falls and Parrot's Nest, both in Cayo, are bargains at US$75 or less for a double.

Another delightful type of lodging in Belize are the casual and small seaside resorts. The best of these, such as Kitty's in Placencia—or, on the budget level, Tradewinds in Placencia Village—are sandy, barefoot spots, with a friendly Belizean feel you won't find in other parts of the Caribbean. A couple can spend a night at the beach for US$50–150.

All around Belize, you can find small places with clean, safe rooms at budget prices. The Trek Stop, Aguada Hotel, and Martha's Guesthouse in Cayo or Tipple Tree Beya Inn in Hopkins are examples. At these places, you can get a nice little room for US$30 or less.

> Whether the owners are Belizean, American, or Canadian, they're almost always friendly and helpful, as well as willing to sit down with you and help plan your day.

At the other end of the scale, for those who demand luxury, a whole wave of up-market hotels have sprung up Belize since the 1990s. No longer is it necessary to stay in a hotel with linoleum floors and mismatched furniture. On Ambergris Caye and other cayes, places such as Victoria House and private island resorts—including Cayo Espanto and Caye Chapel Island Resort—have rooms that could earn a spot in *Architectural Digest,* with rates of US$200–1,500 and up per night. On the mainland, Blancaneaux's villas are luxurious, as are the seafront villas (with furnishings imported from Bali) of Turtle Inn in Placencia. The Inn at Robert's Grove offers all the amenities, from tennis courts to rooftop whirlpool tubs. In a few areas, mainly San Pedro, you can enjoy the extra space of a condo-style unit at a regular hotel-style price. Villas at Banyan Bay and Banana Beach are great versions of the small condotels.

In between are all shapes and sizes of characteristic inns, mostly run by their owners. Many innkeepers struggle to earn a decent income, and they can't always afford to have the softest sheets or new TVs in each room. But whether the owners are Belizean, American, or Canadian, they're almost always friendly and helpful, as well as willing to sit down with you and help plan your day.

The following accommodations listings are a sample of what's available in each area of the country you might want to explore during your fact-finding trip. Note that hotel prices in Belize are almost always stated in U.S. dollars, so that's how they're presented here also.

Northern Cayes
Victoria House (Ambergris Caye)
If you want an upscale but casual resort, this quiet hideaway on 19 acres is just about perfect. Accommodations range from comfy motel-like rooms to thatch casitas to deluxe villas. Gorgeous beachside pool. Rates US$170–390 in season, with discounts off-season.
Coconut Dr. (P.O. Box 22, San Pedro); tel. 713/344-2340 or 800/247-5159; fax 713/224-3287; info@victoria-house.com; www.victoria-house.com

Villas at Banyan Bay (Ambergris Caye)
This 42-unit condotel has two-bedroom, two-bath apartments. Many of the guests are families. Kids love the big pool, and Dad and Mom

Trends Beachfront is a popular small hotel on Caye Caulker.

a view of the Caribbean from a third-floor suite at Banana Beach in San Pedro

go for the fully equipped kitchen. The beach is one of the best on the island. Rates start at US$175–195 off-season.
Coconut Dr. (P.O. Box 91, San Pedro); tel. 501/226-3739; fax 501/226-2766; banyanbay@btl.net; www.banyanbay.com

Banana Beach (Ambergris Caye)
Run by former Montanan Tim Jeffers, Banana Beach has just about everything to make your visit a success: genuinely friendly staff, smartly furnished one- to four-bedroom suites, affordable rooms, and a setting near one of the island's best beaches. US$114 for a room and up to US$557 for a deluxe seafront, four-bedroom suite in season, with lower rates off-season.
Coconut Dr. (P.O. Box 94, San Pedro); tel. 501/226-3890; fax 501/226-3891; bananas@btl.net; www.bananabeach.com

Ruby's (Ambergris Caye)
The favorite of many value-conscious visitors, Ruby's offers basic but clean rooms. Year-round rates: older rooms with fans, US$20–30

double; those in a newer concrete addition on the ocean side sport air conditioning and private baths and go for around US$50. Often full. Barrier Reef Dr. (P.O. Box 56, San Pedro); tel. 501/226-2063; rubys@btl.net; www.ambergriscaye.com/rubys

Iguana Reef Inn (Caye Caulker)

This is Caye Caulker's best hotel. The 12 suites have air-conditioning, Belizean furniture, queen beds, and local artwork. Considering the amenities, the rates—US$107–132 in season, a little lower May–November—are reasonable, and they include a continental breakfast. No children under 10.
P.O. Box 31, Caye Caulker; tel. 501/226-0213; fax 501/226-0087; iguanareef@btl.net; www.iguanareefinn.com

Tree Tops (Caye Caulker)

Tree Tops is beautifully run by Terry Creasy (who's British), his wife, Doris (who's from Germany), and their flock of Jack Russell terriers. Guest rooms are clean as a pin, decorated with mementos from Africa and elsewhere, and two gorgeous third-floor suites were added in 2004. The owners are helpful, and the rooms, at US$40–80 for a double, are well worth the money. Highly recommended.
P.O. Box 29, Caye Caulker; tel. 501/226-0240; fax 501/226-0115; treetopsbelize@direcway.com; www.treetopsbelize.com

Northern Belize

Corozal Bay Inn (Corozal Town)

Owners Doug and Maria Podzun (he's Canadian, she's Mexican) have built 10 new *cabañas,* painted in tropical colors with bay palm thatch roofs, air-conditioning and new 27-inch TVs with cable. They're just steps from the pool and the bay. Rates are US$80 for a double.
Corozal Bay Rd. (P.O. Box 1, Corozal Town); tel. 501/422-2691; fax 800/836-9188; relax@corozalbayinn.com; www.corozalbayinn.com

Copa Banana Guesthouse (Corozal Town)

If you're in town shopping for property around Corozal, you couldn't do much better than this banana-yellow guesthouse, new in 2004. You can cook meals in a common kitchen, and the owners even run a real-estate business, Belize North Real Estate, Ltd. US$55 per night, US$350 per week. The apartments are also available for longer-term stays.

409 Corozal Bay Rd. (P.O. Box 226, Corozal Town); tel. 501/422-0284; fax 501/422-2710; relax@copabanana.bz; www.copabanana.bz

Casablanca by the Sea (Consejo)
This 10-room inn on Chetumal Bay is the place for those who just want to relax and do nothing for awhile. The rooms feature hand-carved mahogany doors and saltillo tile floors. US$75–90 for a double in season, with discounts June–August.
Consejo Village (P.O. Box 212, Corozal Town); tel. 501/423-1018; fax 501/423-1003; info@casablanca-bythesea.com; www.casablanca-bythesea.com

The Last Resort (Copper Bank)
At the mouth of Laguna Secca and the Bay of Corozal, this budget lodge has small thatch cabins with kitchenettes for US$17.50 for a double or US$12.50 for rooms in simple huts with outhouses.
Copper Bank; tel. 501/606-1585

Chan Chich Lodge (Orange Walk District)
Chan Chich is one of the classic jungle lodges of the world. It's run by Barry Bowen, a fifth-generation Belizean who also owns the Coca-Cola bottling franchise and brews Belikin beer. Built literally on top of a Maya plaza, the lodge has 12 thatch-roof *cabañas*. Birding is terrific, and you may even see a jaguar. US$165–250 for a double. Meal packages are US$70 per person.
Gallon Jug (P.O. Box 37, Belize City); tel./fax 501/223-4419; info@chanchich.com; www.chanchich.com

Cayo District
The Lodge at Chaa Creek (San Ignacio)
The Flemings—English Mick and American Lucy—started Chaa Creek in 1980. They've expanded and fine-tuned their operation until it has become one of the best-run lodges in all of Central America. The beautiful grounds cover 330 acres on the Macal River. The 19 large rooms in whitewash-and-thatch duplex cottages, plus up-market suites, have high-quality furnishings. The spa here is the best in Belize. US$170–280 for a double (meal plan US$44 per person). For those on a budget, the Macal River Safari Camp has 10 small "cabinettes" for US$110 including meals.

Chial Rd. (P.O. Box 53, San Ignacio); tel. 501/824-2037; fax 501/824-2501; reservations@chaacreek.com; www.chaacreek.com

San Ignacio Resort Hotel (San Ignacio)
This is the closest thing to an international-style hotel in San Ignacio. The location is convenient, the deluxe rooms are comfortable, the pool is relaxing, and the Running W Steakhouse sizzles. A branch of the Princess Casino adjoins the hotel. US$110 for a double.
18 Buena Vista St. (P.O. Box 33, San Ignacio); tel. 501/824-2034; fax 501/824-2134; sanighot@btl.net; www.sanignaciobelize.com

Aguada (Santa Elena)
This little motel is a real find. You can stay here in a clean, modern room with air-conditioning for US$30–45 for a double. Eighteen rooms, swimming pool, bar, and a good restaurant. Owners Bill and Cathie Butcher—he's American, she's Belizean—and their daughter are doing a super job.
Aguada St., Santa Elena; tel. 501/804-3609; aguada@btl.net; www.aguadahotel.com

The Trek Stop (San Ignacio)
American expats Judy and John Yaeger opened this 22-acre spot in 1998. Budget travelers find cheap sleeps in cozy, neat-as-a-pin cabins (US$20 double), with outdoor composting toilets. Larger cabins with private bathrooms were added in 2004 (US$35 double). Camping permitted.
Benque Rd., San José Succotz Village; tel. 501/823-2265; susa@btl.net; www.thetrekstop.com

Blancaneaux Lodge (Mountain Pine Ridge)
Director Francis Ford Coppola ought to win a sixth Oscar for his incredible lodge. Stay in the villas if you can: They have two huge bedrooms, a screened deck area with views of the Privassion River, tiled Japanese-style baths, and a great room with kitchen. The regular *cabañas,* though less spacious and luxurious, are pleasant and run US$155–210 in season ($120–185 May 1–Nov. 1); as opposed to US$355 for double occupancy or US$415 for four people for a villa in season (US$305 off-season double and $360 quad).

Mountain Pine Ridge (P.O. Box B, Central Farm, Cayo); tel. 501/824-3878; fax 501/824-3919; info@blancaneaux.com; www.blancaneaux-lodge.com

Southern Belize
Hamanasi (Hopkins)
On about 17 acres with 400 feet of beach frontage and a stunning pool, Hamanasi has rooms, tree houses, and condo-style villas. The owners, Americans Dana and David Krauskopf, look as if they just stepped out of a *Travel and Leisure* magazine spread. US$170–300, depending on season and type of room.
Sittee Point (P.O. Box 265, Dangriga); 501/520-7073 or 877/552-3483; info@hamanasi.com; www.hamanasi.com

Tipple Tree Beya Inn (Hopkins)
Looking for an inexpensive little place on the beach? This is it! Rooms are simple but clean. With private bath you'll pay US$40, or US$20 for shared bath. A larger unit for up to four is US$65.
Hopkins (P.O. Box 206, Dangriga); tel./fax 501/520-7006; info@tippletree.com; www.tippletree.com

Inn at Robert's Grove (Placencia)
This upscale seaside hotel on 22 acres is owned by ex-New Yorkers Risa and Robert Frackman. The resort delivers the entire package: beach, tennis, three pools, fly-fishing center, dive shop, spa, tours, and good food. The rooms are sunny and the suites are a delight. US$179–450 in season, with discounts off-season.
Seine Bight; tel. 501/523-3565; fax 501/523-3567 or 800/565-9757; information-request@robertsgrove.com; www.robertsgrove.com

Kitty's Place (Placencia)
It's not the fanciest hotel in Placencia, but Kitty's is just about the perfect Belize seaside resort. It's a barefoot, casual, laid-back, and totally delightful spot. The 350-foot-long stretch of khaki beach is one of the peninsula's best. US$189 for a beachfront cottage; other digs are US$40–$165. Off-season, rates drop a bit.
Placencia; tel. 501/523-3227; fax 800/886-4265; info@kittysplace; www.kittysplace.com

A Day in the Jungle, A Night at the Bar

At Belize's jungle lodges, you can stalk the wild jaguar, the neon blue morpho, and the rare scarlet macaw by day—then enjoy a hot shower, a good meal, and a cold Belikin or Lighthouse beer afterward.

Here are my picks for the best jungle lodges in Belize:

1. Chan Chich Lodge, Gallon Jug, Orange Walk District
2. Lodge at Chaa Creek, near San Ignacio, Cayo District
3. Blancaneaux Lodge, Mountain Pine Ridge, Cayo District
4. Lamanai Outpost Lodge, near Indian Church Village, Orange Walk District
5. Ek' Tun Lodge, near San Ignacio, Cayo District
6. duPlooy's, near San Ignacio, Cayo District
7. Jaguar Paw, near Belmopan, Cayo District
8. Ian Anderson's Caves Branch Adventure Camp, near Belmopan, Cayo District
9. Lodge at Big Falls, Big Falls, Toledo District
10. Pook's Hill Lodge, near Belmopan, Cayo District
11. Black Rock Lodge, near San Ignacio, Cayo District
12. Mama Noots Jungle Lodge, near Dangriga, Stann Creek District

Tradewinds (Placencia)

If you want a beachfront cottage but don't want to pay the higher prices north of the village, Tradewinds is your best bet. The seven pastel-colored cabins on the beach at the south end of Placencia village are cute as a bug's ear. At US$65 in season and US$40 off-season, they're a good value. Placencia Village; tel. 501/523-3122; trdewndpla@btl.net; www.beautifulbelize.com/tradewindshotel

El Pescador PG (Punta Gorda)

The best digs in Toledo are at El Pescador PG. It's primarily a fishing lodge, but you can enjoy it even if you don't fish. Set on a serious hill on 470 acres above the Rio Grande, 12 cottages are nicely outfitted with tile floors and air-conditioning. The lodge also offers pool access, meal packages for US$55, and fishing packages. Rates are US$180 for a single or double November 1 through June 15, and US$140 for all other times of the year.

Five miles north of Punta Gorda (P.O. Box 135); tel. 501/722-0050 or 800/242-2017; fax 501/722-0051; jscott@elpescador.com; www.elpescadorpg.com

Sea Front Inn (Punta Gorda)

Larry and Carol Smith, U.S. expats who have lived in PG for more than 20 years, built a striking four-story building across the road from the sea. Rooms have air-conditioning and cable TV. Rates US$60–75. Front St. (P.O. Box 20, Punta Gorda); tel: 501/722-2300; fax 501/722-2682; info@seafrontinn.com; www.seafrontinn.com

FOOD

I don't know who started the rumor that you can't get a good meal in Belize. The fact is, you can eat gloriously well and at modest prices. Rice and beans is the quintessential Belizean dish, but these are not the rice and beans your momma used to fix—unless she's from Belize or perhaps New Orleans. Beans and rice in Belize are spicy and smoky, with plenty of *recado* (also known as *achiote*) and other seasonings, perhaps flavored with salt pork and some onions and peppers and cooked in coconut milk. Usually these are served with a chunk of stew chicken, fish, or pork. The whole thing might cost just US$5 in a nice restaurant. If you're not happy in Belize, you're probably not getting enough rice and beans.

Along the coast and on the cayes, seafood is as fresh as the salt air. In season (mid-June to mid-February), spiny lobster—grilled, broiled, steamed, or even fried—is fairly inexpensive and good. But a big fillet of snapper or grouper, prepared over a grill with lime juice, is just as tasty and even cheaper. Conch, in season from October to June, is delicious grilled or stewed in lime juice as ceviche, but I like it best in fritters—chopped and fried in a light batter.

Every ethnic group in multicultural Belize has its own taste treats. Among them: *Sere* and *hoodut,* one of the best-known Garifuna dishes, consists of fish cooked in coconut milk with plantains. "Boil up" is a Creole favorite, fish boiled with plantains, yams, and potatoes and served with a tomato sauce and boiled bread. The Maya dish most popular with visitors is *pibil,* pork and other meats seasoned, wrapped in banana leaves, and cooked slowly in an underground oven. Of course, with Mexico next door, Belize has a wide variety of Mexican dishes, including tamales, burritos, *garnaches* (corn tortillas fried and topped with beans, salsa, and cheese), and *panades* (deep-fried tortillas filled with fish).

A few restaurants, such as Macy's in Belize City, serve local game, including iguana, venison, and *gibnut,* a rabbitlike rodent dubbed "the Royal Rat" because it was once served to Queen Elizabeth II.

Most of the beef in Belize is grass-fed and chewy, although you can get an excellent steak in Belize at El Divino in San Pedro and elsewhere. But the pork is heavenly. Pork chops are tender and flavorful—and the bacon is a little different from most I've had, but delicious with fresh farm eggs. Only brown eggs are legal in Belize, by the way, to protect Belize's chicken farmers.

For breakfast, fruit is the thing: fresh pineapple, mango, papaya, watermelon, and oranges. With fry jacks (a sort of fried biscuit, the Belizean version of beignets) and a cup of Guatemalan or Gallon Jug Estates Belizean coffee, you're all set for the day.

For the most part, Belize dining isn't fancy, but even Belize is branching out into some newer worlds of cuisine. Cayo has Sri Lankan dining, and on Ambergris Caye, you'll find excellent Thai, French-Thai fusion, and even sushi. There are a number of Italian restaurants, and Chinese restaurants are everywhere.

To drink, there's nothing more refreshing than fresh lime and watermelon juice. Belikin beer may not be up to the high standards of some of the beers of Mexico and Costa Rica, but it's good enough for most of us.

Iguana Stew and Cowfoot Soup

Belizeans will eat almost anything. At least, it seems that way sometimes. Among the taste treats you can enjoy in Belize are:

Cowfoot soup: To make cowfoot soup, you start with, yes, cow's feet. You boil them for as long as you can stand it, then add potatoes, okra, carrots, and seasonings. It's served with white rice and it's actually pretty good, if you can get by the big hoof in your bowl.

Roast *gibnut:* The paca, or *gibnut* in local parlance, is a brown rodent about the size of a big rabbit. It got its nickname, the Royal Rat, because it was served to Queen Elizabeth when she visited Belize. It tastes a little like venison.

Seaweed shake: Some Belizeans believe seaweed shakes restore a man's virility and can cure just about anything that ails you. Maybe so, but even dosed up with sweetened condensed milk, mangoes, vanilla, cinnamon, and other spices, it still tastes like seaweed.

Stewed iguana: Start by catching, skinning, and cleaning a green iguana. Wash it thoroughly in vinegar and lime. Add carrots, onions, pepper, red *recado* (*achiote* or annatto with herbs), and other seasonings. Tastes like—you guessed it—chicken.

Northern Cayes
Capricorn (Ambergris Caye)
Most people consider this the best restaurant on the island. The founders sold the restaurant and small resort in 2003, but so far, the quality has held up. The seaside setting is cozily romantic but not overdone. You can dine on the veranda or inside. Capricorn can be reached via the golf cart path or by water taxi. Reservations are essential. Very expensive.
About three miles north of San Pedro; 501/226-2809

Papi's Diner (Ambergris Caye)
This is a great local find. There's no water view here, and the atmosphere is a bit like being on someone's back porch, but just about everything on the menu is good—and the prices (fried chicken for US$4 or grilled fish for US$9, both served with a potato and steamed veggies) are a bargain.
Middle St. behind Seven Seas; 501/226-2047

Antojitos San Telmos (Ambergris Caye)
It's just a joint, but a great joint, with snacks such as tacos and burritos for almost nothing.
South on Coconut Dr.; 501/226-2921

Rasta Pasta (Caye Caulker)
Formerly on Ambergris Caye and then in Placencia, Maralyn Gill's Rasta Pasta has always served interesting and delicious fare. Conch fritters are a favorite here. Moderate prices.
Front St.; 501/206-0356

Habañeros (Caye Caulker)
This is Caye Caulker's most upscale dining, and also some of the best. Great fajitas. Moderate/expensive.
Middle St.; 501/226-0487

Northern Belize
Tony's (Corozal Town)
This restaurant in the *palapa* at Tony's Inn is a pleasant place to enjoy the breeze from the bay. The fajitas are the way to go here.
South End; 501/422-2055

Patti's Bistro (Corozal Town)

At Patti's, you can enjoy a huge, filling dinner with multiple appetizers, drinks, and main dishes for almost nothing. Rice and beans with chicken or pork are BZ$6 (US$3), and a fried chicken dinner with mashed potatoes is BZ$6.50 (US$3.25). It's next to the undertakers'. But don't worry—the food is good and a real bargain.
4th Ave.; 501/607-1417

Cactus Plaza (Corozal Town)

Service here is friendly; the tacos, *salbutes,* tostadas, and other Mexican dishes are delicious; and the prices are right—from US$.25 (yes, that's cents) for a small *salbute.* At night, there's a lively bar and club upstairs.
6 6th St. S.; 501/422-0394

Cayo District
Sanny's (San Ignacio)

Considered the best restaurant in San Ignacio, Sanny's serves steaks, chicken, and pork, all with a spicy Belizean twist.
Pelican Ln.; 501/824-2988

Hannah's (San Ignacio)

This is a very popular spot and for a good reason: the delicious food. The owner, originally from Zimbabwe, grows many of the ingredients on his farm.
5 Burns Ave.; 501/824-3014

Serandib (San Ignacio)

You wouldn't except to find a Sri Lankan restaurant in Cayo, but this one has been here for years serving great curries, seafood, and Belizean dishes.
27 Burns Ave.; 501/824-2302

Southern Belize
Bistro at Maya Beach Hotel (Placencia)

Opened in 2004, the restaurant at this small hotel has quickly become one of the most talked about in Southern Belize. You'll enjoy the interesting presentations and sophisticated dishes, such as five-onion cioppino and cocoa-dusted pork on risotto.
Maya Beach; 501/520-8040

Wendy's (Placencia)

There's no atmosphere here, and on a hot night, it can be stuffy despite the air-conditioning. But the service is friendly as lime pie. Wendy's serves simple but oh-so-tasty items such as grilled fish, and even with some beer, you'll pay well under US$10.

Placencia Rd. in Placencia Village, near the gas station

Omar's (Placencia)

The best cheap restaurant in the village, Omar's serves hot and delicious seafood and other local dishes for a few dollars. A good spot for breakfast. Inexpensive.

On the sidewalk across from St. John's Church and school; 501/ 523-3236

Earth Runnins (Punta Gorda)

This hangout is especially popular with expats, and it has good food at moderate prices.

11 Main St., 501/722-2007

Emery's (Punta Gorda)

Fish is the specialty here, and some people think this has the best and most consistent food in town. Inexpensive/moderate.

North St., near the gas station

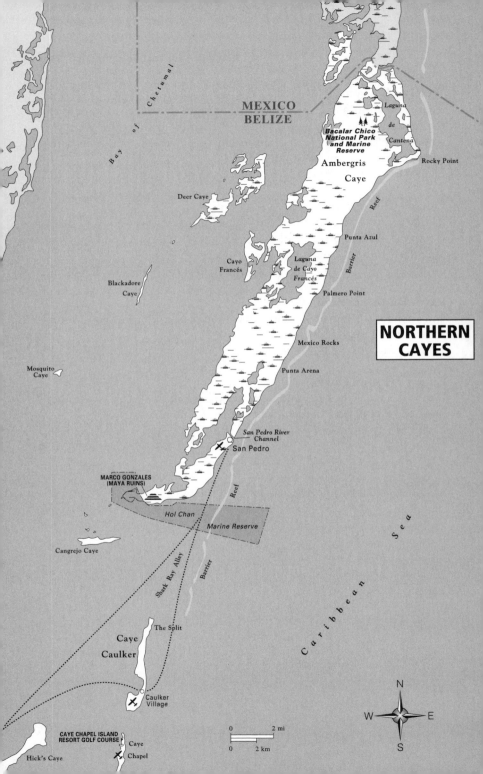

NORTHERN CAYES

MEXICO
BELIZE

Bay of Chetumal

Laguna de Cantena

Bacalar Chico National Park and Marine Reserve

Ambergris Caye

Rocky Point

Deer Caye

Reef

Punta Azul

Barrier

Cayo Francés

Laguna de Cayo Francés

Blackadore Caye

Palmero Point

Mexico Rocks

Punta Arena

Mosquito Caye

San Pedro River Channel

San Pedro

MARCO GONZALES
(MAYA RUINS)

Reef

Hol Chan

Marine Reserve

Cangrejo Caye

Shark Ray Alley

Barrier

Caribbean Sea

The Split

Caye Caulker

Caulker Village

CAYE CHAPEL ISLAND
RESORT GOLF COURSE

Caye Chapel

Hick's Caye

0   2 mi

0   2 km

N
W   E
S

Northern Cayes

Even if you're a world traveler with a bazillion frequent-flyer miles, chances are you'll be impressed by your first visit to the islands of Belize. Set in some of the clearest waters you can imagine, with underwater visibility up to 200 feet or more, scores of travel-poster islands dot the Caribbean along Belize's 190-mile-long barrier reef. The reef is an undersea rainforest of incredible diversity, with wildly colored corals and tropical fish, swooping manta rays, and watchful barracudas.

Ambergris Caye and Caye Caulker are by far the largest and most populated of Belize's cayes, and they attract 99 percent of visitors and expats to Belize's islands. Some other islands are just spits of coral and sand, here today and possibly gone tomorrow, after a tropical storm. Others are mangrove islands. Three—Turneffe, Lighthouse, and Glovers—are Pacific-style atolls, with some of the best diving in the entire Caribbean.

Climate

Ambergris Caye, Caye Caulker, and other northern cayes, though only a few miles from the mainland, enjoy a different microclimate from Belize City, with less rain. In the summer, temperatures often rise into the

90s, with lows in the 70s. In winter, temperatures are cooler: typically in the 80s by day and the 60s by night. A near-constant breeze from the water makes it seem cooler, however, and in winter, a long-sleeved shirt or light sweater may feel good, especially after you've lived on the island for awhile. Occasionally, during the late fall and winter, "Northers" can blow in, bringing several days of rain and rough seas. Like the rest of Northern Belize, Ambergris Caye has a dry season in the spring, from around March to early June. Winds usually kick up during this time, but water visibility is at its peak. Tropical storm season begins in June and runs through November, yet during most of this period, the weather is pleasant, and it's fairly rare to get rain for more than a few hours at a time. On average, Ambergris Caye gets about 50 inches of rain a year, about the same as Atlanta, Georgia.

Hurricanes are relatively rare, but Hurricane Mitch gave the island a scare in 1998, and Hurricane Keith in 2000 did as much as US$150 million in damage on Ambergris Caye alone. Besides Keith, the most devastating hurricanes to hit the island were in 1931, 1942, and 1961.

Ambergris Caye

Ambergris Caye is the largest and most populous of Belize's islands. About 24 miles long and four miles across at its widest point, with a population of around 7,000, it gets more tourists and has more tourism development than any other part of the country. It's also home to the largest concentration of foreign expats, with estimates of around 1,000 on the island, and more arriving daily. Don't worry, though, everything is relative, and this is Belize. While Ambergris Caye—locally pronounced "am-BURR-griss" or sometimes "am-BURR-jess"—is no longer the sleepy island of a couple of thousand people it was 25 years ago, the tallest building is still just three stories—no higher than a coconut palm. Except for some cobblestone paving near the airstrip and in town, the streets are all sand. More cars and trucks have been brought to the caye, but golf carts, bikes, and walking are still the main ways to get around.

American residents say that, real-estate costs aside, they can live on the island for less than what it costs them to live in the United States. While it's not for everyone, it offers the closest thing to "American-style" living that you'll find in Belize.

Expats are attracted to Ambergris Caye for its friendly, laid-back lifestyle, combined with a resort atmosphere with plenty of good restaurants, bars, and shops—and, of course, lots of activities on the Caribbean, from snorkeling and diving to sailboarding, sailing, and sportfishing. The island is usually among the first stops for those thinking about relocating to Belize, even if they end up choosing another area. Real-estate and other costs here are among the highest in Belize, but the level of services is also higher than in many other parts of the country. American residents say that, real-

the grounds of Portofino, a laid-back beach resort on North Ambergris Caye

estate costs aside, they can live on the island for less than what it costs them to live in the United States. While it's not for everyone, it offers the closest thing to "American-style" living that you'll find in Belize.

THE LAY OF THE LAND

The island is shaped something like a banana, hanging from Mexico's Yucatán peninsula. If not for a narrow channel at its northern edge, dug by the ancient Maya, Ambergris would be an extension of the peninsula instead of an island. Much of the development has taken place in and around the island's only town, San Pedro, about three-fourths of the way down from Mexico. Once a fishing village, San Pedro now focuses on tourism, but in a relaxed way. Most of the resorts on the island are owned by American and Canadian investors, but the vast majority of shops, restaurants, and dive shops are run by Belizeans.

Tour of the Island

If you're a veteran Caribbean island-hopper, you'll recognize San Pedro Town immediately. In many ways, it's the Caribbean of 30 years ago, before the boom in international travel—a throwback to the days before giant cruise ships turned Caribbean islands into concrete minimalls hustling duty-free liquor and discount jewelry.

In San Pedro, there are just three north–south streets, mostly still made of hard-packed sand, although in 2005, parts were set to be paved with cobblestones. Wood houses and small shops stand close together, painted in bright tropical colors. Newer buildings are made of reinforced concrete, optimistically girded for the next hurricane.

In an unexpected nod to public relations, a few years ago the local town council changed the names of the town's main streets. Front Street became Barrier Reef Drive; Middle Street was renamed Pescador Drive; and Back Street became Angel Coral Street. Locals, of course, still use the old names.

Many of the town's hotels, restaurants, and tourist shops are on Front Street, er, Barrier Reef Drive. Just beyond the little primary school at the south end of town is the bite-sized San Pedro Library. Here, you don't need a library card to check out books, so even tourists can borrow a volume or two for free. Next door is Ruby's, locally owned and the best cheap place to stay on the island, with budget rooms for under US$25 and air-conditioned rooms on the water for around US$50.

At the Sea Gal Boutique in the Holiday Hotel, gift-shop owner Celi Jean Greif Varela is putting out new inventory bought in Guatemala, Mexico, and Miami. She's the daughter of John Greif Sr., an American pilot in World War II who came to the island in the 1960s and started

Expat Profile: Resort Owner on Ambergris Caye

Many of Ambergris Caye's resorts are owned and operated by expats from the United States or Canada. One is Tim Jeffers, an American businessman who came to Ambergris Caye from Montana to live the island life and to try to make a go of the hotel business. He first built Coconuts, a 12-room hotel on the beach, and then developed Banana Beach, a condotel with 32 one-bedroom suites in a three-story building around a central courtyard. It's about 1.5 miles south of San Pedro, near Mar de Tumbo beach. He has since sold Coconuts.

A couple of years ago, Jeffers roughly doubled the size of Banana Beach, adding 30 rooms and suites, a second swimming pool, and a restaurant and tour shop. Overall, hotels in Belize have averaged occupancy rates of about 40 percent in recent years (on Ambergris, hotels do better, with annual occupancies over 50 percent), but the ponytailed and tanned Jeffers says that, thanks to close attention to management, good marketing through both travel agents and the Internet, and competitive pricing, his Ambergris Caye property enjoys annual occupancy above 80 percent.

the predecessor to what is now Tropic Air, one of Belize's two commuter airlines; and Celi Nuñez McCorkle, who started the Holiday Hotel. The Holiday was one of the first hotels to open on the island in 1965, when a room and three meals were just US$10 a day. A little farther up the street, you can't miss the hulking, concrete Spindrift Hotel and Caliente restaurant, home of the famous "chicken drop"—where, on Wednesday nights, tipsy tourists bet on which square a chicken will poop on. The winner gets US$100 and has to clean up the droppings. Sounds like fun, huh? Actually, it is.

Beyond Central Park—the name is grander than the park, a little square of sand and concrete where kids play basketball and street vendors sell delicious tacos and barbecue for almost nothing—there's Big Daddy's disco, the island's busiest bar and a spot where harder-drinking expats are always to be found. "Paisano," one of the town's well-known street characters, sometimes hangs around here. He claims he was once the island's richest man, but the white-haired gentlemen now naps on the steps of local hotels.

The Catholic church, near the park with a statue of the town's patron saint, St. Peter, out front, is cool and welcoming. Masses are in Spanish and English. There are three banks, about a dozen gift shops, and all along the street are small cafés, where residents and visitors alike stop in for a chat or a cold drink. There are also popular cybercafés where you can check your email.

To the east, beyond the line of low buildings on Barrier Reef Drive and accessible through many alleys, is the Caribbean Sea, in all its mint green and turquoise glory. A narrow strip of beach and seawall between the buildings and the sea is used as a pedestrian walkway.

Many piers jut into the sea. Piers in San Pedro are valuable real estate: Rents for a pier and a shack for a bar or dive shop can run US$5,000 or more a month. The patch of white you see a few hundred yards out is surf breaking over the barrier reef. Don't try swimming out to the reef from the shore. There is a lot of boat traffic inside the reef, and through the years, several swimmers have been killed or injured by boats.

Middle Street, or Pescador Drive, the other main north–south venue, is also busy. Hungry? Cocina Caramba, just up the street, is one of the more popular restaurants, with cheap rum and tonics.

Around the corner, on Caribeña Street, is the island's first casino. The Palace is small and homey, as casinos go, with some slots and a few

© Lan Sluder

a beach south of San Pedro Town on Ambergris Caye

live tables, where the maximum bet on blackjack is US$10. A couple of other small casinos were planned for hotels south of town.

As you go farther north on Middle Street, San Pedro becomes more residential. You'll see the San Pedro Supermarket, the Belize Electric and Belize Telecommunications Ltd. facilities, a small high school, a playground, and then the San Pedro River, actually a channel that divides the larger north of the island from the more developed south.

A little hand-pulled ferry takes you across the river channel to the other side in about 60 seconds. A long-talked-about bridge over the channel may actually be built in 2005 or 2006. Or not. This, after all, is Belize.

A narrow golf cart and walking path wends its way north, mostly on the back side of the island. Stop at Sweet Basil deli for picnic fixings or some of the imported treats you miss. A bit farther north on the water is Capricorn, a resort with just three rooms and the best—if one of the priciest—restaurants on the island. The cart path continues northward for several miles.

Everyone who comes up here asks about the Essene Way, just north of Captain Morgan's. Developed in the mid-1990s by an eccentric health-food magnate from Orlando, Florida, and originally designed as a US$7 million new millennium retreat, the Essene Way is mostly deserted these days. Its solar arrays are idle, its tennis courts and swimming pool are usually empty, and its kitschy Biblical statuettes in a Disneyesque garden of Eden are fading under the sun. It's supposed to be redeveloped as condos. More and more resorts are being built, or at least dreamed about, on North Ambergris. La Perla del Caribe, for example, opening in 2005, is a collection of huge 4,000-square-foot beach houses that go for US$500 a day or more.

Beyond the last resorts is a large undeveloped tract. Through the years, many schemes have been floated for the north end of the island. Much of this area has been saved from Cancúnization, thanks to establishment of the Bacalar Chico National Park and Marine Reserve. The park, which opened in 1996, comprises 12,000 acres of land and 15,000 acres of water. At present, the park is accessible by boat from San Pedro, from the Belize mainland at Sarteneja and elsewhere, and from the Mexican port village of X'calak. The park is home to a surprisingly large population of birds and wildlife, including several of Belize's wild cats, and there are a number of Maya sites.

If you visit North Ambergris, be sure to take plenty of bug spray and wear light-colored clothes, because away from the breezes or the mosquito control efforts of San Pedro Town, the bugs can be terrible, especially in the late summer after the seasonal rains.

If you head south from town rather than north, you'll wind up on Coconut Drive, another mostly sand roadway and the only route to the south of the island. This is an area of intense development. Only about 100 yards of the road, near the airstrip, and another short section at the Island Supermarket, the largest grocery on the island, have been paved. You'll pass clusters of small resorts and hotels.

The beachfront Island Academy (tuition US$250 a month), one of the better private schools in Central America, was founded by Barry Bowen—Belize's beer, soft-drink, and shrimp-farming magnate and one of the country's wealthiest power brokers—as a place for his young daughter to go to school. Barry Bowen has a little 250,000-acre farm in Orange Walk District, where he also owns Chan Chich Lodge and runs Gallon Jug Estates, the only commercial coffee producer in Belize.

To the lagoon side of the road is the San Pablo area, a primarily Belizean residential section, where homes are mostly in the US$50,000–$200,000 range. The development of small, closely spaced houses clustered on a muddy flat was funded and built by the Belize government's now financially troubled DFC as housing for local Belizeans whose homes were destroyed by Hurricane Keith.

There are 12 lagoons on the island, the largest of which is Laguna de San Pedro, just to the west of San Pedro and San Pablo. Considerable development continues along the sea south of town, including deluxe condos going for as much as US$500,000, and a couple of proposed casinos. The beach here, Mar de Tumbo, around Villas at Banyan Bay and Banana Beach resorts, is one of the best on the island.

The hotel sector ends about three miles south of San Pedro Town. If you continue farther south by foot or cart, you're back in a residential area, with a number of up-market houses, including one owned by musician Jerry Jeff Walker, whose song "Another Gringo in Paradise" is the unofficial anthem of local expats. There also are shacks and other assorted digs. As on the north end of the island, mosquitoes are often a problem once you leave the more developed areas in the south.

The San Pedranos

Maya Indians were the first residents of Ambergris Caye. Some of their history is told in remaining small ruins, including the Marco Gonzales site near the south tip of the island and several sites in Bacalar Chico park in the north. There are few Mayas on the caye today, however.

The village of San Pedro was founded in 1848 by refugees from the Caste Wars in the Yucatán. The Caste Wars were a series of successful rebellions by the Maya against the Spanish, and the Indian armies drove thousands of Mexicans south to Belize. The Mestizos who settled San Pedro were mostly fishermen (hence the name of the village, after St. Peter) and farmers, and they continued this work on Ambergris Caye. Many native San Pedranos can trace their ancestry back to the Caste Wars immigration. These families, with surnames such as Guerrero, Gomez, and Nuñez, speak Spanish at home and among themselves, though they are equally fluent in English. They control the island's politics, along with many of its small businesses.

While there is occasional friction between the local and expat communities, usually connected with real-estate development, most foreign residents have high regard for their local neighbors. San Pedranos are known for their friendly, easygoing ways. After years of good lobstering and growing tourism, many San Pedranos are financially comfortable, and a few who run successful businesses or who have sold beachfront land are well off even by American standards. Begging and beach hustling are virtually unknown on the island.

The Expat Community

Ambergris Caye has more foreign residents than any other area of Belize, but no one is sure about the exact number. It's probably somewhere around 1,000, although not all are full-time residents. The problem is: How and whom do you count? Do the snowbird couple from Michigan who own a condo on the island and spend winters in it count as residents or just visitors? How about the students at the offshore med school? Quite a large number of expats on the island are perpetual tourists, in Belize on a visitor's card until their money, or perhaps their livers, run out.

"Lots of people come and go with some regularity, and it seems like there are new gringos everywhere, but it's very hard to say how many actually live here," says San Pedro real-estate investment counselor Jesse Cope. Diane Campbell, another real-estate agent, puts the number of full-time expats at only a few hundred, but "most gringos here aren't full-timers—there are a *lot* of part-timers." Unlike some other areas of Belize, such as Corozal Town, where a majority of expats are here under the Qualified Retired Persons (QRP) program, few "QRPs" live on Ambergris Caye—only a few percent of the area's population, according to Campbell.

Expats also operate bars, restaurants, dive shops, gift shops, sailing charters, the island's ferry boat service, and other small businesses. Several of these businesses are owned by longtime island residents who were grandfathered in before stricter laws were passed against small retail shops being run by non-Belizeans. Selling real estate is a popular option for new arrivals.

Daily Life

Most expats moved here to be close to the Caribbean, and daily life revolves around activities on the water. Depending on their interests, they go fishing or diving, or just swim or beachcomb. Cable television is available (around US$20 a month) with more than 40 channels, mostly from the United States.

San Pedro has dozens of shops and stores, but most of them target visitors. Because of high import taxes and the extra cost of shipping goods from the mainland to the island, costs here are mostly higher than you'd pay in the United States or Belize City. The island's largest groceries (Island Supermarket, Super Buy, and San Pedro Supermarket) have small selections of imported canned goods, cereals, and other items, generally at around 50 percent higher than U.S. prices. Their

Expat Profile: The Island Life

Jennifer McCrary is a young American woman who lived on Ambergris Caye for nine months in 2002. McCrary fell in love with Ambergris Caye long before she ever laid eyes on the island. Within a month of her first trip to Belize, she scheduled a sabbatical and made the move to San Pedro.

"I went to Belize hoping that I would never return. I told the world that I would see them in a year, but I secretly hoped that I would never return. I was a bit naive.

Belize is a beautiful, wonderful country and every time I visit I wonder 'why did I leave?' But moving to an island off the coast of Central America isn't always the answer. I wanted to escape problems and just got the same thing in Belize until I realized that it was probably me. The problems you had back home will most likely follow you. So I did a lot of growing up—more than nine months would ever do in the States. I wouldn't change the experience for anything, even though I experienced some horrible things like Hurricane Iris and the San Pedro jail.

I went planning to work and that worked out fine. As long as you don't fool yourself into thinking you are going to get a high paying job, I found it easy. I worked selling time-share (never sold any), at an Internet café, at a bar, a dive shop, a popular restaurant, and at an offshore medical school. At all of the jobs my pay was around US$150 per week. That was spending money. I brought about US$15,000 with me for my year and spent it all.

How did I work? Without getting into specifics, it is pretty easy to work in Belize. You just have to find the right people and be willing to pay. Some places will hire you without papers as well.

How have I changed? I walk slower, I talk slower, I chew slower, I know I can subsist on rice and beans and no running water for five days. All those toiletries and makeup I packed still sit virtually unused in my bag. I have fought boredom and won, now feeling such contentment on my own that I avoid crowds. I am my own best friend and value everything in my life so much more.

The amazing thing about Belize and San Pedro in particular to me is how people fall in love with her [the land]. I did. Sometimes you have to follow your heart and not listen to all the naysayers telling you why not to do something. Sometimes it is best to find out for yourself."

advertisements in San Pedro

selections of meats and vegetables are limited. Street vendors and a couple of shops sell fresh fruits and vegetables, and seafood is available directly from local anglers. The island has branches of three local banks, Atlantic Bank, Alliance Bank, and Belize Bank (the Belize Bank ATM accepts foreign-issued ATM cards), several hardware and building supply stores, appliance stores, launderettes, and other shops.

There is a privately owned municipal water and sewer system serving San Pedro and surrounding areas, but those living on Northern or far Southern Ambergris have to make do with cisterns, shallow wells, and septic systems. Electricity, most of it supplied from Mexico, costs around US$.20–.21 per average kilowatt—the more you use, the more you pay— about two to three times as expensive as the United States. It's generally dependable, although spot outages do occur. Rates were expected to go up a little in 2005–2006.

Despite the relatively high cost of real estate, imported food, and electricity, the overall cost of living on the island is lower than in the United States, say many residents. In part, that's because you don't need all the things you use in the United States—no heating oil, no cars, auto insurance, or parking fees, and no fancy wardrobe. Seafood and Belize-produced food are comparatively inexpensive. Medical care, insurance, and property taxes are also cheaper than back home.

In the past, expats used to say that their hospitals were TACA, American, and Continental airlines. For top-flight medical care, Americans on the island may still fly to Miami or Houston or at least pop over to Belize City, but there are now full-time physicians on the island, along with a new public medical clinic.

Ambergris Caye residents say island fever strikes from time to time. Most go into Belize City regularly to conduct business, shop for items not available on the island, or get dental care. Many expats take vacations in the United States or long weekends in Cayo District or elsewhere in Belize.

For those who can't find enough to occupy themselves, substance abuse is always a risk, more so in San Pedro's freewheeling resort atmosphere than in most other areas of Belize. "Booze is ubiquitous here, and bar-hanging quite the social custom. And, in San Pedro as much as in most U.S. cities, you can now add other chemicals," says one island expat.

Most residents say they feel safe on the island. Burglaries and petty thefts are unfortunately common, but violent crime is rare.

Recreation

Surrounded by water and just a few hundred feet from the Belize Barrier Reef, Ambergris Caye offers water sports of every kind. You couldn't ask for better fishing. For sportfishing, shallow bonefish and tarpon flats are only a few minutes away. In deeper water around the reef, you can catch grouper, snapper, wahoo, mackerel, jack, barracuda, and more. It doesn't necessarily take a fancy boat or a lot of equipment to catch fish. You can drop your hook off a pier and, chances are, pull in supper. Diving around Ambergris Caye is good, though not as good as around the atolls farther out. Snorkeling, especially off Mexico Rocks on North Ambergris, and in the Hol Chan Marine Reserve, is world-class. In the Shark-Ray Alley and Sting Ray City areas of Hol Chan, you can snorkel with nurse sharks and huge sting rays. Don't worry—they're gentle, at least most of the time.

Few San Pedro families would be caught dead without a boat, which vary from small mahogany skiffs to modern fiberglass speedboats with twin 150-horse Honda motors. Expats have sailed in on everything from island trawlers to big catamarans. The shallow waters, hidden coral heads, and tricky winds and currents mean, however, that boating around Ambergris Caye is not like boating on a calm lake back home.

Even skilled sailors with years of local experience have gone aground on the reef, a sure way to rip the hull of the boat to smithereens—and it doesn't help the fragile reef either.

Kayaking on the lagoon side of the island is popular, and sailboarding between the reef and the shore is a growing sport. January through April have the best conditions for sailboarding, with winds of 15 mph and faster.

Although there is no golf course (other than mini golf) on Ambergris Caye, there is one on Caye Chapel, about 45 minutes away by boat. The Caye Chapel course, which opened in mid-2000, is a par-72 lying beautifully along the Caribbean. It's flat but long and plays more than 7,000 yards, with four par 5 holes. Between the back and front nines is a 23,000-square-foot clubhouse, the equal of any tony country club in the United States. There are a swimming pool, workout center, and tennis complex with lighted courts, all near the clubhouse. Accommodations on the island are limited to 12 3,000-square-foot villas that go for a whopping US$1,000 a night. Current green fees are fairly stiff—US$200 for a full day of golf, including clubs, cart rental, and lunch. If you're interested, Caye Chapel Island Resort is for sale, with an asking price of US$55 million.

Back in San Pedro, tennis buffs will find two courts at the Isla Bonita Tennis Club, along with a small gym and a large swimming pool. There are also courts at the San Pedro High School, Journey's End resort, and the Essene Way.

HOUSING

Real-estate prices on Ambergris Caye are among the highest in Belize. As elsewhere, prices vary tremendously depending on location and specific property. Houses and lots in predominantly Belizean areas, mostly on the back or lagoon/bay side of the island, tend to be much less expensive than seafront property preferred by foreign investors and residents.

Demand in recent years has been strong for beachfront lots and beachfront homes. Appreciation has run 10 percent to 20 percent per year, according to local real-estate brokers. Agents point to beachfront property on North Ambergris that went for US$450 a front foot in the late 1980s and now sells for US$2,000 a foot. In the past five years, beachfront property in some areas has more than doubled in price. Beachfront land within a few miles of town now goes for as much as

US$3,500 a front foot. In great part, real-estate prices depend on the state of the United States economy, as most buyers are Americans and few Belizeans are able—or willing—to pay current prices.

As the U.S. economy rebounded in 2004 and 2005, the island saw a jump in sales, especially beachfront. "The beachfront is selling like crazy, and it's almost gone," said a real-estate agent on the island. That may be an overstatement, but there's certainly been a buying frenzy, with "Sold" signs going up right and left on prime beachfront property, especially within five or six miles of San Pedro.

Condo development continues to be hot and heavy on Ambergris Caye. A number of hotels are converting some or all of their units to "condotel" status. The idea is to sell now for immediate cash, and then make 40 percent to 60 percent of revenues in management fees for running the hotel units for absentee owners. Sales, however, have not always met expectations, as some investors are wary of condominium laws in Belize—condos are fairly new to the country—and some have been burned by disputes with developers.

A few developers offer financing, typically 20 percent down, with the balance payable over 10 years at around 12 percent interest. Usually,

Villas at Banyan Bay, a "condotel" on Ambergris Caye

there's a balloon payment at the end of the term. Unfortunately, there has also been a spate of time-share conversions on the island. Several developers have loudmouthed touts hawking their properties.

Housing Costs

Building lots: Caribbean seafront building lots cost US$1,500–3,500 per beachfront foot. Less expensive lots are generally on the upper reaches of North Ambergris, accessible only by boat or water taxi, and not on the electric grid. Electricity now extends about six miles north of San Pedro. Waterfront lots on the lagoon or Chetumal Bay (back side of the island) start at around US$500 per waterfront foot, with back side lots in nicer areas south of San Pedro at higher prices. Building lots not on the water are much less, starting at around US$15,000, with second-row-back-from-the-water lots with electric service on North Ambergris running around US$25,000, or around US$30,000 south of San Pedro Town. In general, lots one row back from the sea are 70 percent or 75 percent less than those directly on the water. Buyers should be aware that some beachfront lots have mangroves, not sand, on the water side, and a permit is required to cut mangroves.

Homes: Two- or three-bedroom modern houses on the beach on North Ambergris Caye (access via water taxi or ferry) start at around US$300,000. Those south of San Pedro Town on the sea start at around US$250,000. Homes not on the water, but with sea views, are available from around US$100,000. Homes with "sunset views"— that is, on the west side or lagoon side of the island—start at around US$75,000 for a simple house on stilts. At the top end, deluxe, recently built beachfront three- and four-bedroom homes may go for US$300,000–600,000 or more.

Condos: One-bedroom condos near the water but without sea views start at around US$100,000, and those with sea views run about US$110,000–175,000. High-quality, larger condos with sea views range US$250,000–400,000 or more.

Home construction: Building costs on Ambergris are relatively high, because of the need to dig deep foundations and install pilings for stability in the sandy soil, and to build with hurricane protection in mind. Bringing building supplies in by barge also adds to the cost. Expect to pay US$90 a square foot and up for quality reinforced concrete construction. As elsewhere in Belize, labor costs are lower than in the United States, but most building materials are more expensive.

Rentals

Demand is fairly tight for rentals on the island. A "North American–style," unfurnished two-bedroom house rents for US$600–1,500 a month, and a one-bedroom for US$400–800, depending on location and length of lease. Small apartments start at US$250 a month, with modern, furnished one-bedroom apartments going for about US$400–700. A furnished one-bedroom condo in a resort rents for US$700–1,400 a month, including utilities. Off-season rentals are cheaper than during high season.

GETTING AROUND

You can fly to San Pedro or go by boat. Belize's two commuter airlines, Tropic Air and Maya Island Air, have flights to San Pedro at least hourly during daylight hours. It's cheaper to fly from the old Municipal Airport in Belize City (about US$28 one-way) than from the International Airport (about $50 one-way). However, if you're connecting from a flight from the United States, it's easier just to walk a few feet to the domestic terminal at the International Airport than transfer by taxi (US$20) to Municipal. Arrival is at the airstrip at the south end of town.

Water taxis also connect Belize City with San Pedro. The cost is US$15 one-way for the 75-minute trip. Most boats are operated by the Caye Caulker Water Taxi Association and leave from the Marine Terminal on North Barrier Reef Drive, near the Swing Bridge, arriving in San Pedro at the old Sharks Dock near the Holiday Hotel. The fast, open boats, powered by twin outboard motors, make the trip to and from San Pedro six or seven times a day. Boats also stop at Caye Caulker and Caye Chapel.

Water taxis to North Ambergris cost US$5–10 per person each way. Cabs (south of the river channel only) charge US$3–6 to most destinations.

Most expats on Ambergris Caye own a golf cart, either electric or gas. Expect to pay US$2,000–$3,500 for a used cart in good condition. Maintenance—mainly batteries—and repairs can be surprisingly steep, at least several hundred dollars a year. You can buy a new bicycle on the island or in Belize City for under US$150. Too many San Pedranos have cars, but the town council has (at least in theory) placed a moratorium on bringing new vehicles to the island. You'll also need a permit before you can bring a golf cart to the island.

Caye Caulker

Less than 30 minutes by boat from its larger and more bustling neighbor, Ambergris Caye, and 45 minutes from Belize City, Caye Caulker—or Caye Corker as it is sometimes referred to—retains an easy-going, Caribbean atmosphere and homey, village flavor that may appeal to those seeking to escape the rat race back home.

THE LAY OF THE LAND

Caye Caulker, at less than five miles long and a mile wide at its widest point, is roughly one-tenth the size of Ambergris Caye. Hurricane Hattie in 1961 divided the island into two parts. North of "the Split," it is mostly uninhabited mangrove, and part of this area is protected as a land and marine nature reserve. As on many islands, there are basically just three streets running down the island: Front, Middle, and Back streets are the main ones, but there are few street signs, and locals usually give directions by saying something like, "Go down to the yellow house and turn right." Most of the 300 or so listings in the Caye Caulker section of the Belize telephone directory don't even include a street name or address, just the person's name and phone number.

> There are few foreigners living here, except those who own hotels or other tourist businesses. While several dozen Americans and Canadians own houses on the island, most also have a life off the island and spend only part of the year on Caulker.

Nearly all of the island's population of about 1,000 lives in the village on the south end of the island. As on Ambergris, a majority of local residents are Mestizos who originally came to the island from Mexico, and who, until recently, made their living by fishing, but the island also has Creoles, Garifuna, gringos, and others. There are few foreigners living here, except those who own hotels or other tourist businesses. While several dozen Americans and Canadians own houses on the island, most also have a life off the island and spend only part of the year on Caulker.

While it is gradually going up-market, Caye Caulker remains very much a budget island. In the 1960s and 1970s, the island was on the "backpacker trail," a cheap place for long-haired visitors to relax, smoke a little weed, or sip a beer. Today, the most expensive hotel on Caulker goes for around US$130 a night, and most hotels charge under US$50 for a double, with some as low as US$10. Most older houses on the island are wooden clapboard and often painted in tropical colors, but more recently constructed buildings are made of reinforced concrete.

Caye Caulker has much the same mix of tourist-oriented businesses as San Pedro, but in most cases, there are fewer of everything. The island has perhaps 20 simple restaurants—if you include those operating out of somebody's back window—a few casual bars, a handful of dive shops and tour guides, several pint-sized groceries, a few gift shops, one bank, and three cybercafés.

What about beaches? Caulker has much less beachfront, and what beaches it does have don't compare with some of the better stretches of beach on Ambergris Caye. A beach reclamation project in 2000 did widen and improve the beach along the east side of the village (storms have since taken away some sand). Swimming in the shallow water close to shore is mainly from piers and at the Split.

The pipe water, or tap water, on Caulker often has a sulfur smell and comes from shallow wells which may be close to septic systems. Caye Caulker also has sandflies. Especially on calm days, they can be a nuisance.

HOUSING

Most of the land on Caye Caulker is closely held by families that have been on the island for generations, so there is not too much on the market at any given time. Lots in the village, when available, are in the US$50,000 and up range. Beachfront lots north of the Split, where there is no electricity, start at around US$40,000. A large, 53-acre parcel on the north end of the island, part of it a mangrove swamp, with 3,500 feet of beachfront, was being sold for US$1.3 million, or about US$371 a front foot.

In 2005, several small wood homes were for sale in the village, priced at around US$100,000–150,000. Concrete houses of 1,000 square feet or more, not on the water, typically have sold for US$150,000–200,000.

Rentals

A few apartments are for rent on Caulker, starting at around US$300 a month. Houses, on a year lease, go for US$400–600 a month, or less for small Belizean-style houses. For shorter-term rentals (a few weeks), a couple of dozen houses on the island are owned by Americans or others who live on the island only part of the year. They rent their properties by the day or week, starting at around US$300 a week.

GETTING AROUND

You can fly to Caulker's little airstrip on Tropic Air or Maya Island Air from Belize City. The island's airstrip, closed for repairs and up-grading in 2004, reopened in 2005. Flights from either international or municipal airports to San Pedro stop on request at Caye Caulker. Fares are the same as to San Pedro. If you come by air, the airstrip is at the south end of the island. You can walk 20 minutes or so back to the heart of the village, or get a golf cart taxi. Most visitors to Caulker come by boat. The Caye Caulker Water Taxi Association boats make six or eight trips from the Marine Terminal in Belize to Caulker daily. Fare is US$10 one-way, and the trip takes about 45 minutes. Most water taxis dock at the main public pier on the front side of the island. As you come ashore, the pine and green Trends Beachfront Hotel and behind it the Sandbox restaurant are on your right, and Seaside Cabañas are on your left. Walk a few sandy feet, and you'll come to Front Street. Go right, or north, and in 10 minutes or so, you'll end up at the Split. Go left or south, and eventually you'll end up at the airstrip. Many of the island's restaurants, shops, and hotels are on Front Street or on the beachfront.

Like Ambergris Caye, Caye Caulker has streets of hard-packed sand, but with far fewer cars. Almost everybody gets around on foot or by bike, though some residents have golf carts.

Other Cayes

No longer can you buy your own private island for a few thousand dollars, but if you have money to burn and the willingness to rebuild after the next hurricane, one of Belize's remote islands could be yours, beginning in the high five figures and going up to several million.

Developers are also trying to sell lots on several larger islands. Water Caye, less than 10 miles off Belize City, is being filled and developed. Beachfront lots with 100 feet of frontage are being offered for US$95,000, and seaview lots for US$45,000. There are plans for a resort on the island, but most actual development is in the future. Lots on Long Caye at Lighthouse Atoll were, for a time, offered starting at around US$15,000, and many were sold via the Internet. Elaborate plans were laid for resorts and even a medical center, and a few actually came to pass. In 2004, the developer's website began sporting this statement: "Parcels are temporarily unavailable for sale," and the reason given was that it related to U.S. Housing and Urban Development (HUD) registration.

If you are tempted by these offers, by all means go and visit the island first. It's amazing how many people are foolish enough to buy just from an Internet ad. Just getting out to Long Caye, for example, can cost US$200 or more for a boat charter. Imagine the cost of bringing building supplies to a remote island, and approach such sales with caution.

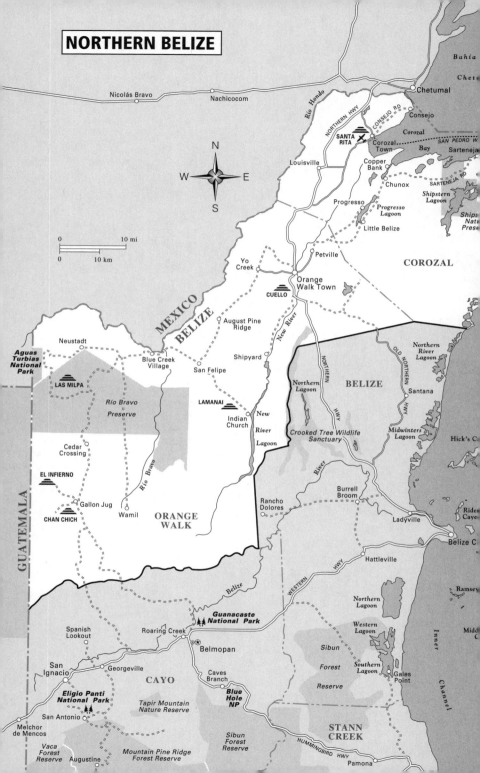

© Lan Sluder

Northern Belize

Northern Belize is a big yawn for most short-term visitors to Belize. But if you're a would-be expat looking for a place to plant yourself for a few months—or forever—you may find this area one of the most appealing parts of Belize. The low-key and friendly ambience, proximity to Mexico for shopping and medical care (the Mexican city of Chetumal has more than two-thirds the population of the entire country of Belize), and attractive housing values have brought hundreds of expats to this area, with more on the way.

Two districts constitute Northern Belize: Corozal and Orange Walk. Corozal District, the northernmost district in the country, has an area of 718 square miles and a population of about 35,000. Orange Walk District, to the south and west of Corozal District, has a population of 40,000 in an area of about 1,800 square miles. In Corozal District, you may want to look at Corozal Town and the nearby Consejo Village area. Eastern Corozal District, an area of farms and small villages, has several small population centers that are just beginning to attract expats—Copper Bank, Progresso, and Sarteneja Villages.

As you read this chapter, keep in mind the distinction between Corozal District (a political and geographic entity somewhere between a

U.S. state and a county) and Corozal, the town. Likewise, we have Orange Walk District and the town of Orange Walk. When you hear people in Belize say "Corozal" or "Orange Walk," chances are they are referring to the towns, but they may also mean the district.

Corozal District can be divided into two hemispheres. Corozal Town and the villages around it anchor the left, or western, hemisphere. The largest populated area in Corozal District by far is Corozal Town, yet its population is only around 8,000. Corozal Town's "suburbs"—the small villages of Ranchito, Xaibe, Calcutta, San Joaquin, and Calcutta, among others—have populations of a few hundred each, and none has more than 1,000.

The main road artery of this hemisphere is the Northern Highway, a good two-lane paved road that runs about 90 miles from Belize City to the border with Mexico. From the southern edge of Corozal District, it is about 28 miles to the Mexican border at Santa Elena.

The right, or eastern, hemisphere, of Corozal District is the Sarteneja Peninsula. This peninsula has far more trees than people. It is an area mostly of swamp and savannah, with the bulk of the peninsula's small population living in villages along the beautiful Progresso Lagoon

© Lan Sluder

Corozal Town may not impress you at first, but you'll find that it is one of the best-kept secrets in Belize.

and on Chetumal Bay, including the villages of Copper Bank and Progresso. The Shipstern Nature Preserve in the northeast part of the peninsula is a 22,000-acre park managed by the Belize Audubon Society. The little fishing village of Sarteneja near Shipstern is charming but remote. An all-weather, mostly unpaved road runs from Orange Walk Town to Sarteneja Village, a distance of about 40 miles. From near Corozal Town, there is also access via a free hand-pulled ferry over the New River.

Mexico looms large to the north. Corozal Town is nine miles from the Mexican border. Just north of the border is the city of Chetumal, capital of Quintana Roo state, with a population of around 200,000, more than twice as large as Belize City.

Much of Corozal District is sugar-cane country. Sugar cane has long been the leading industry in Corozal District, and while sugar-cane fields still honeycomb the district, weak sugar prices have hurt the local economy, and a large sugar cane–processing plant, La Libertad, has closed.

Corozal Town and surrounding villages are on the power grid and generally have municipal water supplies with potable water. Sarteneja and other remote areas have less modern infrastructure.

The climate in Corozal District is closer to that of Central Florida than South Florida. Rainfall is a moderate 50 inches or so a year, less than most other areas in Belize. If you are on or near Corozal Bay, a brisk wind from the water—it usually dies down only in late summer—keeps you cool and also keeps the bugs away.

PEOPLE AND LANGUAGE

The Maya have lived in what is now Corozal since at least 2,000 B.C. The name, Corozal, is from the Yucatec Maya word for the cohune palm, though there are relatively few of these palms in the area now. The Santa Rita archaeological site in Corozal Town, where only a few buildings remain visible today, was an important Maya center because it controlled trade routes up and down the coast and into the Petén. Cerros, across Chetumal Bay, was a busy Maya maritime trade center from around 400 B.C. to A.D. 100. The site apparently suffered an economic decline and was abandoned in the Early Preclassic period after A.D. 250. (An American developer has been trying to sell lots in a "subdivision" near Cerros that is described as being "just 15 minutes from Corozal Town." It is—by boat.)

The Spanish arrived in the 16th century and eventually were successful in conquering the area that is now the Yucatán and northern Corozal District. Modern Corozal was settled mostly by Mestizo refugees from the Mexican Caste Wars of the mid-19th century, when Mayas fought to drive Mestizos from the Yucatán.

Spanish is still the first language in most of Corozal District, especially in smaller villages. In Corozal Town, you can get by with only English. In small villages, it's helpful to have some Spanish, although even in more remote areas, most residents understand some English.

Corozal Town

On the surface, Corozal Town doesn't have a lot of sex appeal. Unlike Placencia or some of Belize's cayes, Corozal has no real beaches, except a couple of human-assisted, sandy bayfront areas, and no nearby dive spots. The shopping in Corozal Town is limited. Somewhat off the beaten tourist track, it sports only a handful of small hotels and restaurants, and they don't compare with the deluxe seaside resorts of Ambergris Caye or the world-class jungle lodges of Cayo District. Aside from some unprepossessing Maya ruins, there are few notable historical or cultural sites.

> Corozal is one of the most pleasant spots in all of Belize and should rank near the top of your must-see list if you're thinking of retiring, relocating, or investing in the country.

Yet, for my money, Corozal is one of the most pleasant spots in all of Belize and should rank near the top of your must-see list if you're thinking of retiring, relocating, or investing in the country. To use a hackneyed but accurate phrase, Corozal is one of best-kept secrets in Belize.

THE LAY OF THE LAND

Despite its lack of beaches, the Corozal Town area enjoys a beautiful setting on Corozal Bay. The waters of the bay are as blue as those elsewhere on the coast or cayes, and the breezes from the water as cooling and constant as any in Belize. If you're an angler, you'll find good fishing for tarpon, bonefish, and permit, and boating is enjoyable on the shallow, protected waters of the bay. Next door is Chetumal, capital of the Mexican state of Quintana Roo, with its good, low-cost

Don't Worry, Be Happy

Margaret Briggs, an American expat who lives in Corozal, surveyed 43 other expats from the United States, Canada, and Great Britain living in Northern Belize. She asked them: "Are you happy that you've moved to Belize?" Of those who answered, here are the results:

11 percent said, "No."
48 percent said, "Yes."
41 percent said, "Yes, but..."

If you combine the "Yes" categories, noted Briggs, you find that almost 90 percent of the expats are happy, to some degree, with their decision to move to Belize. Of those who are completely happy, about three-fourths are also completely retired—as opposed to running some sort of full- or part-time business—and they rent, rather than own, the houses they live in. All but one felt that their decision to live outside the United States, Canada, or Great Britain was the right one. When asked, "If you left Belize, where would you move?" most answered Mexico, Panama, or Costa Rica; only two said that they would return to the United States.

So, the recipe for expat happiness in Belize seems to be: Don't own, don't work, and just hang out!

medical care and inexpensive shopping. Corozaleños are friendly, the crime rate is lower than in other areas of Belize (though burglaries and thefts are an ongoing problem), and the climate is sunny, with less rain than elsewhere in Belize. Best of all, housing and real-estate prices are a bargain.

Margaret Briggs, an American archaeologist living in Corozal Town, says, "People choose Corozal for its waterfront, its climate (less rain than anywhere else in Belize), and its proximity to Chetumal for shopping, restaurants, and movie theaters." Chetumal has an air-conditioned movie theater (the only movie theaters in Belize are in the Princess Hotel and Casino) at Plaza Americas mall, two McDonald's restaurants, and several large supermarket and department stores, including Bodega Aurrera, owned by Wal-Mart, and Chedraui.

Corozal is laid out on a small grid, with its most appealing part along the bayfront, with colorful houses and seawall. A nearly constant breeze off the bay cools the homes and businesses near the water, reducing the need for air conditioning.

Mexico is less than 15 minutes away. As you go north from Corozal Town to the border with Mexico, you pass La Laguna de Cuatro Millas (Four Mile Lagoon) on the right. At the border is the Corozal Free Zone complex (its official name is the Commercial Free Zone, but everyone calls it the Corozal Free Zone), a busy duty-free zone that attracts Mexicans and some international travelers for cheap gasoline and imported goods from China, Taiwan, and other Asian countries. More than 200 stores and other businesses are open in the Free Zone. There is also gambling at two new casinos, including a branch of Belize City's Princess Casino. A third casino was also expected to open. The Free Zone employs about 1,600 Belizeans, making it one of the largest employers in the country.

The border, marked by the Hondo River and the small village of Santa Elena, has a bustling little frontier station on the Belize side. The Santa Elena crossing processes about 300 to 500 arrivals to Belize on a typical day. A few of them are international tourists arriving by bus, but many are Mexicans coming to Belize for the day or Belizeans returning from shopping trips.

In 1955, much of Corozal Town was destroyed by Hurricane Janet. It was rebuilt combining Mexican and Caribbean styles. Tropical storm Chantal in 2001 caused some flooding, but there was no major damage.

Only a few hundred foreigners now live in Corozal Town and environs. One local expat puts the number at 250, others a little more or less. However, as each month passes, I hear of more and more would-be

© Lan Sluder

The waterside atmosphere, low prices, and appealing climate attract retirees and others to Corozal. Shown here is the Corozal Bayfront.

expats who are looking at Corozal as a low-cost and remarkably appealing alternative to the Florida-level prices in San Pedro or Placencia. Real-estate agents also report a spike in the number of lookers and buyers. One first-timer to Belize, looking for a retirement home, told me that he was disappointed by the crowds and the "sky-high" prices on Ambergris Caye and "couldn't wait to get out of there." He's now looking to buy around Corozal Town. Another expat, Rich Zahniser, who had been away in Colorado for about a year, said on his return in 2004 that the number of gringos in town had almost doubled during the time he was away.

Shopping in Corozal Town is limited. There are six or seven small groceries, the best run by Taiwanese families and the largest barely bigger than a convenience store in the United States or Canada. Corozal also has the usual small-town mix of hardware stores and small shops. However, as noted above, nearby Chetumal has plenty of bigger alternatives. Corozal Town has several good, inexpensive restaurants, but many residents also elect to pop over to Mexico to enjoy that city's many fine restaurants.

Three of Belize's banks—Scotia Bank, Belize Bank, and Atlantic Bank—have branches in Corozal Town, but you can exchange money, usually at better than bank rates, at the border.

The town has a Rotary Club and a few other local organizations of interest to foreign residents. An informal expat association meets monthly for lunch. Attendance is usually around 40 to 50 people. Some foreign residents take courses at Corozal Junior College, where tuition costs are nominal. Corozal Town has a small public library. Local cable TV has more than 30 channels, some in Spanish but most in English, for around US$20 a month.

There's no barrier reef here, meaning no diving and snorkeling, but you can swim in one of the lagoons or in the bay. Fishing is excellent, not only in Chetumal/Corozal Bay, but also in nearby rivers and lagoons. The eastern part of the bay is known for its bonefish flats, and you can also catch snapper, jack, permit, tarpon, and snook. Boating is popular on the relatively calm, shallow bay, and you can take your boat all the way to Ambergris Caye or to Mexico's Caribbean Coast, with its wide, white, sandy beaches at Akumal, Cancún, and elsewhere. There is a customs entry point at Chetumal, at X'calak (a tiny Mexican fishing village near Ambergris Caye), and at several other points along the Yucatán coast. If you want to dive, take a day trip to Ambergris Caye or head to the Chinchorra Banks atoll off Mexico.

Two small golf courses (nine holes or fewer) were under construction near Corozal Town, one at Consejo Shores and another at Xaibe.

You can also take advantage of recreational opportunities in Mexico. About 15 miles from the border is Bacalar, a lagoon with excellent swimming. There's a public beach with a *palapa* bar serving drinks and snacks. The city of Chetumal has several museums and historical sites.

Corozal Town has a district public hospital, and the Northern Regional Hospital serving Northern Belize is in Orange Walk Town, a little more than an hour away. Many residents go to Chetumal for medical and dental care, where there are modern hospitals and clinics that charge only a fraction of U.S. prices and even less than in Belize City. However, many local residents go to the Bethesda Medical Clinic, locally known as Dr. Trummer's. There has also been speculation that a new offshore medical school will open soon near Corozal Town. Shipyard, a Mennonite settlement south of Corozal Town, has a low-cost dental clinic, and there are dentists in Corozal Town.

At present, there is no newspaper published in Corozal Town or elsewhere in Corozal District, and no local radio or television stations. Residents get most of their news from Mexican radio, TV, and other media.

HOUSING

Real estate is a bargain in Corozal Town. Belizean-style homes in and around Corozal Town sell for US$20,000–75,000, and attractive modern homes on or near the bayfront, with U.S.-style amenities, are available for US$50,000–200,000.

In 2005, two small thatch houses, built in the traditional Maya style on a lot with mature avocado, mango, *maumee,* orange, soursop, *kinep,* tangerine, banana, and coconut trees, were on sale for US$28,000. A three-bedroom, one-bath concrete bungalow in Corozal Town was on sale for US$65,000, and a two-story, four-bedroom, two-bath concrete house in Corozal Town was available for US$125,000.

Thanks to low labor costs and proximity to Mexico, building costs in Corozal Town are among the lowest in Belize. You can build in concrete here for less than US$50 a square foot. In most cases, you will get more home for your dollar by building, rather than buying. Building lots in

Corozal Town start at under US$10,000, and bayfront lots in or near town are US$50,000 and up, or around US$750–800 a waterfront foot, less than one-half the going rate in Placencia or the Northern Cayes.

Rentals

Corozal Town has some of the cheapest home rentals in Belize. You can find an acceptable small home in Corozal Town for under US$200 per month, and an attractive larger home on or near the water shouldn't cost more than US$600 or so and could be less. Upscale three- or four-bedroom homes in Consejo Shores or other residential areas around Corozal Town rent for US$500–900 a month. You'll do best by spending some time here and finding your own rental, rather than trying to handle it by phone, mail, or email. Foreign residents here say they generally have little problem finding a place to rent, though it's easier off-season (roughly after Easter to just before Thanksgiving).

For a short-term stay while looking for a place to live, several agencies, including Copa Banana and Paradise Bay Villas (see the *Planning Your Fact-Finding Trip* chapter), have weekly or monthly rates for efficiencies or apartments. Expect to pay around US$200–350 a week for temporary accommodations with a kitchen.

GETTING AROUND

From Mexico: ADO and other Mexican bus lines serve Chetumal from various towns and cities in the Yucatán, including Cancún, Mérida, and Playa del Carmen. Fares on first-class and deluxe buses—with reserved seats, videos, and bathrooms—are around US$15–20, depending on the origin and class of service. It's about five hours from Cancún, four from Playa del Carmen, and six from Mérida to Chetumal. At the Chetumal bus station, you change to a bus to cross the border into Corozal Town (fare US$1.50).

From points south in Belize: The Northern Highway is one of Belize's better roads. Figure about two hours by car from Belize City. Novelo's and Northern Transport are the primary Belize bus lines on the Northern Highway, with frequent service in both directions. Fares are around US$6 to Belize City, depending on the type of bus. Maya Island Air and Tropic Air fly from Corozal's tiny airstrip to San Pedro in Ambergris Caye (25 minutes, about US$37 one-way). Both offer four or five flights daily. The airstrip is about two miles south of town, a US$5 cab ride away.

There is no public transportation in Corozal Town, but the town isn't large, so you can walk to most sections. If you don't want to walk, cabs are usually less than US$3 to any point in town, or US$10 to the Mexican border.

A water taxi makes a daily trip in the morning from Corozal Town to San Pedro in Ambergris Caye, returning in the afternoon. The cost is US$22.50. Maya Island Air and Tropic Air each have five flights a day from the Corozal airstrip to San Pedro for around US$35.

Consejo

Consejo is a small village of a few hundred people, seven miles north of Corozal Town on Chetumal Bay. There is a customs office in the village, so you can go by boat (about 10 minutes) across the bay to Chetumal, Mexico.

At the edge of Consejo Village, on the site of an old hotel, a new fertility and genetics clinic, Reproductive Genetics Institute (RGI), has opened in a rather startling juxtaposition of new and traditional. It's one of about 20 clinics in the United States and around the world operated by RGI. The clinic performs in vitro fertilization, embryo transfers, and preconception genetics diagnosis for families at high risk of producing children with genetic disorders, along with other testing for genetic disorders.

WHERE TO LIVE

Near Consejo Village are several developments that attract foreign expats. The largest and best is Consejo Shores, a 350-acre planned development on Chetumal Bay, about seven miles north of Corozal Town. About four dozen homes have been built here so far, occupied mostly by retirees from the United States and Canada, and about half a dozen were under construction as of press time. Lots are large, with most at a half acre or more. The land is higher than in most other coastal areas, which is an advantage during storms. There is electricity (typically US$50–150 a month), piped water (about US$10 a month), telephone and Internet service, and even garbage pickup (US$10 a month). Building lots directly on the water go for around US$35,000–55,000, and those not on the water sell for US$16,000–25,000. Recently built two- and three-bedroom, North American–style homes sell for US$75,000–200,000

A new home is near completion at Consejo Shores.

or more. In 2005, a three-bedroom, two-bath home in Consejo Shores was on sale for US$85,000, and a 2,000-square-foot, custom-built, furnished home on the water on a half-acre lot was on the market for US$285,000, which is near the top end in the area.

Several other promising developments are in the Consejo area, although so far, few have built more than a handful of homes. Wagner's Landing, near the Smuggler's Den hotel, has lots back from the water selling for US$27,500 and up. The waterfront lots have sold out. Mayan Seaside has some waterfront lots available. Most of the "subdivisions" between Corozal Town and Consejo are still vacant land, but electricity and other services are now available in these developments.

Few rentals are available in the Consejo area. When they do come up, rentals in the Consejo Shores development are in the US$500–900-per-month range for a modern house.

GETTING AROUND

There is limited bus service between Consejo and Corozal Town during the school year, September to May. However, expats will want to have a car. The seven-mile road to Corozal is made of hard-packed dirt. A cab into Corozal Town is less than US$10.

Quite a few Consejo residents keep a boat, and it's only 15 or 20 minutes to Chetumal across the bay. There is a customs office, open only on demand, in Consejo Village. You can charter a small boat to take you to Chetumal for US$30, or go over for US$5 per person on a weekly scheduled boat.

Progresso and Copper Bank

Once you leave Corozal Town via a hand-pulled free ferry across the New River (a bridge is planned), or by road from Orange Walk Town, you're in a different world. Few visitors venture here, and locals live a slow-paced life that has changed little since 1950—or even 1850.

> On the east side of the Progresso Lagoon, you will see Mennonites with horses and buggies, and the well-tended farms are reminiscent of agricultural areas in the U.S. Midwest.

This part of Corozal District has a Mennonite farming community of about 2,000 people, mostly conservatives who eschew modern machinery. Here, on the east side of the Progresso Lagoon, you will see Mennonites with horses and buggies, and the well-tended farms are reminiscent of agricultural areas in the U.S. Midwest. The Mennonites here grow corn, beans, onions, and other crops, but chickens are the number one agricultural commodity. The Belize government estimates that about four million chickens in Corozal and Orange Walk Districts are raised by Mennonite farmers and sold mostly in the domestic market.

THE LAY OF THE LAND

A number of small villages are in this part of Corozal District. The primary industries, if you can call them that, are sugar cane and fishing. Copper Bank (locally pronounced "Copper Bonk") enjoys a waterfront location on Chetumal Bay and Laguna Seca. Chunox (pronounced "shoo-NOSH") is nearby. Together, the two villages have a population of around 1,500. On the west side of beautiful Progresso Lagoon is Progresso, another small village with a population of about 1,200. In the Progresso Lagoon and two other nearby lagoons, you'll find crocodiles and even manatees. The ruins of Cerros are on a 53-acre site near Copper Bank. The setting is lovely, with citrus, avocado, and banana trees, but beware the mosquitoes. They can be fierce in this area.

WHERE TO LIVE

American developers have been trying to sell, mainly via the Internet, waterfront lots near Cerros ruins, on Progresso Lagoon, and elsewhere along the peninsula. Most of these lots have no infrastructure, and any promised amenities may be years, even decades, away. You might find a bargain, but *caveat emptor*. You might be better off looking at larger plots along the waterfront. A 40-acre plot with 900 feet of waterfront was sold in 2004 for US$70,000, and a 30-acre tract north of Copper Bank village, with 1,800 feet of waterfront, was sold for less than US$100,000. Homes, either for sale or for rent, are scarce in this area. If you have an interest, the best bet is simply to go door to door and ask if anyone has property for sale or rent. (You'll need to speak some Spanish.)

GETTING AROUND

An automobile is an absolute must for travel in this lightly populated rural area. There are buses on the main road from Orange Walk Town to Sarteneja, but otherwise, there is no public transportation. You can also charter a boat in Corozal Town to take you across the bay to Cerros or other points on the peninsula.

Sarteneja

Near the tip of the peninsula, Sarteneja is a village of about 2,000 mostly Spanish-speaking Mestizos in northeastern Corozal District. The original Maya settlement was built around the site of a well, which is said to have never gone dry, and the town's name in the original Maya language meant "water between the rocks." The Maya deserted the area before colonial times, but Sarteneja was resettled in the mid-19th century by Caste War refugees from the Yucatán. Most of the villagers make their living from the sea, fishing and lobstering in Chetumal Bay. Residents are known in Belize for their boat-building skills. The local style of sailboat is called a "lighter."

THE LAY OF THE LAND

Although it enjoys a postcard setting on the water, Sarteneja has no real beaches. It doesn't have much else, either: There are several churches, one school, two mostly empty guesthouses, one vacant hotel that is for sale, a few little bars and eating places in local houses, and a handful of mini marts. At Easter and occasionally at other times, a sailing regatta is held with local boats—built by hand in the village—and others from Belize City and Ambergris Caye. There's an airstrip, but there's no regularly scheduled service.

The village was nearly destroyed by Hurricane Janet in 1955. About six miles west of Sarteneja Village is the 22,000-acre Shipstern Nature Center, a preserve designed to protect the moist subtropical forest. One of Belize's butterfly farms is here, though it is no longer an active butterfly-breeding center.

Much of the shore around Sarteneja is lined with mangroves, and the water is shallow, with a marl bottom in some areas that is soft and mucky. Manatees are common in the Shipstern Lagoon, and more than 200 species of birds have been spotted.

WHERE TO LIVE

Dwellings here, as in Copper Bank, Progresso, and environs, are mostly simple, Belizean-style properties that sell for less than US$50,000. Rentals, such as they are, are inexpensive, but you will have to seek them out locally, by word of mouth. There is really no organized real-estate or rental market here. In 2005, improved lots with 100 feet of waterfront were being offered in Sarteneja by a developer for US$75,000–100,000, a figure that sounds almost ridiculous given the location, but property from local owners was much less costly. A small, 10-room hotel was on the market for less than US$200,000.

GETTING AROUND

Buses run several times a day from Orange Walk Town to Sarteneja. The daily water taxi between Corozal Town and San Pedro also stops on demand at Sarteneja Village.

Orange Walk District

Your first introduction to Orange Walk District will likely be the sugar-cane fields and concomitant, hulking sugar-cane trucks near Orange Walk Town on the Northern Highway. Orange Walk Town—the name comes from the orange groves in the area—is a somewhat scruffy, bustling place with more of a Mexican than Belizean ambience, having not

Expat Profile: Canadian Reflections

A Canadian expat, who wished to remain anonymous, says that there are two big reasons he chose Belize after looking at other countries:

"After some Internet research, I spent a month each on the Pacific Coast of Costa Rica, in the Lake Chapala area of Mexico, and in Belize. My number one reason for choosing Belize was that most people speak English. People dealing with tourists speak English everywhere. I can buy my vegetables anywhere without speaking the local language. But in Belize, I can talk to the person selling vegetables about anything. I think I have a better chance to become a part of the community, where I can talk to people without struggling with a language. This was not number one on my pre-trip list of important points. I didn't realize how important it was until I spent the time in Costa Rica and Mexico."

This expat's second reason for settling in Belize was "lack of 'petty' corruption. "I won't comment on what senior politicians do. But no Belizean official (police, customs, etc.) has even hinted to me that he would like a bribe. There are probably bad apples, but it is reassuring to occasionally read about cops being charged with shakedowns. I've done business in countries where bribes and payoffs are normal. It is a big negative, especially for a foreigner who doesn't know how to bribe cost-effectively."

a great deal of interest for most visitors or would-be expats. Orange Walk Town could be any number of towns in Mexico. There's a formal plaza, and the town hall is called the Palacio Municipal. The businesses and houses along the main drag—Queen Victoria Avenue, or the Belize–Corozal Road—have barred windows, and some of the hotels and bars are in fact brothels. In this setting, conservative Mennonites who come to town to sell produce look strangely out of place. The town, however, is trying to attract more tourism and other visitor interest. It has opened a museum, the Banquitas House of Culture, to highlight the history and culture of the area. Banquitas refers to the benches in a park on the New River, used for generations by courting couples.

The real Orange Walk is the big, wide, lightly populated area to the west and southwest of Orange Walk Town, up against the Guatemalan border. Here you'll find large tracts of public and private land, teeming with deer, ocellated turkey, toucans, and all manner of other wildlife. Mennonites are a potent agricultural and economic force in rural Orange Walk.

THE LAY OF THE LAND

While Orange Walk Town will interest few, if any, expats, the town of almost 15,000 people is a gateway to a magical area of Belize: the wide sky, fertile land, and unpopulated forests of Belize's northwest shoulder, pressed against the Guatemalan border. The road east from Orange Walk Town, past the Cuello distillery, Yo Creek, and then back south to August Pine Ridge Village and San Felipe Village, leads through agricultural areas to the 240,000-acre Programme for Belize Rio Bravo Conservation area and the 250,000-acre private estate of Barry Bowen. You probably won't see them from the road, but archaeologists say there are many ancient Maya sites in this region. One is well-known: Lamanai, one of Belize's most interesting sites, situated on the New River Lagoon.

Blue Creek is a prosperous Mennonite settlement. About half of the 400 Mennonites in Blue Creek belong to the progressive wing of the Mennonite religion, and the other half belong to the more conservative Kleine Gemeinde community.

One of the more bizarre artifacts of Belize history is in the Blue Creek community: the fuselage of a Lockheed Super Constellation. In 1976, the airliner ran into trouble during a flight to Guatemala City. The pilot attempted to make an emergency landing at the old Belize City airport but missed the runway. The damaged fuselage was trucked to Blue Creek and used as a storage facility by Mennonites.

Beyond Blue Creek is the 240,000-acre Programme for Belize Rio Bravo Conservation Area and the 250,000-acre private estate of Barry Bowen, who owns the Belikin beer brewery and Belize's Coca-Coca bottling company, among other enterprises.

WHERE TO LIVE

Expats looking at Orange Walk District would probably be mostly interested in rural area farmland or along the Northern Highway. There are no housing subdivisions or apartment complexes in this part of Belize. Land in larger tracts is available from around US$300–500 an acre. For example, an 800-acre tract has been on the market for US$280,000, or US$350 an acre. Smaller properties with road access cost US$1,000 an acre and up. In 2005, a 1.8-acre parcel on the New River, with more than 400 feet of river frontage, was on sale for US$15,000.

GETTING AROUND

From Belize City or Corozal Town to Orange Walk Town: Novelo's and Northern Transport offer frequent service—every hour or so—on the Northern Highway to Orange Walk Town, for US$3–5. There is no air service to Orange Walk Town. Taxis are available in Orange Walk Town. Outside Orange Walk Town, you'll definitely need a car.

To Blue Creek, Lamanai, and beyond: To travel by road from Orange Walk Town to Indian Church village and Lamanai, take the all-weather road west to Yo Creek, then southwest to August Pine Ridge and San Felipe, bearing left (southeast) at San Felipe to Indian Church Village near the Lamanai ruins, a total distance of about 36 miles from Orange Walk. Figure about three hours by car from Belize City. There's limited bus service to Indian Church from Orange Walk.

A more scenic option is a boat trip up the New River to the New River Lagoon, which takes about 1.5 hours and costs around US$50 per person. Alternatively, you can go from Orange Walk Town south through the village of Guinea Grass to Shipyard, and take a boat there to Lamanai. To Blue Creek, Programme for Belize, and Gallon Jug, you follow the same route as to Lamanai, but at San Felipe, you turn right and go west to Blue Creek Village, a Mennonite settlement. The Mennonites have paved part of the road here. From Blue Creek, it's about 35 miles to Gallon Jug. Figure about four hours by car from Belize City.

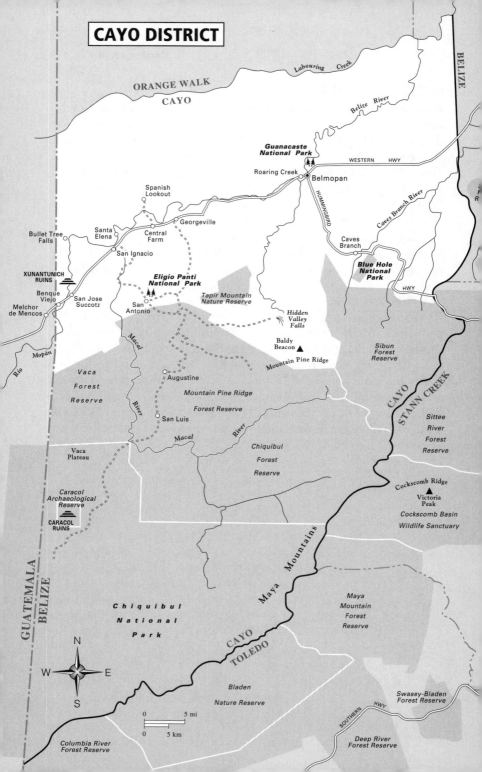

© Lan Sluder

Cayo District

Cayo District, in Western Belize bordering Guatemala, is an exception to most of what you come to expect in Belize. In a country on the Caribbean coast, Cayo (ironically, the Spanish word for "island") is landlocked, with rivers but no lagoons, and it borders on no sea or bay. Instead of low-lying, bug-infested tropical vistas, you'll find rolling hills, low mountains, and few mosquitoes or sandflies in Cayo. While Cayo has some lush broadleaf jungle, it also has piney woods and red clay that may remind you of north Alabama. It has both the hottest and the coldest weather in Belize. On summer days, temperatures can soar to over 100°F, or dip into the 40s on a winter's eve in the 3,000-foot elevations of the Mountain Pine Ridge. Because of the hilly terrain and the rivers, during the rainy season (June to November) the area is occasionally prone to flooding. Rivers can rise with amazing suddenness, creating danger for anyone on or near the fast-moving waters.

As you drive west from Belize City on the Western Highway, you gradually leave the flat savannahs of the coastal plain. The savannah gives way to citrus groves and cattle ranches. You begin to see low limestone hills, some in striking formations, rising out of the plain.

The terrain becomes progressively more hilly and scenic as you go west. Most of the land has been extensively logged in the past, and sizable areas are given up to citrus farms and brahma cattle ranches. This is Belize's "Wild West." While you still occasionally see Mestizo cowboys on horseback, today's ranch hands more often ride in the back of a Toyota HiLux pickup or drive a Land Rover.

The town of San Ignacio, often called Cayo or El Cayo (as with the towns of Corozal, Orange Walk, and Belize City, there can be considerable confusion as to whether one is referring to the town or the district) is the quintessential Western Belize burg. It's the place most people think of first when they think of Cayo District—San Ignacio is a friendly small town set on hills above the Macal and Mopan rivers, and it is the center of agriculture, commerce, transportation, and tourism in Western Belize. Nearby are several small villages and other areas of potential interest for would-be expats, including the Mennonite community of Spanish Lookout and the village of San Antonio. Beyond San Ignacio, at the border with Guatemala, is the town of Benque Viejo del Carmen.

Along the Western Highway, the main road that runs through Cayo District, are a number of small villages and farming enclaves, including Georgeville, Central Farm, and Unitedville. Belmopan City, Belize's little capital, is in Cayo District as well, at the junction of the Western and Hummingbird Highways. Southeast of Belmopan, along the Hummingbird Highway, is some of the most enchanting scenery in Belize. South of San Ignacio, the Mountain Pine Ridge rises. Primarily a forest reserve owned by the government, the Mountain Pine Ridge has a little private property available for those who really, really want to get away from civilization.

Cayo is ideal for anyone who likes the outdoor life, with hiking, horseback riding, mountain biking, canoeing on rivers, and world-class caving. Over time, the limestone terrain here has created extensive underground caverns. Some, such as Actun Tunichil Muknal or "Cave of the Crystal Maiden" (visitors to the cave can still see the calcified skeleton of the Maya maiden, which in lantern light sparkles like crystal) and Che Chem Ha, were used as ceremonial sites by the ancient Maya. Other caves in more remote areas have not been fully explored in modern times.

Orchids and other flowers grow like weeds here. Those in Cayo with a little land and a green thumb can also be virtually self-sufficient with

The rolling hills of Spanish Lookout in Cayo District in Western Belize, home to a large Mennonite population, may remind you more of Pennsylvania than Central America.

food. Tropical fruits such as avocadoes, citrus, papaya, star fruit, passion fruit, and mangoes grow easily. Vegetables from more temperate climates, such as onions, potatoes, corn, tomatoes, peppers, and even broccoli, cauliflower, and kale can also be successfully grown. Central Farm, home of the agricultural research station of the University of Belize, is near San Ignacio, and its staff offer assistance to local gardeners and farmers. There are also several nurseries and garden supply stores in or near San Ignacio.

Even if you're not the active outdoor type, there's plenty to do in Cayo District. The University of Belize has a campus in Belmopan, and a private college, Galen University, is near San Ignacio. You can take classes at either one. The district has three butterfly farms, a botanical garden (on the grounds of duPlooy's Lodge), and many noted Maya sites, including Caracol, Xunantunich, Cahal Pech, and El Pilar. Just a little more than an hour's drive from the Guatemala border is Tikal, the greatest of all excavated Maya sites. For joiners, Cayo has many churches, and there's a Rotary Club in San Ignacio.

For retirees and those with medical problems, the availability of good health care is important. While the options in Cayo are improving—

there are small public hospitals in San Ignacio and Belmopan, and a large clinic in Benque Viejo—local residents still usually go to Belize City or Guatemala City for serious health problems, and most still go to Belize City for dental care.

CLIMATE

Cayo District is generally hotter by day, but cooler by night, than other parts of Belize. From spring to late fall, daytime temperatures around San Ignacio and Belmopan commonly reach into the 90s and occasionally get over 100, with nighttime temperatures mostly in the 60s. In winter, it often drops into the 50s at night, which is cold for Belize, and in the higher altitudes of the Mountain Pine Ridge, a fireplace feels good on winter evenings, with chilly 40-something temperatures. Year-round, it is cooler by five to 10 degrees or so and also less humid in the Pine Ridge than in lower elevations.

From February through May, it is what locals call the dry season in Cayo, with hot, dry weather and rarely any rain. Forest fires are common, especially in the Pine Ridge, where they leave acres of Caribbean pines black and lifeless. The seasonal rains usually begin in June, with heavy black clouds sweeping in from Guatemala.

PEOPLE AND CULTURE

Maya Indians settled the Belize River Valley in what is now Cayo District thousands of years ago. By the time of Christ, sizable cities and large ceremonial and trading centers had been constructed. The Maya began building at El Pilar around 500 B.C. and at Cahal Pech even earlier. During the Maya Classic period, A.D. 250–950, Caracol in the Chiquibul wilderness area beyond the Mountain Pine Ridge was one of the dominant Maya city-states in Mesoamerica. Xunantunich, just west of present-day San Ignacio, was a major ceremonial center.

In the 7th century A.D., the warlords of Caracol defeated mighty Tikal and Naranjo in what is now the Petén region of Guatemala. The Indians developed an immense agricultural system, complete with irrigation and drinking water sufficient to support a large population. Estimates state that 200,000 people lived around Caracol alone, nearly as many people as live in all of modern Belize. The area had so large a population, in fact, that archaeologists think it may have suffered from the Maya equivalent of urban sprawl. Even today, the tallest human-built structure in Belize is Canaa, a temple at Caracol, and the second-tallest is El Castillo at Xunantunich.

After the still mysterious decline of the Maya civilization soon after the end of the first millennium, the number of Maya in the Cayo was much reduced, and it was further reduced when, in the 18th century, some Indians were forcibly removed to Guatemala by white settlers. Now the population is predominantly Mestizo, with a minority of Maya. For many Mestizos, Spanish is their first language, but most, except new arrivals from Guatemala, also speak fluent English. The Maya in Cayo are mostly Mopan Maya, now settled around the village of Succotz west of San Ignacio, and Yucatec Maya around San Antonio, southeast of San Ignacio.

> Today, citrus farming is the main industry in Cayo, and many local residents are employed in agriculture or supporting industries. Nearly 60,000 acres in Belize are planted with citrus fruit, and much of this acreage is in Cayo District.

The first modern settlements of any size in Cayo were logging camps. You'll still see many Cayo place names with "Bank" in them: Banana Bank, Duffy Bank, Macaw Bank, and others. In this sense, "bank" refers to a riverside logging camp. Later, chicle, an ingredient used in chewing gum, was an important revenue source. Today, citrus farming is the main industry in Cayo, and many local residents are employed in agriculture or supporting industries. Nearly 60,000 acres in Belize are planted with citrus fruit, and much of this acreage is in Cayo District. Valencia oranges do particularly well here. Local entrepreneurs have also tried their hand at tourism. Many of the small hotels and lodges around Cayo are run by Belizeans, while most of the larger and more upscale properties are owned by expats.

Expat Community

Most members of the small expat community in Cayo District—the exact count is unknown, but probably numbers in the several hundreds—are involved in either tourism or agriculture. A few foreign retirees have also moved to small ranchettes, where they've built homes and piddle in their gardens and groves.

The pioneers of tourism in this area are Mick and Lucy Fleming (he's British, she's American), who started a lodge at Chaa Creek in 1980, when foreign tourists were almost unknown in this part of Belize. Through the years, they've expanded and fine-tuned the property, on

330 acres on the Macal River, creating the queen of Belize's jungle lodges. Near Chaa Creek is another top Macal River lodge developed by more expatriates, the duPlooys. The late Ken duPlooy came from Zimbabwe, and his wife, Judy, who still owns the lodge, comes from the United States. Farther up the Macal River on about 200 acres, a former Coloradan, Phyllis Lane, helped build the tiny (there are just two *cabañas*) but deluxe and delightful Ek' Tun Lodge. Lane has put her heart and soul into the project, and she has a hard-earned, realistic view of the difficulties of making a go of it in Belize. "I've often thought of writing a book about Belize titled *The Other Side of Paradise,* wherein reality is the focus, and the many frustrations are not overlooked," she says.

More recent comers to the bed-and-bush group are Pamella and Jay Picon, Americans who started Belize's first all-inclusive resort near Benque Viejo. Their Mopan River Resort opened in 1998. Jay first visited Belize in the 1960s to investigate cattle farming but then went to Mexico instead. Pam's first visit was in the 1980s. They became citizens through the Economic Citizenship program in 1988 but only started living in Belize in the mid-1990s, first in Belize City and then in Benque Viejo. Pam offers this advice for those thinking of starting a lodge or hotel in Belize: "Don't do it unless you *like* people. If you see it strictly as a business, you won't enjoy it. Belize has too many average, look-alike facilities. Be prepared to do something different. Be prepared to *work!*... As simple as it sounds, you have to really like Belize for what it is. You must be prepared to adapt your lifestyle to fit Belize—Belize will not adapt to you."

Along those same lines, Pam also offers a bit of advice about how to adapt comfortably into the local community as an expat business-owner: "Although the government encourages foreign investment, many locals will see you only as unfair competition. Choose your type of business and its location with this in mind. Hire as many locals as you can, and be prepared to train them. Again, treat everyone with respect; support local causes nonpolitically."

San Ignacio

About 70 miles from Belize City is San Ignacio and its adjacent twin town, Santa Elena. The two are usually lumped together and simply referred to as San Ignacio or El Cayo. Together, these have outpaced

Orange Walk Town as the largest town in Belize, with a population of around 15,000 in 2005. The Hawksworth Bridge, a 1949 vintage suspension structure over the Macal River, marks the entrance to San Ignacio, although it is one-way, with eastbound traffic only. Nearby, the Mopan and Macal Rivers merge, forming the Belize River, which wends its way northeastward to Belize City.

THE LAY OF THE LAND

San Ignacio, like Rome, is built on seven hills. The views over the river valleys and into Guatemala from some of these hills are lovely. At the top of one of the hills, at around 900 feet, is a Preclassic and Classic Period Maya site, Cahal Pech, a name that unfortunately means "Place of the Ticks" in the Mopan Maya language.

Those looking for a high-energy urban or beachside atmosphere may not want to settle here, but many find San Ignacio, with Corozal and Punta Gorda, to be one of the three most appealing towns in mainland Belize. It's generally safe and easygoing, with a down-to-earth, folksy charm. The residents, mostly Mestizos, with some Mayas and an occasional Creole or gringo, are hardworking and friendly.

San Ignacio is a small town, but it offers the basics most residents need: Caribbean International Bank, Scotia Bank, Belize Bank, and

© Lan Sluder

citrus grove with Maya Mountains in the distance

Expat Profile: Looking for Property

A couple from Nova Scotia, Canada, both in their 50s, began thinking about retirement destinations in 2003. At first, like everyone, they did some online research, but then they talked to a friend who had lived in Belize for two years. In May 2004, Kathleen Owen and her husband took their first trip to Belize for 10 days. Kathleen describes their journey:

"We spent the first couple of days in Belize City and decided immediately this was not the place. We stopped into Emerald Futures while we were there and met John and Madeline Estevan, who were incredibly friendly and helpful and spent a fair amount of time going over our options with us. They hooked us up with their counterpart in San Ignacio, Donna Hill, and we rented a car and drove up to SI. As soon as we got away from Belize City and into the western part of the country, we felt "at home." Even though our time in the country was limited at this point, Donna spent two days with us going to various sites, discussing what we really wanted to do, and exposing us to as much of the Cayo area as possible.

"We came home without making a definite decision, but continued to monitor the various real estate sites online, and Donna kept in touch regularly. Unfortunately, it doesn't matter how many websites you look at, there is no substitute for being there. We requested information on properties via email from some of the other real estate companies and got absolutely no response. We relied on Donna a lot to give us the inside scoop on some of the properties. Apart from Donna, we've discovered that Belizean companies are not very good at responding to emails. We had better luck using the phone if we absolutely had to contact someone.

"We knew we had to go back, so we booked a month off, and Donna found us a perfect small house to rent in San Ignacio for US$400 a

Atlantic Bank all have branches in San Ignacio. Celina's Superstore has a pretty good selection of groceries, plus dry goods and other items. Crossroads Supermarket has better prices on some items. The Saturday market in San Ignacio is one of the best in Belize, with a plentiful array of produce for sale by local farmers. A private hospital, La Loma Luz, is in Santa Elena, along with a public hospital.

In San Ignacio, you can always get a good meal at Sanny's at the western edge of the town. Sanny's takes basic Belize dishes such as pork chops with rice and beans and turns them into something spicy and exotic. Serendib, a Sri Lankan–run downtown restaurant, has authentic curries, along with all the usual Belizean fare. Café Sol and Hannah's are two other local favorites. If you have some extra cash in your jeans,

month. We 'lived like the natives,' i.e., shopped locally, went to the market, cooked for ourselves, etc., and found that San Ignacio is a very easy place to live, once you get used to the traffic and the dogs!

"We found the perfect property on the Hummingbird Highway— [and] in three weeks, we managed to buy the property, buy a vehicle, incorporate a company, open bank accounts, and have meetings with Beltraide and the Department of the Environment (we're building a lodge). Things could not have gone more smoothly.

"I see and hear a lot of negative comments about red tape, and the headaches of dealing with Belize government departments, etc. I can't help but feel that a lot of these problems are self-inflicted. We went down very prepared, knowing what the government regulations were beforehand, knowing what questions to ask, and doing a lot of research on what kinds of documentation to have ready before [we even approached] the government.

"Maybe it comes from our experience in business in Canada, but we know that no matter where you go, there are laws and regulations to follow, and the government does not take kindly to fools coming in empty-handed with nothing but 'ideas' and 'maybes.' Nor do they respond well to the 'I'm going to do this my way and on my timetable' attitude. Sure, they are a little slower than in some other places, and some things are a little hard to understand (the 'safety inspection' on the vehicle we bought was a complete joke), but believe me, in a country as small as Belize, you have to expect some undeveloped areas.

"In some ways, doing business in Belize is a lot like it was in Canada in the 1940s and 50s. It's all personal contacts, word of mouth, and favors among neighbors. Give me that any day over what has evolved in North America."

try the Running W restaurant, specializing in steaks, at the San Ignacio Resort Hotel. Queen Elizabeth stayed at this hotel when she visited San Ignacio in 1994. There's a small branch of Belize City's Princess Casino at the San Ignacio Resort Hotel.

Everyone, locals and tourists alike, eventually ends up at Eva's, a San Ignacio restaurant and bar-cum-cybercafé and community bulletin board, run by an ex-Brit soldier named Bob Jones, who married a local gal and stayed on. Bob claims his place was the first Internet café in Central America. Nightlife in Cayo mostly involves loud music and booze. Several downtown clubs in San Ignacio offer live music on weekends. Less savory are the local brothels, which, in this age of political correctness and AIDS, shall remain nameless.

Spanish Lookout

Northeast of San Ignacio, in and around Spanish Lookout, is one of Belize's Mennonite areas. Farms here, mostly run by the more progressive Mennonites who use tractors and other modern equipment, supply a large part of Belize's produce, chickens, eggs, and cheese. The total population of the Spanish Lookout area is about 2,000.

The well-tended, rolling farmland may remind you of parts of the American Midwest. As elsewhere in Belize, most of the rural roads around Spanish Lookout are unpaved, but the Mennonites, without any government help, have worked together to pave some of the main roads.

Also here are some of Belize's best carpenters and builders, and several companies based here construct prefabricated houses called Mennonite houses, which offer cheap way to get a building up fast. (See the *Resources* chapter for details.)

San Antonio

South of San Ignacio, on the Cristo Rey road on the way to the Mountain Pine Ridge, is the village of San Antonio, with a population of about 2,500. Many residents here are descendents of Yucatec Maya, who moved here after the Caste Wars in Mexico in the mid-19th century. Many still speak the Yucatec Maya language, as well as English and Spanish. San Antonio was the home of famed Guatemalan-born Maya healer Don Eligio Panti, who died in 1996 at the age of 103. His home in the village has become an informal museum.

Also in San Antonio is the Tanah Museum, operated by the Garcia family, who are well-known in Belize for their devotion to maintaining the traditional Maya culture and who help preserve the old Maya art of slate carving. One of the Garcia sisters, Maria, was instrumental in helping to establish the new 19-square-mile Eligio Panti National Park between the Macal River and the Mountain Pine Ridge forest reserve.

Bullet Tree Falls

About three miles west of San Ignacio, Bullet Tree Falls is a small (population about 600) Mestizo village on the Mopan River. With its mellow, laid-back, riverside atmosphere, Bullet Tree Falls has emerged as a budget-level alternative to the upscale jungle lodges in the area. About half a dozen small lodges have set up camp on or near the river. Also in the village are an equal number of bars, so weekends can get lively. Bullet Tree is also a gateway to the El Pilar Maya ruins, which sprawl across the Guatemala border a few miles to the west. Unfortunately, being so close to the Guatemalan frontier, the area occasionally has been the scene of holdups and car-jackings by bandits who cross over from Guatemala and then fade back across the border after doing their dirty work.

Other Villages

Along the Western Highway between Belmopan and San Ignacio, a distance of about 23 miles, are a number of small villages, including (from east to west) Camelote, Teakettle, Ontario, Unitedville, and Georgeville. West of San Ignacio is San José Succotz. To the outsider, there is little to distinguish one of these villages from another. They all have a primary school, a church or two, several small stores in houses along the highway, some chickens, and a lot of barking dogs. Some also have bars with karaoke machines—karaoke is a near-addiction with many Belizeans, especially in this area. For expats, the advantages to living in one of these small villages include low housing costs and easy access to buses on the Western Highway.

WHERE TO LIVE

In this part of Belize, you have a choice of living in a small town or village or in a more rural area. It comes down to personal choice, but most expats who decide to live in or around San Ignacio seem to prefer having some land and being in a rural area.

Ray Auxillou, a Canadian by birth who lived for many years in Caye Caulker, and who now splits his time between Miami and Belize, chose to build a small house in the Hillview section of Santa Elena. He did it for little money, but since building the house, he has had a litany of complaints: about poor road maintenance (off the main highway, most roads are not paved), lack of telephones in the area (there are no telephone lines to Hillview, and cell phones don't work because of the hilly terrain near his house), and not getting mail delivery to his house (there's a long waiting list for post office boxes). By contrast, Dave and Marilyn Eider, wilderness guides in British Columbia, say they have fallen in love with the "jungle" at Bullet Tree Falls, a few minutes west of San Ignacio. "It's a great place with *great* people. We are dealing with a local Mayan gent to purchase 40 acres of his 120-acre homestead. He needs money for improvements, and we like the idea of having our personal jungle," they report. Barbara Kasak, a Texan who runs Barb's Belize, a travel agency specializing in Belize, and who has visited Belize many times, also bought land in Bullet Tree, where she plans to build.

Land is plentiful in Cayo, but the locals have seen you coming, and the cheap land of yesterday around San Ignacio is hard to find. Still, by U.S. standards, land is inexpensive. Expect to pay US$1,000–2,500 an acre for citrus-growing land near San Ignacio with good access. Rougher, more remote land goes for US$500 an acre or less in larger tracts. In 2005, a 32-acre parcel near the village of Georgeville south of San Ignacio was on sale for US$50,000, and a 517-acre working farm, with 150 acres planted with citrus trees and the rest with row crops, was on the market for US$1.65 million. Also in 2005, a 75-acre tract near the Guatemala border at El Pilar was on the market for US$75,000. At Bullet Tree Falls, 14 acres on a hilltop were on sale at an asking price of US$45,000.

Expat Profile: From Tent-Dweller to Lodge Owner

When she first came to Belize, Phyllis Lane lived in a tent. Now she shares space with a howler monkey and runs one of Belize's smallest jungle lodges, Ek' Tun Lodge. Lane came to the Cayo District of Belize from Colorado in the 1980, with her then-husband, Ken Dart. Today, she lives on 200 remote acres adjoining the Macal River in Cayo District, about 12 miles upstream from San Ignacio.

The only way you can get to her property is by small boat, across the river. There guests find two expansive, two-level *cabañas* built of tropical wood in the Maya style. Lane struggles with daily life in the jungle—a generator that goes dead periodically, floods on the river (during heavy rains, the Macal can rise 20 feet in just a few minutes), the frustrating Belizean bureaucracy, that bane of many Belizeans—the BTL phone company, and just the day-in, day-out efforts required to earn enough from her tourism business to make ends meet. Even with rates at US$230 for a double room (including meals), with just two *cabañas,* it's tough to generate enough income to pay the bills.

Lane shares her lodge with a stray howler monkey—unnamed, as she doesn't believe in naming wild things—along with a dog and a variety of creatures from red-rumped tarantulas to rare orange-breasted falcons. An unreconstructed New Ager, she has unconventional ideas on nutrition, politics, and the best way to live life. Given the chance, would she do it all over again in Belize? The answer to that question depends on which day you ask her.

Building lots with electricity and cable TV in San Ignacio and Santa Elena start at US$2,000 and go to US$15,000 or more. Lots in San Antonio Village and other villages near San Ignacio rarely go for more than US$5,000. You'll often get a better deal if you buy from the owner, rather than from a real-estate agent.

Homes in and around San Ignacio start at US$15,000 for small, Belizean-style places and range up to $300,000 or more for deluxe haciendas. Most homes, however, are priced under US$150,000. In 2005, a newly built small house with its own well and a turbine for electricity, on 65 acres overlooking San Ignacio, was on the market for US$150,000.

Many foreigners moving to Cayo build their own homes rather than buy an existing one. Carpenters, masons, block layers, and other skilled construction workers get about US$25 a day. A nicely finished concrete home can be built for US$40–75 a square foot.

Rentals

Rentals in San Ignacio, and indeed throughout Cayo District, start at under US$150 per month for a Belizean-style house, with attractive, North American–style homes available for US$400–800. The fanciest rental in Western Belize in 2005 was a 4,000-square-foot, custom-built home on a five-acre hilltop near Spanish Lookout. On a long-term lease, the monthly rental is US$2,000. Few rentals are advertised or listed with an agent, so you must seek them out yourself on the ground in Cayo.

GETTING AROUND

The main road to Cayo is the Western Highway, a good, paved, two-lane road. From Belize City by car, San Ignacio is about 1.75 hours. Add another 15 minutes to get to the Guatemalan border at Benque Viejo del Carmen. Buses take two to three hours from Belize City to San Ignacio, depending on whether it is an express or a local bus. Novelo's buses run this route at least hourly. Between Belize City and San Ignacio, the cost is around US$5 for an express bus. There is no scheduled air service to Cayo, although there are airstrips at Central Farm near San Ignacio and at Blancaneaux Lodge in the Pine Ridge. Regular taxis and collective taxis are available in San Ignacio (US$10 for a regular taxi to the Guatemalan border, or about US$2 for a collective taxi). Due to lack of bus service except on the Western Highway, most expat residents have a car.

Mountain Pine Ridge

If you drive south from the San Ignacio area on either the Cristo Rey or Pine Ridge Roads, you soon come to the entrance of the Mountain Pine Ridge. "Ridge" in Belizean usage refers not to the geographic feature but to the type of tree common in the area. In this case, it's the mountain pine, which is similar to the Caribbean pine. Unfortunately, an infestation of pine beetles has destroyed thousands of acres of pine forest, but the forest is regenerating quickly. Elevations here range from about 1,000 to 3,000 feet. The elevation means that it is generally cooler and less humid than in the rest of Belize.

THE LAY OF THE LAND

With the adjoining Chiquibul Wilderness, Vaca Plateau, and the northwestern part of the Maya Mountain range, this is the largest protected wilderness area in Belize. While the Mountain Pine Ridge is mostly piney woods, the Chiquibul, Vaca, and Maya Mountains areas have broadleaf jungle. Here you'll find ironwood, cohune palm, sapodilla, and other exotic tropical trees. This region is rough and wild. There are dozens of isolated waterfalls, clean mountain streams (though with the occasional crocodile), and huge underground cave systems. Britain's Prince William spent some time here a few years ago, training with the Welsh Guards.

> With the adjoining Chiquibul Wilderness, Vaca Plateau, and the northwestern part of the Maya Mountain range, this is the largest protected wilderness area in Belize.

Part of the Mountain Pine Ridge is privately owned, mostly in huge tracts once bought for a dollar or two an acre, and part is owned by the government. Controlled logging is allowed, and the roads in the Pine Ridge, some impassable after heavy rains, are all former logging tracks. Except for a small settlement at Augustine/Douglas DeSilva on the road to Caracol, four small jungle lodges, and some isolated enclaves of Guatemalan squatters, few people live in the region. To get tourists to the fabulous Maya ruins of Caracol more quickly, the road to Caracol was improved in 2004, with some of the worst sections paved.

The Mountain Pine Ridge and Chiquibul Wilderness are particularly exciting areas for outdoors types. There are waterfalls seemingly around

At the Macal River in Mountain Pine Ridge en route to the Caracol Maya ruins, the author saw a baby Morlet's crocodile.

every bend—with cool pools for a private skinny-dip—along with cave systems worthy of a *National Geographic* story (of which several have, in fact, been written). This area is also the best in Belize for mountain biking, and one of the best for hiking and horseback riding.

WHERE TO LIVE AND GETTING AROUND

Social butterflies need not apply: The Mountain Pine Ridge is a place for hermits and those who want to be miles from the nearest neighbor. Land in small tracts in the Mountain Pine Ridge is not often for sale. When on the market, it goes for up to US$10,000 an acre. In 2005, 10 private acres with creeks and beautiful trees, ideal for a small resort or private home, were on the market for US$70,000. There are few existing houses and no rentals in the Pine Ridge.

There is no public transportation in the Mountain Pine Ridge. A vehicle, preferably a four-wheel-drive truck with high ground clearance, is a necessity here.

Belmopan

Belmopan City, off Mile 48 of the Western Highway, population 8,130 in the latest census, is hardly more than a sleepy small town. It's truly one of the world's smallest and least imposing capitals.

The new capital was formerly established in 1970, after the devastation of then-capital Belize City nine years earlier. Political leaders envisioned moving all the instruments of government from Belize City to Belmopan, and they foresaw that the population would soon grow to 30,000. This has been slow to happen, as most Belizeans were reluctant to leave their homes, families, and favorite hangouts in the port city, despite the crime and danger of storms that city routinely faces.

Expat Profile: Jungle Fever

In the early 1990s, Cy and Donna Young were living in Florida. Cy had been a beer distributor and owned several video rental stores. Donna was a food and beverage manager for a Greyhound racetrack. They were looking for something different and heard about Belize. Eventually, they bought a 200-acre tract of land in the jungle near Belmopan for US$45,000 and began planning an upscale jungle lodge, one that would have air-conditioning and gourmet food—adventure by day, comfort at night.

Although both were experienced in business, they weren't completely prepared for the red tape and special issues foreigners face in Belize. They initially thought that the lodge, in a remote area near the Caves Branch River, could be built for under US$500,000. They reportedly ended up investing more than three times that amount, spending close to US$100,000 per room for the 16-room project, similar to the costs for a luxury hotel in the United States. The government, according to the Youngs, didn't live up to its promises to extend power and a road to the property, so the Youngs had to buy and run large generators. Officials lost the import paperwork for equipment and materials, which sat in a Belize City warehouse accruing thousands of dollars in storage fees.

In the early stages of getting the project going, the Youngs ran into killer bees and poisonous snakes and even received kidnapping threats from Guatemalan bandits who came across the border. In the end, Jaguar Paw lodge turned out beautifully—and since its opening in 1996 has ranked as among the top lodges in the country. But, according to several reports, it never achieved the consistent large revenue stream it needed to provide a competitive return on the investment. Several years ago, the Youngs put their hotel up for sale, although they continue to operate it and earn rave reviews from visitors to Belize.

Brasilia it ain't, but Belmopan has begun to finally, slowly take off. It was officially designated a city a couple of years ago, a promotion from being just a town.

The University of Belize has established a campus here, and more embassies (including the U.S. Embassy which has broken ground on a 50 million dollar complex) are moving to Belmopan from Belize City. The population grew about 50 percent between 1990 and 2000. The market near the bus station bustles, and some people are making money on their real-estate investments here.

Belmopan does boast several modern stores, among them a branch of Brodies and a Courts appliance store. Belize Bank, ScotiaBank, and First Caribbean International all have branches in Belmopan. Belmopan's few hotels are but modest motels, and its restaurants are equally modest.

LAY OF THE LAND

A ring road encircles the government buildings and some residential areas in Belmopan, but because of the amount of vacant land, the feeling is more of open and underused space than of a busy government center.

Belmopan's most appealing feature is its position as northern access point to the Hummingbird Highway, Belize's most scenic roadway. The Hummingbird, resurfaced a few years ago and now one of the best roads in Belize, wings about 55 miles southeastward, through the Maya Mountains and into Stann Creek District, ending, as the Stann Creek District Highway, at the sea in Dangriga. Along the way are multivariate green hillsides, large orange and grapefruit orchards, and, here and there, old railroad bridges, relics of a railway built in colonial times to transport bananas.

Around Belmopan are more of Belize's top jungle lodges. Most are on one of the many rivers that cut through the country's midsection. Banana Bank Lodge, run by former Montana cowboy John Carr and his artist wife, Carolyn, is on the Belize River. Jaguar Paw, run by two former Floridians, Cy and Donna Young, is on the Caves Branch River. Pook's Hill Lodge on Roaring River is run by Ray and Vicki Snaddon. Longtime Belize residents, both are from other outposts of the British Commonwealth.

A nine-hole golf course, Roaring River, is near Belmopan. The "jungle course" features crocodiles in the water traps. The course is open but currently for sale.

The restaurant pickings are slim in Belmopan, but the Bullfrog Inn has dependable food, and The Oasis is a new place that has its fans. Back toward the Belize Zoo, near Mile 30 of the Western Highway, Cheers is cheap and cheerful.

WHERE TO LIVE

With its recently constructed cinderblock houses set in tidy rows with tiny lawns, Belmopan has the feel of lower middle-class suburbia in Florida, but with more open and unused space. Most of the government buildings are low, ugly, concrete structures of indifferent personality. The main government buildings were designed to reflect the design of a Maya ceremonial center, with structures

a natural swimming hole in Western Belize

© Lan Sluder

grouped around a central plaza, but that design isn't obvious to most who stop by, and the result is more depressing than reflective of the glorious Maya past.

Houses in Belmopan start at around US$30,000 for a small block house and go up to US$200,000 or more for a large, custom-built property on several acres. Most land around Belmopan City goes for US$1,000–4,000 an acre, but lots near commercial or government buildings are much more expensive.

Rentals are affordable in Belmopan. Student housing starts at around US$100 a month, and a middle-class home might rent for US$400–600. As there are no newspapers or other media in Belmopan, and only rarely do real-estate agents handle rentals here, the best way to secure a rental is by word of mouth.

GETTING AROUND

Belmopan, at the junction of the Western and Hummingbird Highways, is about an hour by car from Belize City. Buses come by frequently, about once every half hour during the daylight hours, with most stopping here en route from Belize City and San Ignacio to the Guatemalan border. Some are en route to or from Dangriga and points south. As in other areas of Belize, however, there is no local public transportation system, and to get around, you'll need a car, a few dollars every time you need a cab, or strong legs.

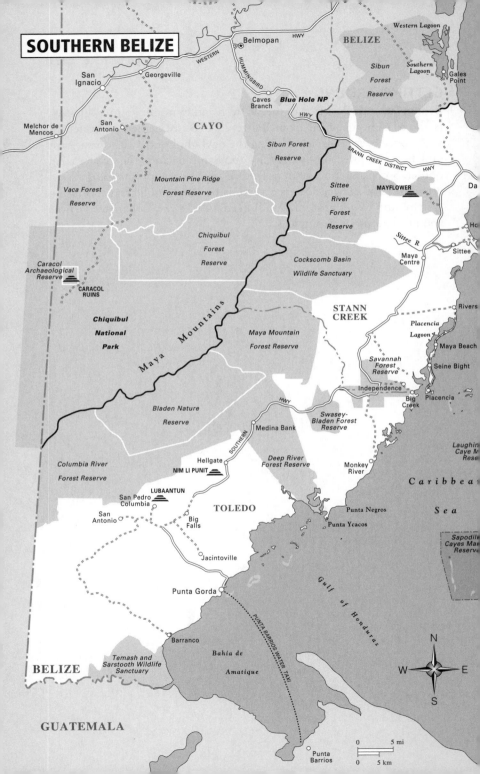

© Ian Sluder

Southern Belize

Southern Belize has the best beaches on the mainland and some of the most dramatic scenery in the country. The region comprises two districts, Stann Creek and Toledo, which together have a population of almost 50,000, predominantly Maya and Garifuna, and also many Creoles and Mestizos. Three areas of particular interest to those relocating, retiring, or visiting Belize for an extended period—or for those looking to buy property in Belize—are the Hopkins Village area, the Placencia Peninsula, and Punta Gorda. The main road through this region is the Southern Highway, almost all of which has been paved and upgraded. It is now the best road in Belize.

Climate is a big draw for Belize, and Southern Belize has the most tropical climate in the country. Generally, the farther south you go, the more precipitation and tropical weather you get. Around Hopkins and Placencia, the summer months of June through August get almost 20 inches of rain monthly. This is more than twice as much as around Belmopan and points north. At Punta Gorda, you might see 25–30 inches of rain monthly during that period. The onset of the rainy season usually begins in early May in Toledo, progressing north to

Placencia and Hopkins in late May or June. July is almost always the wettest month in the far south.

As for temperatures in Southern Belize, you never have to worry about being chilly. Summers see highs near 90, while in winter, highs are usually in the low to mid-80s. Mid-60s are about as low as you'll see, even in the coolest months of January and February. As long as you're on or near the water, the prevailing breezes from the sea keep things more comfortable, although in the summer, the winds may go calm for a few days at a time—at which point, if the humidity doesn't get to you, the bugs will.

All the rain, humidity, and hot weather fuel the growth of flora and create a rich, green environment, especially in the far southern reaches of Toledo. Southern Belize has the country's most extensive rainforests. Even fenceposts sprout new growth. Orchids and heliconia are as common as cucumbers in Connecticut.

Hopkins

Hopkins is a delightfully friendly and still mostly unspoiled village, though it is changing fast—it even has its own Internet café. This is Belize at its most exotic, a Garifuna settlement that may remind you more of a coastal village in Senegal than one in Central America. Nearby are Maya villages that look much as they did hundreds of years ago. A few miles inland from the coast are a wild jaguar preserve and the Maya Mountains. The Cockscomb Basin Preserve west of Hopkins is real rainforest jungle, and the highest peaks in Belize, Doyle's Delight at 3,688 feet and Victoria Peak at 3,675 feet, are in the Maya Mountains.

THE LAY OF THE LAND

Including Sittee River Village and surrounding areas, the population of the Hopkins area is around 2,000, most living on or near the sea and the river. The Hopkins area has real beaches, narrow ribbons of khaki-colored sand, with a good deal of sea grass in the water off the beach. Swimming is possible, especially in areas where the sea grass has been removed, such as the end of a dock. The snorkeling offshore is usually not very good, although you can see some fish and possibly even a manatee. The barrier reef is about 12–15 miles offshore from

Hopkins, so it takes a while to get out to the reef for diving. The Sittee River and the Caribbean waters offer some of Belize's best fishing.

Dangriga, the largest town in the area and about 15 miles by road from Hopkins, is not a popular place for expats, but you'll find some shopping and a regional hospital for medical care there. There are three banks and several groceries in Dangriga, the largest being Southern Pride.

In Hopkins and nearby are several excellent beach resorts, and you'll find some good spots for dining as well. If there's a rub to this paradise, it's the sandflies, which can be fierce.

WHERE TO LIVE

Hopkins, by and large, is a village of wood-frame shacks with thatch roofs and small, simple concrete block houses. Upscale here means there's indoor plumbing. Sittee River Village, a small Creole village nearby, is only marginally more prosperous. If you buy property here, you will most likely construct your own house.

Not too many homes have been built yet in this area by expats, but more building is likely to take place in the next few years. Local land prices have gone up considerably in recent years because of resort development in and around Hopkins and because of promotions by land

© Lan Sluder

a new home owned by an expat near Hopkins

sales companies. For more accom-
modating prices, prospective buyers with cash will want to approach
individual owners in the Hopkins
and Sittee River area.

In the subdivision being developed by Texas-based British-
American Cattle Co., beachfront
lots start at around US$60,000.
Larger lots of more than half an
acre, with both Caribbean and
canal or lagoon access, are close to
US$100,000–120,000. Beachview
lots are around US$25,000, and
lots on the Sittee River are about
the same price. All these lots have
utilities (electricity, telephones,
public water, and cable TV) and

A sandy seafront lot in the Hopkins and
Sittee River Villages goes for less than
US$100,000.

road access. Other beachfront lots in and near Hopkins Village start
at around US$30,000. Small, recently built homes in this area, near
but not on the water, are going for US$125,000–200,000, often with
some owner financing available. Condos are just starting to appear in
this area. Belizean Dreams and Almond Tree, both near Jaguar Reef
Lodge at Sittee River, are two that were finished in 2004–2005. Both
offer luxury condos selling for more than US$200,000. In this area,
rentals are few and far between.

GETTING AROUND

Hopkins has no airstrip, but you can fly into Dangriga. There is bus
service several times a day between Dangriga and Hopkins, but expats
will need a car. The access roads to Hopkins and Sittee River Villages
from the Southern Highway are mostly paved.

Placencia

If you're looking for a little bit of the South Pacific on the Caribbean
coast of Central America, Placencia may be for you. Placencia is a
narrow finger of sandy land between the sea and a lagoon, about 120

miles south of Belize City. If you like the weather in the Florida Keys, you'll probably like the weather in Placencia too. It's humid and hot all year-round, but cooler beachside because of the near-constant breeze from the sea.

Placencia fans boast that it has the best beaches on mainland Belize. The 16 miles or so of beaches on the peninsula are beautiful: a narrow, long stretch of toast-colored sand. Like most beaches in Belize, these are only fair for swimming, as there's a good deal of sea grass, except where hotels have removed it around piers. You can snorkel here and there, but for world-class snorkeling, you'll have to take a boat out to the reef or to one of the small offshore cayes with patch coral, a 10- to 20-mile boat trip. Several marine national parks and reserves are within an hour or two by boat, including Laughing Bird Caye and Port Honduras. The Caribbean is incredibly beautiful above and below the surface. Above, the crystal-clear water sparkles in the sun. Poke your head below, and you find a whole new universe of color and activity, from tiny tropical fish to dolphins, manatees, and whale sharks.

> Placencia fans boast that it has the best beaches on mainland Belize. The 16 miles or so of beaches on the peninsula are beautiful: a narrow, long stretch of toast-colored sand.

Most foreign residents choose Placencia for its quieter, low-stress attitude. The atmosphere is laid-back and focused almost entirely on fishing, boating, and other activities on the water.

THE LAY OF THE LAND

Placencia is a skinny peninsula on the southern coast of the mainland in Stann Creek District. The peninsula, only a few hundred feet wide at some points, lies between the Caribbean Sea on the east and the Placencia Lagoon on the west. The two main population centers are Seine Bight and Placencia Villages, which have fewer than 1,500 people combined. While there are no other villages on the peninsula itself, a number of houses and small hotels dot the unnamed main road that runs down the spine of the peninsula; the largest concentration is in Maya Beach, about nine miles north of the southern tip of the peninsula. Across the lagoon—part of which is being used as a shrimp farm—are several villages, including Mango Creek, Independence, and Big Creek, a deep-water port. These mainland villages get few tourists, but they enjoy a modest prosperity from agriculture (mainly citrus),

Expat Profile: Discovering Belize

Floridian Karen Cochran recalls how she ended up in the Placencia area, across the lagoon in Independence Village:

"For some unknown reason, we just knew that we would not end up in the States. Back in 1989, we saw an ad in the local paper in Ft. Myers, Fla., advertising land for sale in Belize. The deal was that you could buy a certain amount of acres and the developer would match this amount—put so much money down and make monthly payments. This development was north of Crooked Tree in Belize District and called the Revenge Lagoon. Part of the deal was that you had six months to go to Belize (pay your own way) and see if you liked the acreage that you had picked. If you did not and another plot was found and available that you liked, you could switch your choice. So, we first flew into Belize in March 1989. At that time, there were only two hotels listed, the Fort George and the Bellevue. We picked the Bellevue. It was horrible. First evening, the air-conditioning in the room did not work, and we went down to the desk to report the problem. A nice Belizean said to me, 'Well, Miss, perhaps you do not know how to run the air-conditioner.' The result was that about an hour later, they showed up, took the wall unit away, and left. So, there we sat with a hole in the wall.

"The next day, a representative from British American Cattle Co. showed up and took us to see the property that we had selected. He had a regular spiel about how this area would develop and so on and so on. We did see possibilities for the future development of the Revenge Lagoon area. We flew home and thought to ourselves, 'OK, we will keep making our payments and see what happens.'

"Several months later, a gentlemen came to our business in Ft. Myers, and we happened to mention the word 'Belize.' He said 'Hey,

shipping, and shrimp farms. The land everywhere here is low-lying and flat, although the hulking Maya Mountains are visible to the west.

In October 2001, Hurricane Iris did extensive damage to the southern part of the peninsula. But except for a few open spaces where trees have not been replanted or houses rebuilt, Placencia is back to normal now. The peninsula is still in a fairly early stage of development, and contradictions abound. Unpainted wood shacks stand next door to luxury resorts where a week's stay costs more than a local worker might earn in a year. Local families who a few years ago fished for a living have opened restaurants, bars, and hotels, and they don't always have all the management skills down pat. There's a modern water and sewerage system, and

I have been to Belize. In fact, I have a friend who has a Belizean woman visiting, and would you like to meet her?' Sure, we said. It turned out to be a delightful older woman named Mrs. Gertrude Mena from Independence. She said, 'Why don't you come south and visit us the next time that you come to Belize? I think you would enjoy our part of the country.' It turned out she had seven children of her own, plus one boy that boarded with her. We took her up on her offer, and my husband, Bob, and her oldest son formed quite a friendship. The first time down we stayed in a small one-bedroom house and met the Mena family and wandered around the village. So, that is how we ended up in Belize and the Independence area.

"After about 30 visits to Independence over a five- to six-year period, we decided that perhaps we should consider building our own home. At that time, there was nothing that you could buy and there really still is not. [But] a friend was able to get a lot for us, and we went about building our own home. Since Independence is not a town, there is no planning or building department. You just go ahead and do what you want—we ended up with a lot over by the village water tower. Actually, it is a big lot, as lot sizes go in Belize. What started out as a plan to construct a cement house in a year and a half took three. The main problem was that when you show up, most of the construction people are already working, and you have to pull them off whatever job they are on and see if they will come and work on yours. Our house is a simple two-bedroom, one-bath with an eight-foot verandah surrounding half of it. It is elevated and has two rooms underneath. Currently, we try to go to Belize at least four times a year and usually spend 10 to 14 days. The plan is to eventually retire to Belize and live there on a permanent basis."

most of the peninsula is on the power grid, yet local schools barely have any books and, until a Cuban volunteer medical team came to the peninsula, locals had to go to Independence or Dangriga to see a doctor.

Every year in the late spring, usually April through June, large groups of whale sharks *(Rhincodon typus)* appear in an area called Gladden Spit, on the barrier reef about 25 miles from Placencia. These gentle giants—they can reach 40 feet or more in length but eat nothing larger than plankton or tiny fish—are occasionally sighted in much of the tropics and even in colder waters, but Belize is one of only about half a dozen places in the world where aggregations of them predictably appear year after year.

Placencia Village as seen from the harbor

Placencia offers some of the best sportfishing in Belize. Anglers enjoy fly-fishing in Placencia Lagoon and on the Monkey River south of Placencia, fly- or live-bait fishing around the cayes, and open-water spinning and trolling inside and outside the reef. This also is one of the best areas in Belize for permit. There's world-class fishing for tarpon, snook, and bonefish. Inside and around the reef, you can catch barracuda, snapper, king mackerel, wahoo, and yellow- and black-fin tuna, just to name a few. Visitors should expect to pay about US$250 for two people per day, including boat, guide, and equipment.

While there's little to do here beyond water activities, Placencia has some of the best hotels and restaurants in Belize. Most are small places with personality. A restaurant with 10 tables is considered a large operation.

This combination of easygoing resort atmosphere, myriad water activities, and plenty of beachfront has attracted a growing number of potential real-estate buyers, although so far, few of them have built homes or taken up residency.

Placencia and Seine Bight

Placencia Village, at the southernmost tip of the peninsula, is a predominantly Creole village of about 600 people. Most of the area's restaurants and shops are here. To the west of the village is the lagoon; to the east, the sea; and to the south, a small harbor. A mile-long concrete sidewalk runs up the center of the village. A stroll up and down the sidewalk will give you a good introduction to life in the village, which centers around relaxing, tourism, and fishing, roughly in that order. Many of the residents in Placencia Village are related to each other, and you'll hear the same last names over and over again: Cabral, Leslie, Eiley, and Westby.

Seine Bight is a Garifuna village of around 700 people, about five miles north of Placencia Village. This is a place deep in cultural change, with the traditional Garifuna society under siege by tourists, developers, and general modernization. With no small amount of irony, one of the businesses in the village, a combination restaurant, bar, and a place for tourists to experience Garifuna-style music and drumming, is named Kulcha Shak. It's pronounced "culture shock."

Groups of uniformed Garifuna schoolchildren walk along the dusty or muddy road to the new school, a two-story concrete building. In this matriarchal society, Garifuna grannies and moms run their homes and tend small shops, while the men happily fish or hang out at local bars.

The Expat Community

Until recently, the expatriate community in Placencia numbered only a few dozen, and almost all of them were involved in running the peninsula's hotels, restaurants, bars, dive shops, and real-estate agencies. Beginning in the late 1990s, a boom in real-estate sales attracted more Americans and Canadians to this area. However, few have as yet built homes or settled in permanently—but an increasing number of retirees and the almost-retired come down to spend a few weeks or months of the year clearing their lots and making plans to build. Enough construction is going on to keep a couple of building supply companies in business.

The area is attracting a mix of new expats: A few with cash and a dream have opened resorts. Some are middle-class baby boomers buying lots and hoping to build a vacation or retirement home. Others are marginalized escapees from the North American rat race who live hand-to-mouth.

Most foreign residents are still involved in some way with tourism. Among the hotels owned by expatriates are the Inn at Robert's Grove, Calico Jack's, Zeboz Caribbean Resort, Lost Reef Resort, Maya Beach Hotel, Singing Sands, Miller's Landing, Green Parrot, Blue Crab, Nautical Inn, Mariposa, and Barnacle Bill's.

Tourism is still a hit-and-miss thing on the Placencia Peninsula. Except for a few well-marketed properties, annual occupancy at peninsula hotels is under 40 percent. But during the winter, especially around the holidays, hotels fill up and it can be tough to find a decent room. But during the off-season, the peninsula slows down, some hotels and restaurants close, and most of the peninsula reverts to its sleepy self. Many peninsula resorts are, actively or passively, up for sale. Some have been on the market for years; nearly all continue with business as usual, regardless of sale status.

In a previous life, American Mary Toy was an attorney in St. Louis. Now she helps run a travel business in Placencia. Asked whether she would make the move again, if she had it to do over, she says, "Now that's a million-dollar question."

Toy continues, "The first advice I give is come and live here first—for at least six months, but a year would be better. I think it takes that long for us foreigners to begin to develop an understanding of Belize. Belize is beautiful and very seductive for people seeking an escape from the First World rat race. I think the seductiveness stems in large part from its British culture and English as its official language, which makes

Local kids enjoy a swim at Placencia Village.

Belize immediately seem to be a comfortable, safe, and 'just like home' tropical paradise. Trouble is, Belize is not just like home. The cultures and governmental, political, and legal structures are very different. Most foreigners learn this the hard way, after being scammed a few times and finally realizing that they really have no effective redress from the police, elected representatives, or the courts. Usually, unless the foreigner is really stupid or has a lot of money to burn, the scams are small—and are very valuable as lessons in how to survive life in Belize." Consider yourself duly warned.

Local Tips

As in many coastal communities in Belize, daily life for both locals and expatriates revolves around the sea. If you like to dive or fish, this is paradise. Many of the foreign residents own boats or at least small skiffs to poke around the lagoon. The shallow Caribbean can kick up very rough chop, making just boarding a boat on a windy day an adventure. The lagoon side enjoys gentler waters, so if boating is a priority, you'll want to have a dock on the lagoon.

> As in many coastal communities in Belize, daily life for both locals and expatriates revolves around the sea. If you like to dive or fish, this is paradise.

If you don't catch your own, a fishing coop in Placencia Village is a source of inexpensive, ultra-fresh fish. That's a good thing, because local groceries have a limited stock of foodstuffs. The biggest and most popular grocery, Wallen's, is the size of a small convenience store in the United States. The owners, Harold and Lucy Wallen, moved to Placencia in 1974 from Evergreen, Colorado, just after Hurricane Fifi. Initially, they sold vegetables and lobsters from their house, later expanding to a location in Placencia Village across from the football (soccer) field. In late 1999, in what made headlines in the local monthly newspaper, Wallen's opened the first air-conditioned market in Placencia, adjacent to the old store, which is now used to service wholesale customers. The grocery stocks basic canned foods, some frozen meats, and plenty of rum. During the busy tourist season, and especially around Christmas, the shelves get bare by late in the day. Prices, except for rum, are roughly about twice what you'd pay in a supermarket in the States. Wallen's and the area's other groceries don't usually have much in the way of fresh fruits and vegetables. Most expatriates buy produce from trucks that come down once or twice a week from Dangriga.

The Placencia area has six churches, including ones of Anglican and Catholic denominations. Sadly, the area also has its share of drug problems. The lack of local industry, except for tourism, means that many locals lack gainful employment. Crime, including theft and burglaries, but mostly smalltime pilfering from tourists or building sites, are increasing. As there are no movie theaters, bowling alleys, or health clubs in Placencia, what social life exists for expats revolves around casual encounters in Placencia Village, visits to each other's homes, or meals at local restaurants.

Shops and services are mostly clustered in Placencia Village, though a few are in Seine Bight and Maya Beach. Atlantic Bank and ScotiaBank have offices in Placencia. There is a gas station in Placencia Village, a fairly well-equipped building supplies store, Professional Builders Supply, and an Internet café called Purple Space Monkey. A small medical clinic is near the school in Placencia Village, and another clinic is in Seine Bight. Cuban doctors, on loan from Fidel, may still be in residence when you are there. Otherwise, you may need to go to Dangriga for medical attention.

© Ian Sluder

Prices for beachfront lots in Placencia are near US$2,000 a front foot.

Placencia is famous for its sidewalk, a mile-long ribbon of concrete through the middle of the village (reputedly one of the longest continuous sidewalks in the world). Stroll the sidewalk once or twice, and you'll meet most of the people in the village and be up-to-date on local gossip and news.

Nearly all of the peninsula is now on the power grid, and residents of both Seine Bight and Placencia Village enjoy good drinking water piped in from the Maya Mountains. A garbage dump been established off the peninsula, and along with regular garbage pickups, this has improved the appearance of residential areas.

WHERE TO LIVE

Real estate is booming on the Placencia Peninsula. With limited land on the narrow peninsula, and considerable demand from Americans seeking a place on the Caribbean, prices have zoomed upward in recent years. Desirable beachfront lots are now going for close to US$2,000 per front foot, or around US$140,000 for a deep lot with 75 feet of beachfront, while lots a row or two back are US$30,000–60,000. Lagoon and canal lots are US$25,000–50,000.

Wood homes in the village may be available for under US$100,000, but modern reinforced concrete homes farther north on or near the beach are US$200,000–300,000 and up—often way up.

The few upscale condos are also fairly pricey—US$185,000–210,000 for a one-bedroom and US$215,000–240,000 for a two-bedroom. The newest "Hacienda" units at the Inn at Robert's Grove are even more expensive: up to US$489,000 for a 2,000-square-foot, three-bedroom unit. Condos at Zeboz resort north of Maya Beach range from around US$100,000 for a studio apartment to US$225,000 for a three-bedroom condo.

There aren't many rentals on the peninsula. You may be able to find a rental in Placencia Village for around US$200–500 a month. A nicer home north of the village may rent for US$600 and up.

GETTING AROUND

Placencia is about 3.5 hours by car from Belize City, or less than an hour by plane (tickets run about US$70). The Placencia airstrip has a dramatic setting right on the sea, and Maya Island Air has built a new but small terminal. There is bus service, twice a day, between Placencia and Dangriga, but no local bus service on the peninsula. An alternative is to take a little ferry, aptly named the *Hokey Pokey,* across Placencia Lagoon and catch a bus on the Southern Highway at Independence. Taxis are expensive—US$15 from Placencia Village to Maya Beach. Unless you live in Placencia Village and spend all your time there, you'll need a car.

Punta Gorda

Many people, even in Belize, will tell you that Punta Gorda is the end of the earth. You may be surprised, then, to discover how inviting a town it is. With around 4,000 people, it has a mix of Mopan and Kekchi Maya, Garifuna, and a dollop of Creoles, Lebanese, and Chinese, plus a few American expats, missionaries, and dreamers. PG, as it's known in Belize, is colorful and friendly. There's usually a breeze blowing from the Bay of Honduras. Four days a week, and especially on Saturdays, the downtown market draws Maya from surrounding villages. PG's waterside setting is, like that of Corozal Town, truly pleasant and even beautiful, though there are no real beaches here.

THE LAY OF THE LAND

The Maya have lived in this part of Belize for millennia. Among the Maya ruins here is Lubaantun ("Place of the Fallen Stones"). Lubaantun was occupied only from around A.D. 700–900. The famous, or infamous, "crystal skull" was supposedly discovered here in 1926 by F. A. Mitchell-Hedges, on assignment from the British Museum. The head is still in the possession of F. A.'s now elderly daughter, Anna Mitchell-Hedges, who lives in Canada. Nim Li Punit ("Big Hat") was occupied about the same time as Lubaantun, in the Late Classic Period. At its height, several thousand people may have lived there. The Maya were joined in the early 19th century by Garifuna from the Bay Islands of Honduras and, after the American Civil War, by a group of former Confederate soldiers and their families, who attempted to settle here with relatively little success. In modern times, Punta Gorda has held an attraction for missionary groups, mostly fundamentalists from the United States.

Business activity in Punta Gorda is not exactly hot and hopping. Hotels in and around PG stay empty most of the year. The official occupancy rate is less than 20 percent. Even if some operators fudge the numbers a bit to save on taxes, clearly most rooms are empty most of the time. As yet, only a few tourists make it all the way down the Southern Highway from Belize City or Placencia. Some backpackers do pass through on their way to cheaper towns in Guatemala and Honduras. With the paving of the Southern Highway, conventional wisdom is that PG will explode with new hotels, real-estate developments, and other businesses. I'm not so sure that will happen to any great extent, but things are certain to get busier eventually.

Reality Check

Yes, the weather is warm and the Caribbean is blue, but Belize has its downsides, too. Here's a reality check.

"There is a negative about Belize we didn't find out until we had spent more time there, and finally knew people well enough that they would tell us the truth. There is an animosity, distrust, dislike, call it what you will, of the locals for expats that is exacerbated by the Belize government. For example, if I want to build a pier in front of my business/house and a Belizean wants to build one in front of his, the Belizean will get permission within two weeks, while I may get an OK in two years, if I'm lucky. There is an attitude of 'We like your money, but we don't much care for you.'"
—*Catherine McCabe, a Californian who decided to build a house in Roatán, Honduras, rather than in Belize*

"Anti-gringo, and especially anti-American, sentiment [has grown] here, and it is vocal. It is tiresome to be snubbed and cheated in the local stores, panhandled on the streets, shaken down by government officials, and robbed in your home, whether by real thieves or just dis-

honest workers, on a daily basis. Many of our retirees come from the Midwestern U.S., from small communities where no one even locked their doors. I'll bet that this is the first time many of them have been on the receiving end of such wholesale discrimination."
—*Margaret Briggs, an American who runs a website for expats in Corozal Town*

"Crime is definitely a big problem. The cheaper hotels in San Pedro are always having thieves break into their rooms. You can't leave anything of value in your golf cart, or guaranteed it will be gone when you get back."
—*Kathy Wangsgard, San Pedro*

"I'm getting sick and tired of people telling me that we 'foreigners' take advantage of Belizeans. I earn a decent amount of money in my business, but I also work seven days a week, usually from 6:30 or 7 A.M. to at least 6:30 or 7 P.M. (more often than not, 9 P.M. or later)—and I came here with a few thousand dollars, not thousands, and definitely not hundreds of thousands. What I have, I earned here."
—*Mary Toy, an attorney from St. Louis who now runs a travel business in Placencia*

Bay of Honduras at Punta Gorda

© Ian Sluder

Belize Bank has a branch in PG. For groceries, Wallace Supaul Store on Main Street and Southern Grocer on King Street may have what you need. Punta Gorda Hospital (south end of Main Street) can provide basic emergency care; for something more serious, you may want to upgrade to the Southern Regional Hospital in Dangriga or to hospitals in Belize City.

Outside of PG, the land in Toledo District is lush, wild, and wet, fed by 160 inches or more of rain each year—the only dry months are February through May. Emerald-green valleys lay between low peaks of the Maya Mountains. Rice grows in flooded fields, and giant bromeliads line the roads. The rocky shorelines are cooled by near constant breezes from the Bay of Honduras. Offshore are isolated cayes and the straggling end of the barrier reef.

WHERE TO LIVE

Toledo does not have a very active real-estate market, and it is difficult to establish market values. Accessible land in smaller tracts (under 50 acres) often goes for US$500–2,000 an acre. Larger parcels with access and river frontage are usually under US$1,000 an acre. In 2005, a 40-acre parcel near San Antonio Village with a stream and electrical service was on the market for US$70,000. At the same time, a 100-acre tract eight miles from Punta Gorda was for sale at an asking price of US$95,000. A 200-acre tract on the Moho River, with dirt road access and on the electric grid, was offered for US$150,000.

Building lots in or near Punta Gorda but not on the water are inexpensive—usually no more than a few thousand dollars, at least for Belizean buyers, but waterfront lots are more costly. In 2005, a two-acre waterfront site in Punta Gorda was on the market for US$180,000. Smaller

Hard-Earned Wisdom

Here's some advice from expats about how to make it in Belize.

"The very best piece of advice is to 'try before you buy.' Rent a place, stay a while, see if this life is for you. Because it's not for everybody."
—Margaret Briggs, an American in Corozal Town who has lived in Belize since 1997

"To live in Belize, you need to have a sense of adventure. Also, you have to have some skills. You need to be able to change a tire, have some mechanical skills, and some basic knowledge of how things work. I would be the first to admit that the only skill I have is I could walk 10 miles for help if I had to but possess none of the others. Good thing that I have my husband, Bob, because he knows all of these things. He knows cars, plumbing, electricity, cement, fiberglass, boating, lawn mower repair, weed eater repair, cabinets, how to tile, just lots of things."
—Karen Cochran, an American who owns a house in Independence Village

"Most gringos do not initially understand that Belize has a relationship-based culture. For instance, being respectful of an employee will get you 100 percent farther than offering a raise in pay."
—Diane Campbell, real-estate developer on Ambergris Caye, originally from California

"The less you expect from life here, the more often you are pleasantly surprised. I love the exotic climate, the birds, the flowers, the rain, the wonderful ladies who work for me with smiles on their faces all the time."
—Pamella Picon, resort co-owner in Cayo District, originally from Colorado

"It's a mistake to be too generous. Generosity can backfire and become an obligation if not dealt out sparingly. Never pay in advance for goods and services. Always hold out at least 20 percent until you are satisfied."
—John Burks, the head of the realty department at Regent Realty in Belize City. He's an American who first came to Belize in 1972 as a cattle rancher.

concrete houses on the bay in PG have sold for under US$50,000. Near PG, a 20-acre tract with a two-bedroom house was offered in 2005 for US$72,000.

In the Maya villages in southern Toledo, many homes are traditional thatch huts and have virtually no value beyond that of the land. Small concrete block homes in the Maya villages may sell for a few thousand to US$50,000.

GETTING AROUND

By road via Belmopan, Punta Gorda is almost 200 miles from Belize City, and even with the improved highways, it's a long trip—four or five hours or longer. By bus, it's a cheap trip (less than US$14), but a long one—seven hours or longer if you don't get an express. Most people prefer to fly. Flights take less than an hour and cost around US$80–100, depending on which Belize City airport you leave from. In PG, taxis are plentiful, with most trips around town costing less than US$3. However, most foreign residents find it essential to have a car, as there is only limited bus service to the surrounding areas of Toledo.

Daily Life

Making the Move

Before you even think about moving to Belize, spend some time in the country. Come experience the country firsthand, so you can make an informed decision. So, let's say you've done your due diligence, and you're ready to make the move. How do you go about doing it? There are three main options for those wishing to live or retire in Belize or spend extended periods of time in the country: You can enter on a tourist card or as a Qualified Retired Person (if you fit the bill), or you can apply to become an official permanent resident. Each status has advantages and disadvantages. These choices—as well as other handy information on the hurdles you must cross to make your big move to Belize—are detailed in this chapter.

Red Tape

VISAS AND IMMIGRATION

For many people, the easiest and cheapest way to live in the country for a while is to be a perpetual tourist, which requires no long-term commitment. Nationals of countries not required to have a visa to enter

Belize—including the United States, Canada, the United Kingdom, most other British Commonwealth countries, and EU and Caricom countries—get a free visitor entry card. However, nationals needing a visa to enter Belize can face high visa application charges. Under changes in effect in early 2005, citizens of the People's Republic of China, Pakistan, Bangladesh, Sri Lanka, and Nepal must pay a US$2,000 visa application fee. Visas for nationals of other countries cost US$100.

Upon entry, you receive a visitor permit good for up to 30 days. After 30 days this permit can be renewed for up to 12 months. The renewal fee was increased in 2005 to US$25 per month for the first three months, then US$50 per month thereafter. To renew it, you'll need to visit a government immigration office in Belize City or Belmopan or a police station in district towns. You are supposed to show that you have sufficient resources to maintain yourself in Belize, at least US$60 a day, but this requirement is rarely enforced. If you are staying more than three months, you are supposed to obtain an AIDS test, but again, this rule is not always enforced. After 12 months, you must leave the country and start the process over again.

If you fail to renew your permit in a timely way, or if you overstay your allotted time, you are technically in violation of Belize law and can be deported. As a practical matter, if you can offer a good reason why you failed to follow the law, you'll probably be let off with a short lecture from the immigration official, plus payment of any fees due.

QUALIFIED RETIRED PERSONS (QRP)

The Qualified Retired Persons Incentive Act, passed by the Belize legislature in 1999 and initiated in 2000, is being implemented by the Belize Tourist Board (BTB). The program is designed to attract more retirees to Belize. The Belize Tourist Board says that only about 200 people, mostly Americans, have been enrolled in the program to date. Interest in the program appears to be fairly high, but because of the income requirement, inability to work for pay in Belize, and other factors, the actual number of retirees in the program is as yet relatively small.

For those who can show the required monthly income from investments or pensions, this program offers the benefits of official residency and tax-free entry of the retiree's household goods and a car, boat, and even an airplane. This program also eliminates some of the bureaucratic delays built into other programs. The BTB says that most applications are approved within three months from the date of application.

QRP Facts

Who qualifies? Anyone at least 45 years old from anywhere in the world can qualify for the program. A person who qualifies can also include his or her dependents in the program. Dependents include spouses and children under the age of 18. However, it can include children up to the age of 23 if they are enrolled in a university.

Benefits: Besides prompt approval of residency for qualifying applicants, import duties and fees for household goods and a vehicle, airplane, and boat are waived.

Duty-free import of personal household effects: QRPs in the program can qualify for duty and tax exemptions on new and used personal and household effects that are admitted as such by the Belize Tourism Board. A list of all items with corresponding values that will be imported must be submitted with the application. A one-year period is granted for the importation of personal and household effects.

Duty-free import of a motor vehicle: Applicants are encouraged to import new motor vehicles under the program, but the vehicle must be no more than three years old. A QRP may also buy a vehicle duty-free in the country.

Duty-free import of a light aircraft: A Qualified Retired Person is entitled to import a light aircraft less than 17,000 kg (about 37,500 pounds). A QRP is required to have a valid private pilot's license to fly in Belize. This license can be obtained by passing the requirements set by the Civil Aviation Organization. However, if the participant has a valid pilot's license, that license only has to be validated by the Civil Aviation Department in Belize.

Duty-free import of a boat: Any vessel that is used for personal purposes and for pleasure will be accepted under this program.

If, for whatever reason, a QRP decides to sell, give away, lease, or otherwise dispose of his or her approved means of transportation or personal effects to any person or entity within Belize, all duties and taxes must be paid to the proper authorities. The Belize Tourist Board states: "Qualified Retired Persons must note that only after three years and upon proof that the transportation that was previously imported to Belize was adequately disposed of, will another concession be granted to import another mode of transportation."

Expats and the QRP

The following recent comments address the Qualified Retired Persons incentive program. The names of the individuals, most resident in Belize under the QRP program, have been withheld because of possible repercussions from Belizean authorities.

"My experience with the Qualified Retirement Persons program was great, but that was in 2000. Now I hear bad things. Mostly that program administration is unresponsive, doesn't answer the phone or email. This was supposed to be the reason for putting it [under] Tourism, not Immigration. You need to bring more money in, and you need a lot more paperwork. Probably unrealistic paperwork for someone like me, who relies on investments, rather than pension. In my view, QRP—reasonably and fairly administered—can be good for Belize and retirees. I don't count what I paid for my lot because that went to the foreign owner. But building the house, furniture, [and] landscaping, plus what I bring in, has added up to well over US$100,000 in foreign currency so far. That is equivalent to a whole boatload of cruise tourists. I wonder what would happen if the Belize government thought about it that way: One QRP brings [in] more than the benefit of one Carnival ship.
—*A Canadian expat in Corozal*

"I find the new people in the Belize Tourist Board and QRP program much less helpful than the former group. They won't give out information and seem afraid to answer questions."
—*A prospective QRP applicant from the United States*

"My husband and I started the QRP process [six months ago] and are still not done [with] the mess. We bought a house in Placencia and paid cash for the thing, so we have already "invested" in the country. [Then came] national security, an inquiry we were told was actually sent to Interpol. That came back clean. Next thing, even though we proved we can comply with the required amount of funds to be deposited in a Belize bank, [was] they still needed printouts of

Income requirement: To be designated a Qualified Retired Person under the program, the applicant must have a monthly income of at least US$2,000. A couple does not need to show US$4,000 a month—just US$2,000, as the applicant is normally an individual, and the applicant's spouse is considered a dependent of that individual under the program.

our savings account balance. In short, they want to know when you went to the bathroom last."
—*An American retiree in Placencia*

"Make sure all your paperwork [is] "originals"—no copies. There has been a problem with QRPs being available on the black market here, so the processing time has increased from a few weeks to several months. The weather and the sea are the chief reasons I came to Belize, and remain the chief reasons I stay."
—*An American living in Belize City*

"I was told by a government rep that you CAN earn income from a business activity that takes place within Belize and still participate in the QRP program, so long as your income is from a passive investment, like real estate (something that you do not need a work permit to make money from). Of course, that is a matter of "interpretation" and could change at any time (including retroactively)."
—*A former U.S. investor in Belize, now living in Panama*

"As with everything involved in Belize bureaucracy, it's a plodding pace once you get started, and full of exasperating waits and delays. Allow plenty of time and patience."
—*An American in Belize*

"Do not think that, just because you did your research and have your budget and know exactly what the laws and regulations are here in Belize, you will have smooth sailing. One couple (Belizean wife, U.S. husband), who applied for the retired status [and] followed every regulation to the T, have become VERY upset at the trouble and inconsistencies they have found in this system. And this is for a couple where one was born and raised and worked in Belize until she was 25! Many things they were told [at] the beginning of the process by government officials have changed or been "redefined." They are ending up spending more than if they just moved here on tourist status. So, do your homework, but don't think that it will be easy, nor by the books."
—*A resort owner in San Pedro*

The income rules for QRPs are, like many things in Belize, a little confusing. On first reading, it looks as if the income must derive from a pension or annuity that has been generated outside of Belize. The rules do not specifically say so, but according to Belize Tourist Board officials, U.S. Social Security income can be included as part of this pension requirement. This pension and annuity information then has

Fancy a tropical beach like this? It's an option in Belize.

to be substantiated by a Certified Public Accountant, along with two bank references from the company providing the pension or annuity. These substantiations may not be required if your pension and/or annuity is from a Fortune 500 company.

That is one way to show that you have the necessary income. However, there is another way. You can demonstrate that you have the necessary income by providing documentation that you have deposited the money in a Belize bank in either a Belize dollar or U.S. dollar account. Several retirees have told me that they were able to include other forms of income, including investment income, in the US$2,000 figure. In this latter case, the US$2,000-per-month income (US$24,000 a year) can be substantiated by showing records from a bank or other financial institution in Belize where the retiree has deposited the necessary money. As a practical matter, some retirees say that they have not been asked to provide documentation—at least not yet.

Background check: All applications are subject to a background check by the Ministry of National Security.

Application: Applications for the program must be made to the Belize Tourism Board in Belize City and include the following:

Birth certificate: A certified copy of a certificate for the applicant and each dependent.

Marriage certificate: If the applicant is married and wishes to register a spouse as a dependent.

Authentic police record: A police record from the applicant's last place of residency issued within one month before the application.

Passport: Certified color copies of the complete passport (including all blank pages) of the applicant and all dependents. The copies must have the passport number, name of principal, number of pages, and the seal or stamp of the certifying Notary Public.

Proof of income (choose one of the following):

1. An official statement from a bank or financial institution certifying that the applicant is the recipient of a pension or annuity of a minimum of US$2,000 per month.

2. A financial statement from a financial institution, bank, credit union, or building society in Belize certifying that the applicant has deposited the sum of a minimum of US$2,000 per month or the equivalent of US $24,000 per year.

Medical examination: Applicants must undergo a complete medical examination, including an AIDS test. A copy of the medical certificate must be attached to the application.

Photos: Four front-view and four side-view passport-sized photographs that have been taken recently of the applicant and dependents.

The application form for the Qualified Retired Persons program is available for download on the Belize Tourist Board website.

OFFICIAL PERMANENT RESIDENT

Requirements and benefits are similar to those described in the Retired Persons Incentive Act. For example, as a regular permanent resident, you can import household goods and a personal vehicle duty-free. The application process and supporting documents needed are virtually the same as for retired residency. Here are the main differences:

• As a regular permanent resident, you do not have to deposit any particular sum in a bank in Belize. However, you do have to show financial resources sufficient to obtain residency status.

• You can work for pay in Belize.

• You must live in Belize for one full year before you can apply for regular permanent residency. During this period, you cannot leave the country for more than 14 consecutive days.

• It is more expensive to apply for regular permanent residency than for retired residency. Application fees were increased in 2005 and vary according to your country of citizenship. Nationals of Caricom countries pay US$250, citizens of the United States pay US$1,000, and Commonwealth country citizens also pay US$1,000. If residency is granted, you pay a fee of US$62.50 for a residency card.

• For permanent residency, you must apply to the Belize Immigration Department rather than to the Belize Tourist Board. Note that during 2004, very few permanent residency applications were approved. Many applicants waited for six months or longer without hearing anything from Belmopan. As of press time, since application fees were increased, applications seem to be processed and approved much more quickly. For more information contact the Immigration Department (see *Contacts* in the *Resources* section for more information).

The controversial Economic Citizenship program, also known as the "buy-a-passport" plan, has been discontinued. It was started by the previous United Democratic Party government and continued under the present People's United Party government. It provided for Belizean citizenship, including a Belize passport, by "investing" in Belize. In reality, that just meant paying a big chunk of cash—US$50,000 or more—to the government of Belize and a smaller chunk to someone with ties to the government.

In addition to these programs, regular citizenship in Belize is a possibility for those living in Belize for a long period. To acquire citizenship, applicants must have been a resident or have held permanent residency status for a minimum of five years. Applicants for citizenship need to provide essentially the same supporting documentation as those applying for permanent residency.

WEIGHING YOUR OPTIONS
Tourist Card
Pros: No commitment, no financial requirement, flexibility, little red tape.

Cons: No tax advantages, no official status, inconvenience of having to renew and leave the country periodically, cost of US$25 per person per month for three months, then $US50 per month afterward, adds

Wish You Were Here

Here's a sampling of what expat residents in Belize say they miss from their previous lives back in the United States or elsewhere:

"Four to five percent mortgage money, L. L. Bean, championship wrestling, Blatz beer."

"Live jazz and artichokes—but we got a flat of fresh artichokes for the first time last week. Now all we need is a personal visit from Tony Bennett."

"I enjoy prowling a big U.S. store or supermarket when I'm there, but don't miss it when I'm gone."

"*The New York Times* on Sunday."

"Pumpernickel bread, real Wiener schnitzel, chianti from Italy, a bookstore."

"I would have to say Trader Joe's!! Oh boy, what I would do for a TJ's to land anywhere in Belize."

"I miss Wal-Mart and Home Depot like you wouldn't believe."

"I can't find a good selection of quality women's lingerie for sale here."

"I would kill for an Arby's beef and cheddar right now. I was never a fast-food person, but now that I can't get it, I'm craving it!"

"Friends and family back home, of course."

"Actually, nothing."

up over time, there's a possibility the rules may change, you can't work for pay in Belize, and after one year you must leave the country and then return to restart the process.

Qualified Retired Person

Pros: Quick (as little as three weeks) approval, application through Belize Tourist Board rather than Immigration Department, tax-free entry of household effects, car, boat, and airplane.

Cons: You must deposit US$2,000 a month in a Belize bank, you can't work for pay in Belize, you must be 45 or older. In mid-2005, the Belize government stated that QRPs were not residents of Belize, but had the status of a long-term tourist.

Permanent Resident

Pros: Full residency rights (except voting—unless you're a citizen of another Commonwealth country, which entitles you to vote in Belize), you can work, it's open to anyone regardless of age, tax-free entry of household effects and car.

Cons: Yearlong residency before applying, a costly application process, more red tape.

Moving with Children

Belize is a country of young people—the average age of the population is only 19—so your children will probably have many opportunities to meet other children their age. Belizeans love children, and children are welcome almost everywhere. It's rare to find a restaurant or any other business that doesn't allow children to enter. In many respects, most of Belize is the way the United States was in the 1950s or earlier: Children play outside all the time, walk or ride bikes to the store or school, and hang out with friends. There are very few "soccer moms" in Belize who spend their days driving their offspring here and there.

> Belize is a country of young people—the average age of the population is only 19—so your children will probably have many opportunities to meet other children their age.

Whether your children adapt well to Belize or not depends on what expectations that you both have. If their lives have revolved around going to the mall, seeing movies every weekend, and eating fast food, they're probably facing a serious adaptation problem—there are no malls or fast-food places in Belize and only one movie theater in the entire country. On the other hand, if they like to be outdoors, and especially if they enjoy activities on the water (no place in Belize is more than a few miles from the sea, a lagoon, a bay, or a river), they'll be in heaven.

Young children do have to be watched, as they may not recognize the dangers of scorpions, snakes, Africanized bees, and other wild creatures. In some neighborhoods in Belize City, children may be endangered by gangs and drugs.

Finding toys, children's books, and children's clothes may be a challenge in Belize, especially in rural areas. Libraries are few and far between, and none is large.

Schooling is obviously a concern for expats with children. About 85,000 Belizean children are enrolled in schools of all types, including almost 65,000 in primary schools and 14,000 in high schools. Schools vary widely in quality of teachers, equipment, and facilities. In rural Toledo, your local school may have few textbooks, no library, and perhaps not even electricity or running water. In Belize City, the best schools are quite good indeed, and motivated students will be well prepared for a rigorous college. Most Belizean schools do teach religion as part of their daily curriculum, and that may be an issue for some families. Some expats home-school their kids. (For more information, see the *Language and Education* chapter.)

Moving with Pets

Dogs and cats can be brought into Belize without quarantine. Owners must get a certificate from a veterinarian after an examination not more than 48 hours before to shipment stating that the animal is free from infectious diseases and has been vaccinated for rabies not less than one month and no more than six months before departure.

Bringing a pet into the country falls under live animal importation and is regulated by the Belize Agricultural Health Authority (BAHA). Domestic pets are allowed to enter the country provided their owners have a valid import permit, international veterinary certificate, a valid rabies vaccination certificate, and that their pets have been inspected by a quarantine officer. There is a US$12.50 entry fee, plus a US$12.50 fax fee.

> In rural areas, you will see a number of wild animals, such as howler and spider monkeys and the smaller wild cats, kept as pets (even though it is often against the law).

To apply for an import permit, request an application form from the Permit Unit of the Belize Agricultural Health Authority, and then return the completed form to the same agency. The date of arrival must be specified. Approved permits will be faxed to the applicant at a cost of US$12.50 to be paid at the point of entry on the day of arrival. If you don't follow this application process, you will be subject to a US $100 violation fine in addition to the US $12.50 entry fee.

Small dogs and cats can usually be carried in the cabin of scheduled commercial airlines. For larger animals, American and Continental are two of the airlines flying into Belize that ship pets. Pets are transported in pressurized cargo holds. Charges vary depending on the weight of the animal. Continental charges about US$200 to fly a 50-pound dog from the United States to Belize. There are also cargo airlines that transport pets, including AmeriJet, which has service from Miami to Belize. You can also drive through Mexico with your pets.

Not all pets adapt well to Belize's subtropical climate. Mange and venereal disease are endemic. Rabies occasionally shows up in rural areas, vectored by vampire bats and other wild things.

BELIZEAN ATTITUDES TOWARD PETS

Belizeans generally do not have the same view of pets as Americans do. They rarely allow dogs in the house, for example. Dogs are used more as watchdogs than companions. You don't see many cats in Belize. It's possible they've been eaten by the dogs or wild animals. In rural areas, you will see a number of wild animals, such as howler and spider monkeys and the smaller wild cats, kept as pets (even though it is often against the law).

What to Bring

Foreign residents in Belize are split on how much to bring to the country. Some see a savings in bringing everything you may need, especially if you have a duty exemption on household goods.

On the other hand, many who have moved to Belize say it's best to bring as little as possible with you. After all, you won't need a lot of clothes. You can buy furniture cheaply in Belize, and you can find appliances and other household goods either in Belize City or Chetumal, Mexico. Amazon.com and other companies will ship books, CDs, and other items to Belize. You may want to store most of your household goods in a storage facility back home. Then, after you've been in Belize for a while, you can return to your storage space to pick up the items you decide you really need.

You will probably want to bring the following items to Belize if you are setting up housekeeping, as these are hard to find or expensive there, or will be expensive to ship later.
- Good-quality sheets and towels
- High-quality mattresses
- Dishes
- High-quality pots and pans, silverware, and other kitchenware
- Hobby equipment

- Specialized hand and power tools
- Fishing and diving gear
- Top-end electronics
- Books

Belize Customs Duties on Imports

Here are examples of import duties you'll pay on goods brought or shipped into Belize. Duties on most goods imported into Belize range from 0 to 45 percent, with the majority attracting a 20 percent duty. The duty rate is based on the value, plus freight and insurance. In many cases, in addition to these duties you'll also pay sales tax at 11percent and on some items a replacement duty of 5–25 percent. Goods from Caricom countries generally are duty-free, though replacement taxes may apply. Import duties are complex and change frequently—contact the Belize Customs Department for information.

Automobiles New or Used:
(Customs uses U.S. Blue Book value as basis,
plus evaluation by customs officer)

4-Cylinder Auto under 3000 cc	60% duty including taxes
4-Cylinder Pickup Truck	22% duty including taxes
Golf cart	25% duty
Motor Scooter (under 50cc)	0% duty
6- or 8-Cylinder Auto over 3000 cc	68% duty including taxes

Household Appliances:

Dishwasher	20% duty
Refrigerator	0% duty (no tax if under 15 cubic ft.)
Stove	0% duty (no tax)
TV	20% duty
Vacuum Cleaner	20% duty

Power Tools and Building Supplies:

Building Supplies (Various)	15%–20% duty
Drill/Saw/Sander	20% duty
Hand Tools	0–5% duty
Hurricane Shutters	15% duty

Other:

Books	0% duty
Computer	0% duty
Computer Software	110% duty
DVDs/Video Tapes	0% duty
Office Equipment	0–5% duty
Most Staple Foods	0% duty
Musical Instruments	0% duty

SHIPPING OPTIONS

You can ship bulky items by sea or overland. Small items can be shipped via the postal system. You can drive your vehicle down through Mexico or ship it by sea.

Ocean and Overland Freight

Sending goods in a 20-foot container from Miami is likely to cost you about US$2,000, not including import duties. A 40-foot container may cost you US$4,000 by the time you get it to your home in Belize, again not including any import duties.

Hyde Shipping is probably the most used and recommended shipping company serving Belize. It offers freight sailings from Port Everglades near Miami to Belize once and sometimes twice a week. Both 20-foot and 40-foot containers are available. Tropical Shipping also offers weekly freight service from Miami to Belize.

There are freight consolidators in Miami who will assemble your goods, crate them where necessary, and put them in a full or partial container—for a price. Small items can be shipped to Belize by air or surface mail, which is fairly dependable, or by fast but expensive airfreight services such as FedEx or DHL. Speed Cargo in Miami can ship small boxes via freighter: A 20-cubic-foot box might cost under US$100.

You can also move goods to Belize overland from Texas. One recommended mover is Elbert Flowers at Cayo Adventure Tours.

Ferry

Yucatan Express has offered on-again, off-again pedestrian and vehicle ferry service on the Canadian ferry ship *Scotia Prince.* For a short time, it ran in the winter from Tampa, Florida, to Mérida, Mexico, and to Puerto Moreles near Cancún. However, this service has at least temporarily been discontinued. It is possible service will resume in late 2005, but this time from Corpus Christi, Texas, to Veracruz, Mexico.

CUSTOMS BROKERS

Customs brokers in Belize can be very helpful in smoothing the way and getting materials quickly released from customs. They will meet your goods when they arrive in Belize, fill out the paperwork, and have the goods forwarded to their final destination in Belize. It will make your life a lot easier if you have a local customs broker

The 10 Commandments of Expat Life in Belize

1. Test-drive the country *before* deciding to move to Belize permanently. Come for a long visit before you spend time dreaming of a paradise that may not exist for you, and rent before you even think about buying.

2. Keep a financial and legal lifeline to your home country. The United States, Canada, and other prosperous Western countries are islands of stability in an ever-changing world.

3. Learn some of the local lingo. Even in Belize, where English is the official language, working knowledge of Spanish or Creole—or, in some areas, Garifuna or a Maya dialect—is an asset.

4. Understand that, as a foreigner with a totally different background and set of experiences, you will probably never be 100 percent accepted as a part of the community, and you may even experience some resentment from locals.

5. Even so, work to become accepted by volunteering your talents and becoming involved in the daily life of your new community.

6. Do not try to duplicate your lifestyle as it was "back home." In many cases, it will cost more, and it will certainly not let you benefit from local ways of doing things.

7. Be prepared for culture shock to hit, usually after a year or so in the new setting. Belize may at first look like back home, but it's not.

8. Be aware that as a "wealthy" foreigner, you may be the target of all kinds of scams and thefts, from real-estate rip-offs to neighbors ratting to the police or tax authorities about you to burglaries and robberies. You must protect yourself.

9. Don't limit yourself to the local expat community. Get to know the local folks.

10. Enjoy the wonders of your new home to the fullest—life is not a dress rehearsal.

working for you. Be sure to check references. (See *Contacts* in the *Resources* section for some recommended brokers and freight-forwarding agents.)

STORAGE IN BELIZE

If your home isn't ready for occupancy yet, what do you do with your goods after you get them to Belize? Storage facilities in Belize, other than those owned by the government, are few and far between. Edgar's Mini Store in the Vista Del Mar area of Ladyville, near Belize City, was the first ministorage facility in the country. Dave Edgar established it in 2002. As of press time, it was for sale. Another storage facility is on Ambergris Caye. Caye Mini Storage offers monthly storage for US$.15 per cubic foot—an eight-foot-wide, 12-foot-deep, and 10-foot-high container is US$144 a month.

Many homes in Belize are decorated with locally available Guatemalan fabrics like these.

No Litta

Supported By
The Ministry of Tourism &
the Environment
Funded By . NARMAP

© Lan Sluder

Language and Education

You don't need to learn a new language to live in Belize. English is the official language of the country, and all legal documents and public records are in English, along with most newspapers and broadcast programs. In contrast to other popular retirement and relocation destinations in the region, such as Costa Rica and Mexico, that's one of the great benefits of Belize. Even if you already know some Spanish or are willing to spend time learning it, it can take years for an adult to become truly proficient. After all, it's one thing to know how to ask for directions to the bathroom—and it's entirely another to discourse in Spanish on the intricacies of the game of baseball or the jargonized details of your profession.

With immigration, legal and illegal, from neighboring countries, Spanish is becoming more widely spoken in Belize, and it is the first language of about two in five Belizeans.

Creole, a colorful language combining elements of English with African grammar and syntax, is spoken as a first language by perhaps a fourth of Belizeans, mostly in Central Belize, in and around Belize City.

Many Belizeans are bi- or trilingual, fluent in English, Spanish, and Creole. Several Maya dialects are also spoken in Belize, along with the Garifuna language, and, in Mennonite areas, a version of Low German. Because of the influx of Taiwanese into Belize since the 1980s, Mandarin Chinese is spoken by several thousand people in the country.

Languages

SPANISH

If you *habla Español,* or have always wanted to, never fear. Spanish is widely spoken in Belize, and in some areas of northern and western Belize, it is the first language. In Mestizo-dominated tourist areas, such as Ambergris Caye, locals speak English in public but Spanish at home or among friends. Many, though not all, Spanish-speakers in Belize also speak English. The current prime minister of Belize, Said Musa, has said he believes all Belizeans should know Spanish as well as English.

Latino culture and traditions are becoming increasingly important in Belize. Beginning with the Caste Wars immigration in the 19th century and now with contemporary waves of legal and illegal immigration from Guatemala and other countries in Central America, Latino culture, language, attitudes, and food have gradually gained influence. Today, Belize looks both to the Caribbean and Latin America for role models in language and culture, as well as trade and politics.

Unlike in Guatemala and some other countries in the region, there are few private classes or schools where you can learn Spanish in Belize. But some colleges, such as Corozal Junior College, offer Spanish-language classes that are open to anyone for a small fee.

CREOLE

Creole, sometimes referred to as Belize Kriol, has long been the country's lingua franca, spoken by people of every background and social class, though with the increase in Spanish-speakers, it is becoming less widely used than in the past.

In colonial Belize, as in Jamaica, elsewhere in the Caribbean, and also in antebellum America, a new vernacular developed in the intersection of languages spoken by West African slaves and the English, Spanish, and other languages spoken by slave masters and colonizers. Words from Moskito, a language spoken by Indians in Nicaragua and Honduras, were also incorporated. Now, as during slave times, Belize Creole uses many common English words, but the syntax and much of the grammar derive from African languages. When you hear Creole spoken, you can grasp quite a few of the words, but the way the words are put together make it impossible for an outsider to understand entirely. It is easier to understand when written, and some local newspapers have a few features in Creole.

Creole, sometimes referred to as Belize Kriol, has long been the country's lingua franca, spoken by people of every background and social class, though with the increase in Spanish-speakers, it is becoming less widely used than in the past.

After emancipation, former slaves in America lost much of their Creole patois, except in the remote coastal islands of Georgia and South Carolina, where dialects such as Sea Island Gullah and Geechee are still used today. But the language stayed alive in Belize and some other parts of the British Empire in the Caribbean. The best estimates claim that more than 50,000 Belizeans, mostly around Belize City, speak Creole as a first language, and another 90,000 or more speak it as a second or third language. Sir Colville Young, governor-general of Belize by appointment of the queen of England, is the author of several texts on Creole, including *Creole Proverbs of Belize.* Until about 30 years ago, Creole was a spoken language only. In the 1970s, an effort was made to standardize Creole and to put it in written form.

Sometimes, Creole is a kind of litmus test for determining how much of a Belizean you really are. A few words in Creole, spoken at the right moment, go a long way. Certainly learning some Creole and Spanish is helpful, especially when dealing with domestic or other workers. With a little effort, you can pick up enough of these languages to impress your visiting monolingual friends from the United States.

There are no Creole schools in Belize, but a website created by the National Kriol Council of Belize is a helpful resource on the language.

MAYA LANGUAGES

The Maya, including the million or so who lived in what is now Belize during prime time for the Maya empire, must have had many geniuses in mathematics, architecture, engineering, astronomy (or at least astrology), religion, and the military arts, although we know very little about individual Maya. Of the thousands of books the Maya must

Creole Words, Phrases, and Proverbs

You don't need to speak Creole to get along in Belize, but knowing at least a few words helps you fit in. Because it's primarily an oral language, written versions of Creole vary. To hear part of the Bible, some children's stories, and other examples of spoken Creole, visit the Belize Kriol website at www.kriol.org.bz.

backra: white person, as whites in tropical climates get raw backs from sunburn
brukdong: breakdown, a traditional type of music
chinchi: a little bit
da: is, am, are
deh: there
di: the; also indicates verb tense, as in "Yu muma di luk fi yu" ("Your mother is looking for you")
noh: don't, as in "Noh mek dehn get weh" ("Don't let them get away")

fowl caca white an tink e lay egg: Literally, "A chicken mistakes her white droppings for an egg"; said of a politician or other self-important person
gyal: girl; as opposed to bwah, boy
rompopo: eggnog drink with rum
So yu si, yu get save troo Gaad jeneros gif wen yu bileev. Dis noh hapm sake a eny a fi yu werk, aal a dis da wahn gif frahn Gaad: A translation from the Bible of Ephesians, chapter 1, verse 8: "For by grace are ye saved through faith; and that not of yourselves. It is the gift of God."
unu: y'all, second person plural; as in "Weh mek unu lef me alone? ("Why don't y'all leave me alone?")
wen puss no deh, rat take place: when the cats are away, the rats play
yerisso: gossip; from "Ah yer so" ("So I hear")

have created, only four have survived into modern times, the so-called *Dresden, Madrid, Paris,* and *Grolier Codices.* These works, of which the *Dresden Codex* is the finest example extant, were written on long strips of bark, folded, and covered with a protective material. Along with these four remaining books, many Maya inscriptions remain on stone stelae and on buildings. It took archaeologists many decades, but finally the Maya glyphs writing system was decoded, and now most Maya writings can be deciphered.

We do know, as Michael D. Coe, a curator of the Peabody Museum at Yale and author of *The Maya,* states, that "during a span of six centuries, from about 250 to 900 A.D., the Maya ... reached intellectual and artistic heights which no others in the New World, and few in the Old, could match at that time."

One of the great intellectual achievements of the Maya, insofar as we can determine from their written records, was a complex astrology and numerology, in which movements of planets and stars, along with their supposed impact on human affairs, were measured by a sophisticated calendar. The Maya, like the Aztecs elsewhere in Mesoamerica, thought along the lines of a series of cyclical creations and destructions, occurring over long periods of time. According to some interpretations of Maya cosmology, the present universe was created in 3,114 B.C. at the beginning of the 13th era, an approximately 5,200-year period called a *baktun,* and that Armageddon will overtake the degenerate peoples of this world on the last day of the 13th *baktun,* or on December 23, 2012. Make your reservations now, as this could be even bigger than the advent of the new millennium.

In Belize, you'll find Kekchi, Mopan, and Yucatec Maya, and their languages are spoken in Toledo, Cayo, and Corozal districts, among other places.

GARIFUNA
Other cultures brought their own oral and written traditions to Belize. Originally from St. Vincent in the Windward Islands, the Garifuna came to Belize in the early 19th century via Honduras. Today, they are concentrated in a few towns and villages in southern Belize. They have their own oral language—a written version is being developed. Hopkins, between Dangriga and the Placencia Peninsula, is where you will hear Garifuna spoken most widely by residents.

Education

Belize's educational system is based roughly on the English system. Students move through forms, from first form in primary school to sixth form (a kind of junior college), although some schools, following U.S. and Caribbean community practices, use the grade system: grades one to 12. The Catholic Church, through an agreement with the government, operates many of Belize's public schools. Nearly two-thirds of Belize's population are teenagers or younger, so in every part of Belize, you'll see schoolkids in their khaki or blue uniforms. In Belize City and elsewhere, there are both Catholic and government-run high schools. A few private or parochial schools run by Protestant denominations also exist. The best schools are in

The Catholic Church, through an agreement with the government, operates many of Belize's public schools.

Belize City and larger towns, and many of the worst schools—with untrained teachers and few books or equipment—are in the far south. One recent study found that lack of supplies was a major problem for schools in Toledo, and that about one-half of the teachers in the district had no educational training beyond high school. Only one in two Toledo children even finish primary school. You can help improve education in Toledo by donating school supplies or money to Teachers for a Better Belize, a alliance of Belizean and American teachers.

In 2004, more than 85,000 students were enrolled in Belize schools and colleges at all levels, including almost 4,000 in preschools, 63,000 in primary schools, and more than 13,000 in high schools. Close to 5,000 students were in postsecondary studies.

For contact information on colleges and schools in Belize, including those discussed below, see the *Resources* chapter.

PRIMARY AND SECONDARY EDUCATION

Primary education is free and compulsory through age 14. However, a sizable minority of Belizean children do not complete primary school. Only about 60 percent of teachers are professionally trained, though the number is growing. Secondary education, consisting of a four-year high school, is competitive, requiring passage of a comprehensive exam. A student's percentile ranking on the admissions test in part determines which school he or she can attend. Charges for books and fees at secondary schools are beyond the reach of many Belizean families. About three-fourths of primary school students do go on to secondary schools, but not all graduate. The typical tuition cost for private schools in Belize is around US$15 per month. The Belize government pays this tuition if the student is a child of a citizen or permanent resident.

Public schools vary but are generally best in Corozal and Belize City and worst in the far south. In villages and rural areas, schools are usually small concrete buildings with open windows and a pump for water. Some expats choose to home-school their children instead. Private schools are available in a few areas, but they can be pricey. For example, the Island Academy on Ambergris Caye, which goes through grade eight, charges US$2,500 a year per student. This school has an excellent reputation. Belize Elementary School in Belize City is one of the best private elementary schools on the mainland. Saint Catherine Academy for girls and St. John's High School for boys, both in Belize City, are recognized as among the best high schools.

© Lan Sluder

The Island Academy, a private school in San Pedro

Belize also has community colleges and junior colleges. Despite the name, community colleges such as Corozal Community College and Toledo Community College, and also some other schools with "college" in the name, are usually secondary schools (high schools). Junior colleges may have secondary school programs, but they also offer tertiary, post–high school programs. Most are patterned after the "sixth form" in Britain. They usually offer associate or two-year college degrees. St. John's College in Belize City has educated many of Belize's leaders. Corozal Junior College in Corozal and Muffles College in Orange Walk Town are other examples. Corozal Junior College and St. John's Junior College also offer evening and extension programs directed primarily at adults.

The literacy rate in Belize has been touted as being more than 90 percent, but this is misleading, as a large number of Belizeans, especially recent immigrants from Honduras and Guatemala, are functionally illiterate and may read and write no English at all. A more accurate number is about 70 percent. Still, compared with neighboring countries, Belize has a high literacy rate and a well-educated population.

UNIVERSITIES

Until the 1990s, Belize did not have a true four-year university system. The colleges in Belize City and elsewhere were more like American high schools or two-year community colleges. However, in 2000, provisions were made for the development of the University of Belize, which combines several existing Belize educational facilities. A small private college, Galen University, opened in Cayo. In addition, several small offshore medical schools have set up base in Belize—one in Belize City, one near Belmopan, and one on Ambergris Caye.

University of Belize

The University of Belize (UB) has campuses in Belize City and Belmopan, with satellite campuses in Punta Gorda and Central Farm in Cayo and a marine studies program on Calabash Caye on Turneffe atoll. About 2,100 students are enrolled at the University of Belize. The strategic plan of the university calls for Belmopan to be the main campus, and in 2004, much of the administrative functions of the university were moved to Belmopan from Belize City. Student dormitories and other facilities are also under construction in Belmopan.

UB offers associate and baccalaureate degrees in engineering, information science, nursing, education, and other disciplines, along with other training programs. The university also has a limited number of graduate programs, including a Master's in Business Administration program in coordination with the University of the West Indies. About 20 Belizean students a year graduate with MBAs through this program.

Student dormitories are available on the UB campus in Belmopan. Housing and meal rates are affordable. Dormitory housing is in one- to four-bedroom units and ranges US$70–200 per person monthly. Meal plans including breakfast, lunch, and dinner are US$6 per day. Private student housing is also available in Belmopan with local families for around US$200 a month, including room and board.

Belizean citizens and residents can attend at modest rates, as low as US$10 per credit hour for associate degree programs and adult education and US$45 per credit hour for four-year programs.

Galen University

Galen University, a small college based in San Ignacio, offers undergraduate and some graduate programs. It has degree programs in an-

The Price of Education

Here's a sampling of what an education costs in Belize. All figures are given in U.S. dollars.

Primary Schools

Island Academy, San Pedro (private school): $2,500 or more a year

Public schools (often run by the Catholic Church): Free, except for uniforms and books

High Schools

Mount Carmel High School, Benque Viejo: $300 a year (tuition)

Saint Catherine's Academy, Belize City: $500 a year (tuition and fees)

Junior College (Sixth Form)

St. John's Junior College, Belize City: $600 a year (tuition and fees)

Four-Year Colleges

Galen University, San Ignacio: $3,000 a semester (tuition for 15 credit hours)

University of Belize, Belmopan and Belize City: $675 a semester (tuition for 15 credit hours)

Offshore Medical Schools

CAHSU Belize Medical College, Belize City: $6,050–6,690 a trimester (tuition and fees)

Medical University of the Americas, San Pedro: $5,500–6,950 a semester (tuition and fees)

St. Luke's University School of Medicine, Belmopan: $8,595–9,875 a semester for foreigners; $4,300–4,900 for Belizeans (tuition and fees)

thropology, hospitality, tourism management, marketing, international business, and management.

The tuition cost for most undergraduate programs is US$200 per credit hour. For a year's program (30 semester hours), you'd expect to pay about US$6,500 for tuition and fees. There is no student housing on the small campus, so students live in rental housing around San Ignacio. Cost for student rentals range US$200–500 a month. In addition, there are food costs, personal living costs, and medical insurance, which is required by the college. Altogether, you'd expect to pay US$12,000 or more for a school year at the college.

The student body, which numbers only in the dozens, is drawn from Belize and foreign countries, including the United States. For foreign students, Galen obtains student visas from the Belize Department of Immigration. Admission requirements are relaxed. Students need only have completed their high school education and be in the top 50 percent of their class. About two-thirds of the student body work at local jobs to help pay for their education. Scholarships of up to 50 percent of tuition are available to students based on grade performance at Galen.

Many Belizeans who pursue advanced education do so at universities in Cuba, Jamaica, and elsewhere in the Caribbean, Guatemala, the United States, and England. Many lawyers in Belize have been trained in England, and many physicians in Guatemala or the United States.

OFFSHORE MEDICAL SCHOOLS

At present, Belize is home to three offshore medical schools, and a fourth is being planned. These and the score of other offshore medical schools target students who, although they may be motivated and talented, cannot gain admission to medical schools in the United States. Typically, the curricula at these schools parallel those in American medical schools. The basic sciences program is five semesters and can be completed in as little as 20 months. The clinical medicine program involves about 72 weeks of clinical rotations at hospitals in the United States or elsewhere.

Although these offshore schools offer an alternative to other types of medical education, some of them come and go. Grace University School of Medicine in Belmopan left Belize in 2003, and St. Matthew's University School of Medicine moved to Grand Cayman from San Pedro.

Medical School of the Americas

This school, which has about 50 students, has a small campus on south Ambergris Caye. The main school building is a large, square, wood-frame structure around a central open courtyard. Medical School of the Americas (MUA) is no longer associated with the Medical University of Americas in Nevis. Tuition and fees run around US$6,000 per term (MUA is on a trimester system). The school says it has a student/faculty ratio of 6:1. Students say that living costs on the island run about US$750–1,000 a month, depending on living arrangements. This sum includes rent of about US$450 for a one-bedroom apartment, US$150 for water, telephone, and electric service, and US$200 or more a month for food. Sharing a two-bedroom apartment will cut expenses somewhat.

St. Luke's University School of Medicine

St. Luke's is a small school in Belmopan with fewer than 75 students. Tuition at St. Luke's ranges US$8,600–9,900 per semester; Belize nationals pay roughly one-half this rate. The school estimates that housing costs in Belmopan for students will range from US$150 for a one-bedroom house to $500 per month for a three-bedroom.

Central America Health Sciences University (CAHSU), Belize Medical College

Founded in 1996, Central America Health Sciences University (CAHSU), Belize Medical College has its campus, a modern group of buildings, on the Northern Highway just north of Belize City. Tuition and fees are around US$6,000 a semester. The school estimates monthly living expenses for students will be US$700–1,000. Students must also buy required medical malpractice insurance (US$1,000 a year) and face other costs.

A fourth medical school, still unnamed, which is planned to provide specialties and techniques not currently available in Belize, reportedly will begin operations soon, probably in the Corozal Town area.

© Ian Sluder

Health

In many ways, Belize is a very healthful place. The country has little manufacturing and relatively few automobiles, so the air and water are clean. The pace of life is more relaxed than in most developed countries, so you aren't stressed out all the time. The weather is warm, so you can be active and outside in the fresh air year-round. If you live on an island or in an area where you don't need a car very much, you're likely to walk more and get more exercise.

But health standards and health care in Belize present a mixed picture. On the one hand, health and hygiene standards are considerably higher than in most other countries in Central America. On the other, Belize is a developing country; its medical resources are in no way comparable to those offered in the United States, Canada, and Western Europe.

Yet the situation is improving. One longtime expat had serious surgery in 2004 at Universal Health Services, a private hospital in Belize City, and he had high praise for the professionalism, capabilities, equipment, kindness, attention, coordination, and qualifications of the hospital and its staff. He also noted that the cost of his treatment was about one-tenth of U.S. fees for the same procedure.

If you are older and especially if you face chronic health problems, you will have to look closely at the tradeoffs—a healthier way of living, lower medical costs, and more personalized care in Belize versus the high-tech, impersonal, high-cost of health care and health insurance back home.

Living Conditions

Overall, the standards of health in Belize are remarkably high. In developed areas of the country, where tourism plays a key role in the economy, conditions are similar to those in the United States. You could almost be in Florida or California.

LIFE EXPECTANCY

Life expectancy at birth in Belize is about 71 years, not too different from that in the United States. Heart disease is the leading cause of death from illness for both males and females, but Belizeans, like Americans, have started paying more attention to the causes of heart disease, such as smoking, lack of exercise, and a diet high in fats, and the incidence of death from heart illnesses is declining.

Belize also has an ambitious, if underfunded, program to immunize children. Between 1993 and 1998, measles were eliminated, and the

Malaria

If you're worried about contracting malaria in Belize, take comfort from these statistics on reported cases in selected countries. Even considering Belize's small size, its rate of infection puts it on the low end of the list.

Country	Reported Malaria Cases in 2002
Cuba	29
Canada	740
Belize	928
United States	1,000
Costa Rica	1,021
Mexico	4,289
Honduras	17,223
Guatemala	35,540

Source: Pan American Health Organization

Measles, Mumps, and Rubella (MMR) vaccine was widely introduced in Belize. Vaccination rates for common childhood diseases now are well over 90 percent. The infant mortality rate in Belize is about 33 per 1,000 live births, a rate that compares well with those in Central America, but it is still considerably higher than among most countries in the Caribbean Basin.

TRAFFIC ACCIDENTS

The overall leading cause of death in Belize is not illness, but traffic accidents, which cause about one-fourth of all deaths in the country. Rarely a weekend goes by without news reports of a deadly car crash. The high rate of traffic deaths is remarkable, given that the vast majority of Belizeans don't have cars. Often the cause of accidents is alcohol-related. Belizeans, unfortunately, are all too prone to drink and drive. The speed limits that do exist in Belize—and most roads have no posted limit—don't mean much, because there are very few traffic enforcement officers. The use of seat belts is now required, but this rule too is rarely enforced. Finally, many Belizeans simply aren't good drivers. Driver-education programs are virtually unknown. Some people get their driver's licenses simply by showing up at the local Works Department office with the necessary materials: a certificate from a doctor that states the individual is in good health, two passport-sized photos, and US$30. Driving test? What's that?

> The overall leading cause of death in Belize is not illness, but traffic accidents, which cause about one-fourth of all deaths in the country.

AIDS

Local health officials say AIDS has become a serious epidemic in Belize. UNICEF estimates that 2.3 percent of the adult population in Belize is HIV-positive, and the Belize government says that almost 3,000 Belizeans have AIDS. However, AIDS workers estimate that the number could be considerably higher. Even at the lower official numbers, Belize has the highest per capita incidence of AIDS in Central America. HIV/AIDS is the second-most commonly treated communicable disease at Karl Heusner Memorial Hospital in Belize City.

In Belize, nearly 75 percent of HIV infection is spread by heterosexual contact. The highest number of reported AIDS cases are in

Belize and Stann Creek Districts. All blood for transfusion in Belize is screened for HIV, and the cost is absorbed by the government.

Visitors to Belize who are staying more than 90 days are now supposed to have an AIDS test, but this rule isn't always enforced. Those applying for permanent residency or residency under the Qualified Retirement Persons program must also have an AIDS test.

ENDEMIC DISEASES

Exotic and unpleasant tropical diseases are present in Belize, but the numbers are generally low and shouldn't be a concern for the average expat. Every year, hundreds of cases of malaria are reported in Belize. In fact, at one time, Belize had one of the highest incidences of malaria in the world on a per capita basis, and the highest in Central America. However, thanks to a widespread program of spraying for mosquitoes and other pest-control efforts, the incidence of malaria in Belize has been declining from its peak of more than 10,000 reported cases in 1994. In 2002, there were just 928 reported cases in Belize. That's actually fewer than in the United States, where about 1,000 cases are reported annually.

Another positive development is that more than 95 percent of the malaria cases in Belize come from the *Plasmodium vivax* strain, which is less dangerous than *Plasmodium falciparum* and can be prevented with the use of chloroquine, a time-tested and fairly inexpensive drug.

Most of the cases of malaria in Belize are in remote areas of Toledo, Stann Creek, and Cayo Districts. In Toledo District, the annual incidence of malaria has ranged from about four per 1,000 people to as high as 18 per 1,000 in the mid-1990s. Children and young men, often immigrants from Guatemala or elsewhere in Central America, are most at risk. One study found that villages within two kilometers (about 1.2 miles) of a river had higher incidences of malaria than those that were not near a river.

Three mosquito species are considered potential malaria vectors in Belize: *Anopheles albimanus* is the most widely distributed mosquito in Belize; *Anopheles darlingi,* primarily a riverine mosquito, has been found year-round in shaded patches of floating debris and submerged plants along creek and river margins; and *Anopheles vestitipennis,* found throughout the year, is most abundant during the wet season in swamp forest and marsh habitats.

Dengue fever is transmitted by another type of mosquito. It causes flulike symptoms that are unpleasant, but, in most cases, not life-threatening. Dengue has been reported in Belize—there were 42 cases reported in 2002—but it is not as common as in other parts of Central America. For example, Guatemala had more than 7,500 reported cases in 2002, Mexico had 10,000 cases, and Brazil had more than 780,000, according to the Pan-American Health Organization. There is at present no preventative medication for dengue, but its symptoms can be treated effectively with Tylenol or a generic equivalent. Avoid taking aspirin if you think you have dengue, as aspirin can exacerbate internal bleeding sometimes associated with dengue.

Both cholera and typhoid fever are occasionally present in Belize, but only a handful of cases have been reported in recent years.

BUGS AND CREEPY-CRAWLIES

Belize is a subtropical to tropical environment, and that means you have to coexist with a lot of life forms, including bugs and various other nasties. Mosquitoes are not a big problem in Belize City or in most towns, thanks to mosquito-control efforts. They're also not a problem on the coast or cayes close to the water when a breeze is blowing, which is most of the time. But inland, especially in the far south and around standing water, they can be ferocious. Bug juice with 30 percent DEET helps. For skeeters and other kinds of bugs, some people also swear by Vitamin B6 in doses of 100 mg/day.

Even worse are sandflies and sandfleas. These little monsters are common on beaches and in grassy areas near the coast. They affect some people more than others. I'm told you eventually build up a resistance to them, although I know lifelong Belize residents who still get badly bitten. Baby oil, Avon Skin-So-Soft, or other oily lotions drown 'em, and DEET also helps. Many people swear by a product called Cactus Juice, an insect repellent that seems to work on sandflies and on mozzies, too.

The botfly is an obnoxious creature, though it's not deadly. With the help of a mosquito, it lays an egg under your skin. The wormlike larva then digs it way out of your body. You can kill it by putting Vaseline or other gel over the opening in your skin. This suffocates the larva, and you can then remove it.

Killer bees are a common problem, especially if you're out clearing land. All regular bees in Belize are now Africanized, though a variety of small, stingless bees in Belize escaped Africanization. The sting of an Africanized bee isn't any worse than that of a regular bee, but when disturbed, the bees tend to be very aggressive and can kill cattle and other livestock. And you. If attacked, try to get into water or under a shed. Some people advise standing dead still.

Scorpions and tarantulas are common. Neither is deadly, though their bites can be painful. Belizean schoolkids sometimes keep them as pets.

Belize has about two dozen species of poisonous snakes. The good news is that only nine are deadly to humans, and Belize hospitals usually have antivenin medicine for fer-de-lance and other snakes. Bats are the most prevalent mammal in Belize, and among the ones present are vampire bats. But unless you make a practice of sleeping naked outdoors, you shouldn't be bothered by them.

Frankly, though, none of these pesky critters is even remotely as dangerous as commuting on the New Jersey Turnpike.

Health-Care System

Belize has a mixed public and private health-care system. Most Belizeans get medical care through a system of government-run hospitals and clinics. The country spends only about 4 percent of the GDP on health care, about a fourth of what is spent in the United States.

PUBLIC HEALTH CARE

There are eight public hospitals in Belize. Karl Heusner Memorial Hospital in Belize City functions as the main public hospital in the country and as a national referral center. There are also two regional hospitals: the Southern Regional Hospital in Dangriga and the Northern Regional Hospital in Orange Walk Town. In addition, there are district public hospitals in Belmopan, San Ignacio, Punta Gorda, and Corozal Town. Rockview Hospital in Belize City is a psychiatric center. Altogether, there are about 600 public hospital beds in Belize.

The public hospitals provide the four basic medical specialties: internal medicine, surgery, pediatrics, and ob-gyn. Karl Heusner Memorial also provides neurosurgery, ENT, physiotherapy, orthopedic surgery, and several other services.

The quality of these hospitals varies considerably. Karl Heusner Memorial—named after a prominent Belize City physician—opened

Bad Tooth

It was Friday night. I was sipping a Belikin at Cheer's, just up the road from the Belize Zoo, when I felt it. Zowee! It was a pain in my tooth, one that I'd chipped a few days earlier. This was no garden-variety type of hurt. It was deep-down, festering, I'm-sorry-I-didn't-floss bad tooth pain.

I pretended the pain wasn't there. I sipped another Belikin. But over the weekend, it got progressively worse. By Sunday night, I was gulping aspirin by the fistful and soaking my tooth in rum. The only good thing was that my entire jaw was beginning to go numb. But the tooth itself, a pesky lower molar, still felt like Jimi Hendrix was playing riffs on it with an ice pick.

After getting some advice about dentists from friends in San Ignacio, I called Dr. Osbert Usher in Belize City. His receptionist gave me an appointment that same afternoon. I drove to the Usher Dental Clinic on Magazine Road.

Dr. Usher's office looked about like any dentist's office in the United States. It was packed with patients: two nuns, several Creole kids, a Mestizo woman dressed to the nines, a Mennonite woman in a calico dress, and a British businessman. I answered a couple of questions from the receptionist—none of them about money, waited 10 minutes, and was ushered into one of the patient rooms and seated in a standard dentist chair. Dr. Usher's dental diploma from a university in Guatemala City was on the wall. The doctor, a trim man in his late 30s, wasted no time taking X-rays or getting my dental history. He just looked at the tooth, probed

it, felt my cheek, and said, "That's a bad one."

But, he said, it was no problem. He'd take care of it. He'd save the tooth. Soon he was sticking me with Novocaine, wielding a drill—the old kind with a comforting low-speed sound—and filling my mouth with cotton. This was dental care the way it used to be: no happy-face newsletters to generate referrals, no mood music on the stereo, no assistants lined up to do charts, no expensive film, and no second opinions.

In 45 minutes, the root canal was done and I was on my way, with the pain a fading memory and another appointment later in the week for a follow-up check on infection. Appointments, I noticed, were available on Saturdays and on evenings during the week. Dr. Usher gave me a prescription for antibiotics and painkillers, which I filled at Community Drugstore for less than US$6.

On my second visit, Dr. Usher finished prepping the tooth for a crown; I was on my way to the States and would have the final work done by a family dentist in North Carolina. I asked what I owed. Dr. Usher declined any payment, saying that since I had been nice enough to send him some copies of my books for his waiting room, he wouldn't let me pay. I insisted on paying something, and finally he agreed to take US$50 for the two appointments. For completing the job, the dentist in North Carolina charged me something in the three figures. If you need a dentist in Belize, may I recommend Dr. Osbert Usher?

in 1997 and has modern equipment, such as a CAT scan, though some Belizeans and expats complain that even this hospital is chronically short of supplies—even, at times, toilet paper. In 2004–2005, it added facilities, including ones for neurosurgery and trauma care. The Southern Regional Hospital in Dangriga, which opened in 2000, is another modern facility, with many of the same medical technologies and pieces of equipment you'd find in a community hospital in an American town. However, other hospitals leave a lot to be desired. The one hospital in Orange Walk, for instance, though it is being upgraded, still looks more like a refugee camp than a hospital, with low, concrete-block buildings and limited equipment. A new hospital has long been planned for Ambergris Caye, but it has yet to become a reality. A 24-hour medical clinic, however, opened in 2004 in San Pedro.

Besides these hospitals, Belize has a network of around 60 public health clinics and rural health posts in many towns and villages, providing primary medical and dental care. Most of these suffer from inadequate staffing, serve too many patients for their available resources, and lack equipment and medicine. Doctors may diagnose health problems accurately, but they may not be able to provide the proper medications to cure them.

Government figures show Belize has less than one physician per 1,000 people, or about 205 practicing physicians for a population of 270,000. This works out to less than half of the U.S. rate. Belize has about 465 nurses, or one nurse per 580 people. Altogether, there are perhaps 700 or 800 trained medical personnel in Belize. They are not distributed evenly around the country, however. More than half are in Belize City, which has only about a quarter of the population. About three-fourths of trained medical people work in the public sector and the rest in the private sector.

Starting in the late 1990s, health care in Belize got a boost, thanks to the arrival of a group of several dozen medical volunteers from Cuba. Currently, almost 100 Cuban nurses and physicians are in Belize. They were assigned to clinics in areas of Belize that did not previously have full-time medical personnel available to the local people. These hardworking Cubans, who exist on stipends of only a few dollars a month, have won many new friends for Fidel in Belize, regardless of what Belizeans may think of his politics. Medical and dental volunteer teams from the United States and Canada also regularly visit Belize to provide short-term care. Nigeria has been helping provide medical care for Belize, too. In late 2004, 17 Nigerian medical technicians arrived in the country to assist in public health clinics.

Medical-care professionals in Belize earn very modest incomes compared with those in the United States. Physicians employed by the government start at under US$15,000 a year, although they may supplement their incomes with private practice. Nurses start at US$6,000.

Most physicians and dentists in Belize are trained in the United States, Guatemala, Mexico, or Great Britain. There are three so-called offshore medical schools in Belize (see the *Language and Education* chapter), but their graduates are unlikely to practice in the country. A nursing school, which is affiliated with the University of Belize, trains nurses for work in Belize.

What you won't find in Belize is top-notch emergency care. While Karl Heusner Memorial has added a trauma care center, and there are ambulances and even an emergency air transport service operated by Wings of Hope, a U.S.-based charitable organization with an operations center in Belize City, Belize's spread-out population means it could take hours to get you to a hospital.

In terms of specialist care, such as for heart disease or cancer, Belize is behind the United States, Canada, and even its larger Latino neighbors, such as Mexico, Guatemala, and Honduras. One expat, who owns a lodge near San Ignacio, notes that for people in Western Belize, Guatemala has "excellent care and is the quickest place to get to in an emergency."

While many expats do go to Guatemala, Chetumal, or Mérida, Mexico, for specialized treatment, others who can afford it go to Houston, Miami, New Orleans, or elsewhere in the United States. When Barry Bowen, the wealthy Coca-Cola distributor and Belikin beer brewer, had an automobile accident on the way to his shrimp farm in Placencia, he was first treated and stabilized at Karl Heusner Hospital. Then he and his family opted to have him flown to Miami, where he underwent treatment for his back injury.

PRIVATE CARE

In addition to these public hospitals, Belize has three private hospitals: La Loma Luz, a nonprofit hospital in Santa Elena near San Ignacio; and Universal Health Services and Belize Medical Associates, two for-profit facilities in Belize City. All together, these hospitals have fewer than 60 hospital beds.

La Loma Luz is operated by the Seventh Day Adventists. It has 17 hospital beds, a primary care clinic, and 24-hour emergency services.

Owned by a group of Belizean physicians and businesspeople, Universal Health Services has up-to-date equipment and technologies. It has a primary health-care clinic on the south side and a surgical center with CAT scan equipment, ultrasound, cardiac, neurological and ENT labs, a kidney dialysis center, a pharmacy, and private hospital rooms.

Established in 1989, Belize Medical Associates has a 25-bed hospital, along with two surgical suites, X-ray and ultrasound machines, a clinical lab, emergency services, and a pharmacy. It is affiliated with Baptist Health Systems of Miami.

ALTERNATIVE THERAPIES

The use of herbal remedies is common in Belize. Bush doctors or snake doctors often have an extensive knowledge of plants with healing properties. Don Eligio Panti was one of the best-known herbal healers. He was a Guatemalan by birth but a longtime resident of Cayo in Western Belize, and he died in 1996 at more than 100 years of age. His work was popularized by Rosita Arvigo (with Nadine Epstein and Marilyn Yaquinto) in the 1993 book, *Sastun: My Apprenticeship with a Maya Healer.*

TYPES OF INSURANCE

Even if medical care isn't always up to snuff in Belize, at least it's cheap. Even for Belizeans not in the pilot project for National Health Insurance, almost all health care is provided at no charge. Belizeans who can't afford to pay are treated in about the same way as those with more means. Only a tiny percentage of Belizeans have medical insurance. Private medical insurance coverage in Belize begins at US$100–200 a month, far above what the average Belizean can pay. But nowhere in the public health system in Belize will anyone be turned away for lack of cash or insurance, as thousands routinely are in the United States every day.

Public hospitals and clinics may bill nominal amounts for tests and procedures—one woman's clinic in Northern Belize charges US$5–20 for a Pap smear, cervical exam, and breast exam, and less than US$15 for an ultrasound—or they may ask for a donation. In some waiting rooms, you will see a box where you can leave money if you wish. But even visitors are routinely treated for free. A friend of mine, a guidebook writer, was injured in a boating accident off Dangriga. In great pain, he was taken to the hospital in Dangriga, where he was diagnosed as having broken ribs. He was then transported by air to Belize City, where he was hospitalized for several days. His total bill, including X-rays, hospital stay, transport, and medications: zero.

If you can accept long waits and less than state-of-the-art medical technology, you won't have to spend all your savings to afford health care. "Medical, dental, and eye care are a fraction of the cost of the U.S. I have my teeth checked and cleaned for US$40, pay US$10–20 for an office visit to my physician, and medications are cheap," says one Californian who now lives in Belize full-time.

Even if you opt for private care, office visits to a physician generally are just US$10–20. A root canal with a crown might cost US$250–500, although some Belize dentists charge more. Hospitalization runs less than US$100 per day, even at private hospitals. Prescription drug costs vary but generally are less expensive than in the United States. A few years ago, I paid just US$5 for a course of antibiotics. Pharmacies can be found in Belize City and all towns. (By the way, prescription drugs in Belize are usually dispensed in plastic baggies or envelopes, rather than bottles.)

While it is difficult to compare costs between Belize and the United States, since the quality of care is different and the amount of medical tests done in Belize pales beside those routinely ordered in America, it's probably fair to say that even in the private sector, overall costs for health care in Belize are one-fourth to one-third that in the United States—and may be even less.

National Health Insurance

The medical-care system in Belize is in a transitional period. A National Health Insurance scheme, proposed in the 1990s, is gradually being put in place. It is being tested in pilot projects in Belize City, with medical-care coverage provided in both the north and south sides through the Belize Social Security system. Under the scheme, all Belizeans and permanent residents would get medical care through a system somewhat similar to that used in Britain.

Eventually, the scheme calls for individuals and businesses to pay into the Social Security system for health care. The benefit would be comprehensive universal medical care, paid for at least in part, at either public or private hospitals and clinics.

A pilot project in Belize City, started in 2002, was initially funded by the government and was free to all residents of the Belize City south side. Later, residents of the north side were added. It provided for care at a group of clinics, free drugs from participating pharmacies, and free lab tests at participating clinics.

Unfortunately, the Social Security system in Belize has been in crisis for several years, with charges flying back and forth about management and financial accountability of the system. The Belize government is also running a high budget deficit. Together, these factors are hampering and delaying expansion of the NHI.

As of press time, the NHI was in existence only in Belize City and applied only to public health facilities there. It is unclear how or when the NHI will be rolled out nationally, and exactly how it will be funded.

Insurance Policies

For routine primary care, most foreign residents in Belize make do with the low-cost public system, or they go to a private physician, dentist, or clinic. Mostly, they pay cash. Many "self-insure," taking a calculated risk that what they save in medical insurance premiums will more than pay for their actual medical costs in Belize. Health insurance policies for care in Belize are available through several insurance brokers in Belize.

F&G is based in Belize City and has six other offices around Belize, including branches in Corozal Town, Belmopan, Punta Gorda, Dangriga, Placencia, and Orange Walk Town. Among international health insurance programs used and recommended by expats in Belize, and by Belizean nationals, are British Fidelity Assurance, Amedex, and Capitol Life.

Several international insurance companies write health-care policies for expatriates, with the premiums sometimes covering medical transportation back to the home country, along with actual health care. Amedex specializes in coverage for foreigners living in Latin America and the Caribbean, including Belize, and has gotten good reviews from those in Belize who have used it. The company says it has more than one million policyholders in Latin America and the Caribbean, with a 90 percent renewal rate. Policies cover direct payment to any hospital in the world, 24-hour medical assistance, and medical evacuation. You cannot live in the United States for more than six months in a year. Premium costs vary based on age, but an individual $5 million major medical policy with a US$1,000 deductible for a person age 50 would be around US$1,600–2,000 annually.

British Fidelity Assurance provides both standard major medical and hospitalization programs, with fixed daily payments for hospitalization. Based in Barbados, it has representatives in Belize. Major medical insurance with coverage of up to 85 percent of hospitalization and physician costs has premiums in the range of US$150 month for a couple.

Capitol Life is an international insurance broker used by some Belize residents. It offers international medical insurance for expats through several large insurance companies, including Allstate, Specialty Risk International, and Allnation.

Medicare

Medicare and Medicaid do not pay for medical care outside the United States, except for limited situations in Canada and Mexico. The U.S. Department of Veterans Affairs will pay for coverage outside the United States only if you are a veteran with a service-related disability. For Americans, this is a major drawback of expat life in Belize, or indeed anywhere outside the United States and its territories. For visitors and short-term residents, some private insurance policies do cover you regardless of where you become ill or have an accident. Also, some credit cards—American Express's Platinum Card is one—pay for medical evacuations back to the cardholder's home country.

Pharmacies and Prescriptions

There are drugstores in Belize City, all towns, and some villages. Many prescription drugs cost less in Belize than in the United States, but pharmacies may not stock a wide selection, and some drugs cost more in Belize than in the United States or Canada. In general, prescriptions are usually not needed for antibiotics and some other drugs that require prescriptions in the United States, even some painkillers containing codeine. However, pharmacies owned by physicians or operated by hospitals, a common situation in Belize, may require or suggest a consultation with the doctor.

Among the larger drugstores in Belize are Community Drug Stores, which has three locations in Belize City; Val-U-Med, Family Health Pharmacy, and First Choice Pharmacy, all in Belize City; and The

Pharmacy in San Ignacio. Also, Brodies supermarkets in Belize City and Belmopan have pharmacies.

In addition, especially if you are in Northern Belize, crossing the border to Chetumal is an option. Chetumal has large *farmacias* that have most medications at prices significantly lower than in the United States, and often lower than in Belize.

If you are taking prescription medications, you should be sure you have the generic name of the drug when you come to Belize, as local pharmacies may not have the same brand names as back home.

Medical Records

If you have preexisting health conditions, you should bring a copy of your medical records with you when you move to Belize or come for an extended stay. It is also a good idea to have a letter from your physician outlining your conditions and past treatments.

Preventive Measures

If you decide to live in Belize City, Belmopan, Corozal, Placencia, around San Ignacio, or on one of the cayes, you face little more risk from exotic diseases than you would living in Florida. The biggest health problem you'll probably face, other than those that you would have back home, is sunburn. Since Belize is only 16 to 18 degrees from the equator, the sun is strong, and on a clear day, you can burn in a surprisingly short time.

In remote bush areas near rivers, especially where mosquito-vectored diseases are more common, you should have good screens on your windows and consider sleeping under a mosquito net.

VACCINATIONS

The only vaccination required for Belize is for yellow fever, and then only if you are coming from an area where this tropical disease is endemic, such as parts of Africa. However, many physicians recommend tetanus-diptheria; Hepatitis A and B; Measles, Mumps, and Rubella (MMR); and perhaps other vaccinations for all travelers, or even if you are just staying at home. (See the sidebar *Recommended Vaccinations* for more information.)

Recommended Vaccinations

Based on the current medical practices in the United States, the following vaccinations are recommended for adults. The prudent visitor or would-be resident of Belize would be advised by many physicians to get the full spectrum, just in case.

Tetanus-diptheria—One-dose booster every 10 years

Recommended for those who may not have been vaccinated earlier:
Varicella—Two doses (4–8 weeks after original dose)

Measles, Mumps, and Rubella (MMR)—One or two doses for those age 18–49

Recommended for those who may be at risk:
Hepatitis A—Three doses (at 1–2 months and 4–6 months after original dose)
Hepatitis B—Two doses (second dose at 6–12 months after original dose)
Influenza—One dose annually
Meningococcal—One dose
Pneumoccoccal—One dose

The U.S. Centers for Disease Control and Prevention specifically recommends Hepatitis A for visitors to Belize and Hepatitis B if you might be exposed to blood, have sexual contract with local people, stay longer than six months, or be exposed through medical treatment. A pre-exposure rabies immunization series is also recommended if you expect to spend time in caves or come in routine contact with domestic and wild animals. Typhoid might be advised for those spending time in remote rural areas and villages who are exposed to local conditions for long periods. Both the oral and injected vaccines have only a 50 to 80 percent effectiveness in preventing typhoid, however.

Health workers, pregnant women, and others in special risk categories may have different vaccination needs. Children require a different schedule and series of vaccinations. For the latest information, check with the Centers for Disease Control and Prevention.

ANTIMALARIALS

The Centers for Disease Control and Prevention recommends that visitors to Belize, except Belize City, take chloroquine phosphate. The brand name is Aralen, but there are generics. For adults, the dosage is 500 mg once a week. Take the first dose a week before arrival, then once weekly on the same day while in the malaria risk area, and then again four weeks after leaving. It should be taken on a full stomach to lessen nausea. Chloroquine has been used for a long time and has relatively few side effects. The most common are nausea, headache, dizziness, blurred vision, and itching.

All that aside, the vast majority of visitors to the most popular destinations in Belize, such as Ambergris Caye and Placencia, do not take any antimalarials. Probably fewer than one in 10 visitors to these areas takes chloroquine.

In addition, very few expats, retirees, students, or long-term visitors take any antimalarial drugs. I don't think I've ever met a single expat who takes such medication regularly. However, archaeologists and others working in remote bush areas do take the drugs. I also know of a few long-term expats, all in Toledo and Cayo Districts, who have contracted mild cases of malaria, but probably 99 percent say they have not.

Environmental Factors

A truly positive side to the typical Belize lifestyle, especially outside urban areas, is that compared to the usual way of living in developed countries, you tend to walk and exercise more, get more fresh air, and eat simpler, healthier meals of complex carbohydrates and fresh fruits. One Canadian, a chef in Placencia, says that after a year in Belize, he went for a health checkup. He found his blood pressure was down 15 points and his weight down 15 pounds. "But what do you expect?" he asks, smiling. "I live on the beach, walk 25 feet to work, and eat almost nothing but fresh fish and fruit."

AIR QUALITY
With little manufacturing and few cars, and with brisk winds blowing off the Caribbean Sea most of the year, Belize generally has crystal-clear air. What pollution there is comes from smoke from burning land for milpas (small corn plots used in traditional Maya slash-and-burn agriculture.) This usually takes place in the spring, typically in April. A little air pollution also floats in from Mexico and Guatemala.

WATER
Bad water and poor sanitation are major causes of illness in much of the Third World. In Belize, happily, these are less of a problem than in the country's larger neighbors, such as Mexico and Guatemala. Es-

sentially, all residents in Belize City and in nearly all towns have access to safe and adequate water supplies, or "pipe water," as it's called in Belize—and close to 82 percent of rural residents do also, according to UNICEF. Belize City, major towns, and quite a few villages, including those on the Placencia Peninsula, have safe, treated water systems.

Thanks to the plentiful rain in Belize—from 50 to 200 inches or more per year—drinking water literally falls from the sky. So, even if you decide to live in an area without a community water system, you can collect drinking water in a cistern. Concrete or plastic cisterns, with accompanying pipes and drains to gather rain from your roof, are sold in building supply stores or can be constructed by local workers if your home does not already have one. To be safe, this "sky juice" should be treated by filtering or with a disinfectant, such as chlorine bleach. Overall, about 91 percent of Belizeans have access to potable water. In short: In most areas of Belize, including nearly all areas of interest to expats, you can drink the water and not worry about getting sick.

> Thanks to the plentiful rain in Belize—from 50 to 200 inches or more per year—drinking water literally falls from the sky. So, even if you decide to live in an area without a community water system, you can collect drinking water in a cistern.

© Lan Sluder

a water jug from an old bleach bottle

SANITATION

Sewage disposal is less adequate. The Water and Sewerage Authority (WASA), which was privatized in the spring of 2001, with majority ownership by a European consortium, operates sewerage systems in Belize City, Belmopan, San Pedro on Ambergris Caye, and a few other areas. There is still a lack of facilities in rural areas, and three-fourths of rural Belizeans lack adequate sanitation, according to UNICEF; even in urban areas, about one-fourth of houses do not have adequate sanitation, according to Belize government figures. In rural parts of Belize, refuse disposal is not organized at the community level; households are responsible for the disposal of their own solid wastes. While many homes have reasonably effective septic systems, or at least well-maintained pit latrines, Belizeans dump their household waste into rivers or the Caribbean Sea in poorer areas.

SMOKING

There are no reliable statistics on how many Belizeans smoke, although one school survey in the mid-1990s found that about one-fourth of boys age 10–18 smoked, as did about 15 percent of girls in that age group. Certainly, the antismoking crusade hasn't progressed as far as it has in the United States. Few businesses, public buildings, or restaurants are smoke-free, and many Belizeans think it is their right to light up anytime and anywhere. My own very unscientific survey of foreign residents in Belize suggests that a large percentage, maybe as many as a half, smoke. Perhaps some of these folks came to Belize just to be able to smoke without being harassed by the lifestyle police? However, with local brands of cigarettes costing around US$15 a carton and imported brands US$20–25 or more, many Belizeans can't afford the habit. Additional tobacco taxes were imposed in early 2005.

Safety

"Is Belize safe?" That's one of the most common questions I hear from would-be expats, retirees, and prospective-real estate buyers. It's a question with a complicated answer, one that depends on all of the following factors.

PROPERTY CRIME

An American couple who own a second home on Ambergris Caye posted a plaintive note in late 2003 on one of the message boards on www.ambergriscaye.com, stating that their house had been broken into yet again—after a similar break-in just a few months earlier. They tried hiring caretakers, going through six of them in five years, but those people also stole from them. Their neighbors experienced similar problems.

Point-Counterpoint on Crime

The following are two diametrically opposed views about property crime from two expats, both living in the same area of Northern Belize.

Point: "Expats here talk a lot about crime against property. You would think that unless you have 24/7 security staff, if you go out to dinner you will return to find your house stripped to the bare concrete. I've had no problem. I did give thought to security when I built, and I do put valuables in a safe room when I go away for six months. Where I've lived for the last five years (Consejo area in Northern Belize), there have been four or five break-ins per year for about 45 houses—about 10 percent annually. This is substantially less than in a relatively wealthy neighborhood in Toronto, Canada. Furthermore, the average loss [was] under US$500, including damage repairs. None of the snowbirds here have security while they are away. Year-round residents do use housesitters, but this is mostly to look after pets.

Counterpoint: "Are we concerned about crime? Are you kidding? We all live behind locked burglar bars on every window and every door, upstairs and down. We all have fenced yards with large dogs and expensive security lighting. In short, we live in fortresses, just as our Belizean neighbors do. The difference is, Belizeans seem resigned to living this way, and we are not. We are proactively organizing neighborhood watches, monitoring cases in the courts, and quietly obtaining gun permits. Some of us, after all, are Texans."

This kind of comment, unfortunately, is common among those who own vacation or second homes in Belize. And it's not unheard-of among expats who live full-time in Belize. Gaz Cooper, who has lived on Ambergris Caye for many years and operates a small hotel and dive shop on North Ambergris, says, "My house has been broken into four times and if I were to reveal the whole story it … would make your hair curl. One guy got caught in the house and still got away with it, God knows how." Another resort owner on the south end of Ambergris Caye said her house was broken into while she was sleeping, and her wallet was stolen.

These accounts reflect a similar situation in most parts of Belize. When I meet homeowners in Placencia, Cayo, or Corozal Town, often the talk turns to the latest break-in at a neighbor's home.

So, as you've guessed by now, burglaries and petty theft are disturbingly common. Of course, this isn't unique to Belize. There were 2.2 million burglaries reported in the United States in 2002. When you add together burglaries, auto thefts, and larcenies/thefts, the total in 2002 for the United States was 10.5 million. That's one theft-related crime for every 10 households.

But the situation is more acute in Belize, in part because the police often do nothing about the problem. This may be because they are incompetent, lack the necessary training or, in some cases, know the culprits and refuse to arrest them. Most often I think it is due to lack of resources. In many cases, constables don't even have the basic tools to do their jobs. There have been a number of reports about police cars that simply sat at the police station because there wasn't money to buy gas for them.

In many cases, the local authorities do have a good idea of who is responsible, but in a society such as Belize—where most people in a village are at least distantly related—police have to go along to get along, and this may mean turning a blind eye if they think a cousin is doing the stealing or drug-dealing.

Avoiding Burglaries

What can you do to avoid being a burglary victim in Belize? Several things can help:

Put burglar bars on your windows and doors. These are available from local hardware stores and cost around US$50–75 per window. If your house is in a remote area, the bad guys may just attach a chain to the burglar bars and pull them off with a truck, but in most areas, the bars offer a good first line of defense.

Get a dog. A dog is the single most effective deterrent to break-ins in Belize. It doesn't have to be a vicious dog, but it should sound vicious. A black dog is best, as many Belizeans think black dogs are mean.

Put a fence or wall around your property. This won't deter serious thieves, but it may slow them down.

Hire a caretaker you can trust. Though there are irresponsible or crooked caretakers, there also are many who are dependable and will look out for your property when you are away. Ask around, especially at local churches, for an honest individual or family. Remember, the mango doesn't fall far from the tree. You will usually have to provide free living quarters and a monthly stipend, typically about US$50–100 a month, depending on what you require of the caretaker.

Install an alarm system with motion detectors. Belize has several security companies that install and monitor residential security systems.

The largest such company in Belize is KBH Security Systems, with offices in Belize City, Belmopan, Corozal, Punta Gorda, Orange Walk Town, San Ignacio, and San Pedro. Another is AAA Security Services Corp., offering First Alert brand systems. AAA has offices in Belize City, Belmopan, Corozal, and Dangriga.

Start or get involved in a neighborhood watch program. A neighborhood watch program has begun on North Ambergris Caye, with residents using walkie-talkies to alert each other and the police of problems.

PERSONAL SAFETY

It's difficult to compare crime statistics from one country to another because of different reporting and record-keeping systems, but the murder and violent crime rate in Belize is higher than in large urban areas of the United States. Typically, there are 50 to 70 murders a year in Belize. In 2002, the murder rate in Belize was 26 per 100,000 people, or about five times higher than the average in the United States, which has an annual rate in the range of 5–6 murders per 100,000 people (and that statistic in itself is very high compared to Canada or Western Europe). The majority of the murders are concentrated in Belize City.

To put the Belize crime rate in perspective, Guatemala City sees about 60 murders a *week.* Also, Belize does not have the severe youth gang problems that plague Mexico, Guatemala, Honduras, El Salvador, and even Costa Rica. In Central America alone, it is estimated that there are 250,000 members of *maras,* the Spanish term for a species of swarming, aggressive ants. While there are gangs in Belize City, the situation is nothing like that in Honduras, where the number of gang members is higher than the total population of Belize City.

While most expats are concerned about burglaries and thefts, most retirees and foreign residents in Belize express little concern about their personal safety. Certainly, it's wise to use common sense: Don't walk in unlit areas at night; don't pick up strangers in your car; put up exterior lighting around your home driveway and entrance.

Even those who do express concern about the high rate of crime are still generally happy with their decision to move to Belize. American expat Margaret Briggs asked about 30 expats living in Corozal Town if they were happy that they moved to Belize. About nine out of 10 said they were.

ARE YOU READY?

SEA RIOUS
ADVENTURES

TOUR CENTER

© Lan Sluder

CC 05 ZEIDITA

Employment

I magine you're living beside the blue Caribbean Sea. You spend your days snorkeling, diving, and fishing. Now imagine you get money to do this. You pay your way through paradise by working as a dive master, guiding tourists, or tending bar in a little thatch hut.

In reality, Belize has an unemployment rate in the low double digits. The few good jobs available are mostly reserved for Belizeans. Many occupations, including tour guiding, waiting tables, and barkeeping, are reserved for Belize citizens. Work permits for most foreigners cost US$1,500 a year and are hard to get. Residents under the Qualified Retired Persons Incentive Act can't work for pay at all. Even if you were able to get a job legally, salaries in Belize are far below those in the United States, Canada, or Western Europe, and even physicians, college teachers, and other professionals may earn under US$15,000 a year.

Despite these grim statistics, I do know quite a few expatriates who have carved out a comfortable niche for themselves in Belize, either working for an established Belizean company or running their own businesses. It is possible to make a living here, but it's not easy.

After all, the United States is the mecca for job-seekers and entrepreneurs. Millions of people around the world vie for a green card to let them live and work in the States. More than 100,000 Belizeans have left Belize to work and find their fortunes, legally or illegally, in the United States.

Why leave the United States, Canada, or Western Europe—with all their opportunity, capital, and huge consumer bases—to set up shop or find a job in poor little Belize, with its tiny population and small-town economic resources? What's wrong with this picture?

There are good reasons why you or I might decide to move to Belize and work or invest there, mostly having to do with quality of life, but economic rewards and an easy road to fortune are not among them.

Even if you can't get a high-paying job in Belize, you may find a rewarding volunteer position or decide that enjoying a low-stress life on the Caribbean coast is more important than making a lot of money.

The Job Hunt

In theory, unless you are a Belizean citizen or a permanent resident under the regular permanent residency program, you cannot work in Belize without a work permit from the government. You are also supposed to have a Belize Social Security card. As a permanent resident under the Qualified Retired Persons Incentive Act, you can't work for pay.

In practice, I know a few foreigners without work permits who have part-time jobs and take in-kind or cash payments. Foreigners usually seek out jobs in tourism or real-estate sales.

Maybe there's no need to worry, but I recommend erring on the side of caution—if you're caught working without a permit, both you and your employer could be in trouble. Rules for work permits have been tightened because of concern about illegal immigrants from other countries in Central America taking jobs from Belizean citizens. Fines are imposed on employers found with illegal workers.

Except for self-employment work permits, employment permits are obtained by an employer and employee jointly. The employer has to prove that he or she has exhausted all avenues for finding a qualified Belizean applicant, including advertising the position for at least three weeks. Examples of jobs that may require a foreign applicant are hotel restaurant chef or specialized computer software engineer. Work permit applications have to be submitted to the Labour Department, an office of which is in each district or town, along with a copy of the prospective employee's passport and three photos. After about six weeks, the Labour Commissioner can approve the permit, but the final decision for approval lies in the hands of the Director of Immigration.

Although fees for work permits were increased in 2005, the new work permit fee schedule implemented by the Belize government is subject to review and may change. For professional workers—almost anyone with a college degree—the fee is US$1,500 per year; for technical workers (without a degree), which covers most other jobs, the fee is US$1,000 a year. Permits must be renewed annually and new fees paid. With rare exceptions, work permits are not granted for waiters, domestic workers, and anyone involved in retail or other types of sales.

If that sounds like a lot of red tape, it is. The Belize government is trying hard to discourage foreigners from working in jobs in Belize that Belizeans can perform. One American, who moved to Ambergris Caye from Florida, said that her Belizean husband had no trouble finding work as a bartender, but businesses were very reluctant to hire her without a permit in hand—the high cost of securing foreign workers is prohibitive, as is the necessity of proving there is no qualified Belizean to take the job instead.

Sometimes it does work out for the best, though. Another American, who was an executive in the music business in New York City before moving to Belize, recalls the frustrations of trying to get a work permit: "It was not at all difficult adjusting—Belize was a perfect fit for me. Finding work wasn't a problem for me, either. Getting a work permit was, however, and it took a tremendous amount of stick-to-it-ness, patience, and energy. But I finally got that, then my residency, and now I'm seconds away from being a citizen."

FOREIGN PROFESSIONALS IN BELIZE

Lawyers, physicians, dentists, accountants, and other foreign professionals generally find it difficult, if not impossible, to become licensed and set up practice in Belize.

For attorneys, having a JD degree isn't sufficient. Belize attorneys, in most cases, must be Belizean citizens and have a Legal Education Certificate (LEC) from a Caribbean law school. This typically requires a year's study at an accredited Caribbean law school, in addition to the regular law degree requirements in the United States, Canada, England, or elsewhere. At present, the only three law schools that offer the LEC in Belize are Norman Manley Law School in Jamaica, Hugh Wooding

Earning Your Keep

As in most other countries, salaries and wages in Belize vary widely, even for the same position. Overall, wage levels in Belize are about a third to a fourth of those in the United States, or even lower, although a few businesspeople, professionals, and entrepreneurs in Belize make as much or more than their American counterparts.

In general, wages are highest in Belize City and San Pedro and lowest in remote rural areas. All figures are given in U.S. dollars. The work week in Belize for many people is six days long.

Maid/Domestic Worker	$10–15 per day
Day Laborer	$12–20 per day
Carpenter or Mason	$20–30 per day
Lodge/Resort Workers	$10–25 a day
Nurse	$6,000 per year
Doctor in Public Health Care	$12,000–25,000 per year
Primary School Teacher	$5,500 per year
High School Teacher	$7,000 per year
Sixth Form or College Professor	$13,000 per year
Shop Clerk	$90–140 per week
Office/Clerical Worker	$90–150 per week
Minimum Hourly Wage	$1.13 per hour

Law School in Trinidad, and Eugene Dupuch School of Law in the Bahamas. There are additional hoops that foreign attorneys must jump through before being permitted to join the prestigious, and usually lucrative, Belize bar. Since there are relatively few attorneys practicing in Belize, Belizean lawyers are typically able to charge higher fees than American attorneys.

An American physician with a home in Belize said, "I've been trying for years to become licensed in Belize, and I have had no success, and no other U.S doctors I know of have, either." The situation is similar for dentists.

In Belize, professional accountants are called Chartered Public Accountants, as in Canada, Britain, and some other Commonwealth countries. Further information is available from the Institute of Chartered Accountants of the Caribbean (ICAC).

Self-Employment

With well-paying jobs few and far between, most foreigners who want to generate an income in Belize will need to consider operating a business. In theory, the Belizean government welcomes investors who can contribute to the country's economy and provide work for citizens, particularly in tourism, agriculture, and manufacturing. But, theory in Belize is about as worthless as a Belize dollar outside the country. It's rarely simple or easy to do business here. A timeworn local saying is that if you want to make a small fortune in Belize, better start with a big one. The country's small domestic market, inefficient distribution and marketing systems, heavy-handed government red tape, and other factors make it difficult for entrepreneurs to achieve great success in Belize.

> With well-paying jobs few and far between, most foreigners who want to generate an income in Belize will need to consider operating a business.

Work permits are also required for those operating their own business, although generally self-employment work permits are easier to get than regular work permits. This category applies to foreign investors and others seeking self-employment or looking to start a business in Belize, where it is assumed that the venture will lead to the creation of jobs for Belizeans. The applicant has to show proof of adequate funds for the proposed venture, such as a bank statement. Also, the applicant has to have a reference from the relevant government ministry or other organization showing that the venture is reasonable. For example, if you're opening a tourist operation, a reference from the Ministry of Tourism or the local village or town council where the operation is to be located may be required. For the temporary self-employment certificate, the usual six-month residency period is waived. Self-employment work permit fees are US$1,000 a year.

Overall, Belize's business environment is above average in the region. The 2005 Index of Economic Freedom rating by the Heritage Foundation, a market-oriented think tank in the United States, gives Belize a score of 2.66 on a five-point scale, with a score of 1 meaning that the economy is entirely free. Belize rates as "Mostly Free," ranking 47 out of 155 countries for economic freedom. Hong Kong and Singapore are rated No. 1 and No. 2, the United States is tied with Switzerland for 12th place, and Canada ranks 16th. The Heritage Foundation looks at 10 key indicators: trade policy, fiscal burden of government, government intervention in the economy, monetary policy, capital flows and foreign investment, banking and finance, wages and prices, property rights, regulation, and informal (or black) market activity.

TYPES OF BUSINESSES

Once again, in theory, non-Belizeans can invest in or open almost any kind of business in Belize. In practice, though, several types of businesses require special permits or licenses, and these may not be granted to non-Belizeans so as to prevent non-Belizeans from taking jobs from locals. The following businesses, in varying degrees, generally are not open to foreigners:

- Commercial fishing
- Sugar-cane cultivation
- Restaurants and bars (not associated with a resort)
- Legal services
- Accounting services
- Beekeeping
- Retail shops
- Beauty shops
- Internal transportation
- Sightseeing tours (only Belizean citizens or permanent residents can be tour operators)
- Tour guides (only Belizean citizens can be tour guides)

Businesses that are most likely to succeed in Belize have their main markets outside Belize. The Belize market itself is small and spread out, and with a per capita income of just a fraction of that in the United States, the average Belizean doesn't have the income to buy much beyond the basic necessities of life. Opportunities include any kind of export-oriented business, from agriculture to manufacturing. Niche products, such as specialty or organic agricultural products, may have a future. Potential successes also include businesses that target bringing international tourists to Belize. There are potential opportunities to supply products to tourist businesses—for example, to sell specialty herbs, fruits, and gourmet vegetables to larger resorts.

Aquaculture has also taken off in Belize in recent years, with shrimp farming becoming a major industry. Shrimp farming generated nearly US$50 million in export earning for Belize in 2004.

Tourism

Tourism is the Belize industry that most attracts foreign interest. The country has more than 450 hotels, and a majority of the larger properties are owned by United States, Canadian, and other foreign nationals, although some of these owners have become Belizean citizens. You can find some real success stories among these entrepreneurs, but also many failures. In the former category are people such as Mick and Lucy Fleming, who pioneered tourism in Cayo in the early 1980s. They built the Lodge at Chaa Creek into one of the premier jungle lodges in the region and now employ about 70 people. Tim Jeffers is a Montana native who came to Belize in the 1990s and built two successful beach resorts on Ambergris Caye. His latest project, Banana Beach, with more than 60 beachside units, is one of the largest hotels on the island and enjoys one

Tourism Industry

Tourism is Belize's biggest industry. Yet, as these figures show, tourism is hardly big business in the country. Microsoft, by way of comparison, grosses more in *eight hours* than all the hotel operators in Belize gross in room revenue in an entire year.

33.6 million	Total annual room revenues (in U.S. dollars) of all hotels in Belize
820,000	Cruise-ship day-trippers to Belize in 2004 (estimated)
233,000	International overnight visitors to Belize in 2004 (estimated)
70,022	Annual revenue of average hotel in Belize (in U.S. dollars)
23,388	Most international visitors to Belize in a single month (March 2002)
5,050	Hotel rooms in Belize
466	Hotels in Belize
271	Average daily visitors to Altun Ha Maya (Belize's most visited Maya site)
85	Lodging facilities on Ambergris Caye
60	Lodging facilities on Caye Caulker
41	Annual occupancy rate of Belize hotels (percentage)
28	Average daily visitors to Belize's most popular national park (Cockscomb jaguar preserve)
23	Average daily visitors to Caracol Maya site
19	Lodging facilities in Corozal Town area
4	Average daily visitors to Crooked Tree Wildlife Sanctuary
1	Average daily visitors to Cerros Maya site

Source: Belize Tourist Board (data from 2002–2004; some figures extrapolated or projected from previous data)

of the highest occupancy rates in Belize. New Yorkers Bob and Risa Frackman first came to Belize in 1994, fell in love with the Placencia Peninsula, and opened the Inn at Robert's Grove in 1997. That hotel has been wildly successful since its opening and has grown to 52 seaside units. It's often full, even off-season. Film director Francis Ford Coppola has developed two very successful hotels in Belize, Blancaneaux Lodge in the Mountain Pine Ridge and Turtle Inn in Placencia. He also bought and is expanding a hotel near Tikal in Guatemala.

According to Belize Tourist Board statistics, the typical Belize hotel has just 11 rooms. Total annual revenue for an average hotel is only US$70,000, not including revenue for any meals, tours, or other sales. Thus, the typical small hotel in Belize can't afford to do the international advertising and marketing necessary to compete with larger, better capitalized resorts in other parts of the Caribbean.

The difficulty of making a go in tourism is shown by the number of hotels that are on the market at any one time. Probably about one-sixth of the properties in Belize are actively for sale, and other owners would quickly sell for the right offer. Hotel occupancy rates in Belize have increased with the growth of tourism, but in most areas of the country, tourism is seasonal. Annual hotel occupancy rates in Belize now aver-

Caracol is viewed as the number one Maya site in Belize, yet in 2003 it averaged fewer than 30 visitors a day. The numbers could increase with the boom in cruise tourism.

age about 40 percent, still a third less than average occupancies in the United States. Many hotel operators, while enjoying a pleasant lifestyle, are barely breaking even and holding on, hoping to turn a profit from their real estate when the property is sold. Only in San Pedro, which gets a regular flow of tourists year-round, do hotels appear to be consistently profitable. Some of the well-managed properties in Belize City, Caye Caulker, Cayo, and Placencia also show a profit.

TRADE AND INVESTMENT

Belize has several incentive schemes designed to encourage investment in the country, including the Fiscal Incentives Act, the International Business and Public Companies Act, the Export Processing Zone Act, and the Commercial Free Zone Act. However, as a U.S. Commerce Department advisory notes, "Many foreign investors have complained that these investment promotion tools are rarely as open and effective as they are portrayed." The government organization set up to provide one-stop information and assistance on trade and investment is Belize Trade and Investment Development Service, known as Beltraide.

The government programs of most interest to those thinking of starting a business in Belize are the Fiscal Incentives Act, the Export Processing Zone Act, and the Commercial Free Zone Act. The International Business Companies Act (IBC) makes it possible for foreign companies to get tax exemptions on all income of the IBC, all dividends paid by an IBC, all interest rents, royalties to non-Belizean residents, and capital gains realized. There are several thousand companies registered as IBCs in Belize. However, IBCs are not available to residents of Belize. Some entrepreneurs may also be interested in casino gambling and offshore banking operations. Information on any of these programs is available from Beltraide, although it may take a while to get response.

FISCAL INCENTIVES ACT

The Fiscal Incentives Act was designed to encourage genuine investment in Belize through tax holidays and duty exemptions. It was amended in 2002 to encourage small and medium-sized enterprises. Tax holidays (reductions in Belize income taxes) may be granted for up to five years, with extensions of up to another 10 years. Tax holidays of up to 25 total years may be available for companies engaged in agribusiness, food processing, manufacturing, and aquaculture. Import duty exemptions are available for up to 15 years, with extensions of up to another 10 years.

Tax holidays and duty exemptions are less generous for small and midsized businesses but still may be attractive to entrepreneurs. Small and midsized businesses must be involved in agriculture, forestry, agro-processing, auto rental, arts and cultural activities, fishing, computer and information technology, health-care services, hotel, restaurant, and other tourism activities, or handicrafts.

Some foreign investors have taken advantage of these incentives to open resorts and hotels. The minimum investment is usually US$125,000. The exact benefits depend on the size of the investment. A fee of several thousand U.S. dollars must accompany the application, and those who have used the incentives and concessions say there's a good deal of red tape involved.

COMMERCIAL FREE ZONES

The Commercial Free Zone Act of 1994 was established to attract investment in manufacturing, wholesaling, processing, and related activities in a duty-free zone. There are exemptions, for up to 25 years, from Belize income taxes and other taxes. A Commercial Free Zone (CFZ) is a place where visitors to Belize (but not Belizean citizens or residents) can shop for duty-free goods, and goods can be manufactured, processed, or stored duty-free if they are destined for export. All imports into and exports out of the zone are tax- and duty-free.

The first CFZ was developed at Santa Elena at the Mexican border north of Corozal Town. The Santa Elena Free Zone consists of around 300 acres, half of which are developed. More than 200 companies are doing business in this CFZ, mostly in the import/export sector, but there also are restaurants and retail businesses. A casino targeting Mexican visitors—Mexico does not permit casino gambling—recently opened. The Santa Elena CFZ employs about 1,600 Belizeans. Another Belize CFZ for Cayo District near the Belize-Guatemala border is in the works.

EXPORT PROCESSING ZONES

An Export Processing Zone (EPZ) is an area where goods destined for export are manufactured, processed, packaged, or distributed. Three locations so far have been designated as EPZs, one in Corozal District and two near Belize City. Businesses in an EPZ receive a

Barrier Reef Drive in San Pedro is one of the busiest tourist spots in Belize.

Belize tax holiday of 20 years. During the tax holiday period, an EPZ business is exempt from income tax, withholding tax, capital gains tax, or any new corporate tax. So far, the track record of EPZs in Belize has been spotty.

CASINO GAMBLING

Casino gambling is now permitted in Belize, and casinos have opened in Belize City, San Ignacio, the Corozal Commercial Free Zone area, and San Pedro. Licenses, good for up to five years, are available to foreigners who qualify. Casinos generally must be in a "large" hotel, which usually means one of 50 or more rooms. For information and application procedures, contact Beltraide or the Ministry of Finance.

OFFSHORE BANKING

Offshore banks were authorized by the Banks and Financial Institutions Act of 1995, the introduction of the Offshore Banking Act of 1996, and the Money Laundering (Prevention) Act of 1996. By law, these banks cannot serve customers who are citizens or legal residents of Belize. The 1995 legislation defines offshore banking as "receiving, borrowing, or taking up foreign money exclusively from nonresidents at interest or otherwise on current account, savings account, term deposit, or other similar account and which, according and subject to arrangement, is repayable on the check, draft, order, authority, or similar instrument of the customer, and investing the foreign money so received by lending, giving credit, or otherwise exclusively to nonresidents; or carrying on exclusively with nonresidents such other activities as are customarily related or ancillary to offshore banking." There are two categories of Belize offshore banks: "A" Class—Unrestricted and "B" Class—Restricted.

"A" Class—Unrestricted

The holder of an "A" Class offshore banking license needs to establish, maintain, and operate a business office in Belize. It is permitted to transact offshore banking business through its business office in Belize without restrictions on that business. The annual license fee is US$20,000. Authorized and paid-up capital of at least US$3 million must be maintained if the license is for a local company, or US$25 million in the case of a foreign bank.

"B" Class—Restricted

A holder of a "B" Class offshore banking license also needs to establish, maintain, and operate a business office in Belize, but it is limited to transacting only such offshore banking business as is specified in its license. "B" Class offshore banks cannot solicit or accept deposits from the general public and cannot provide any current deposits or checking accounts to depositors. The annual license fee is US$15,000. Authorized and paid-up capital of not less than US $1 million must be maintained if the license is for a local company, or US $15 million in the case of a foreign bank.

IBCs

Belize's International Business Companies (IBCs) Act was designed to attract sophisticated offshore investors to Belize, especially those who want to maintain as much secrecy as possible, and, of course, generate new fee revenue for the Belize government in the process. The bank accounts and names of beneficial owners of IBCs are generally not disclosed. IBCs chartered under this act are exempt from all Belize income taxes, dividend taxes, and capital gains taxes. There are no currency restrictions, and meetings of shareholders and directors can be held in any country. IBCs can be owned by one or more people anywhere in the world, except those resident in Belize, but IBCs must have a registered office and agent in Belize (typically a Belize legal or accounting firm). A Belize IBC cannot carry on business in Belize or own real estate in Belize.

Companies specializing in creating IBCs for foreign businesspeople usually charge US$1,500–2,000 to create the IBC, but with fees, annual administration charges, and other charges, the total may be more.

LABOR ISSUES AND WORKER RIGHTS

Besides the small size of the market and large doses of red tape, entrepreneurs in Belize face several problems related to the labor market. Unemployment in Belize is stubbornly high, yet many of the best-trained and ambitious Belizean workers have moved to the United States. This brain drain means that it's difficult to find skilled, motivated employees. In rural areas, many Belizeans have never held a regular job. Training must start with the basics, such as showing up on time and coming to work every day. Another problem is that the cost of labor in Belize, while low compared with the United States, is relatively high compared with other Third World countries. The minimum wage in Belize is under US$1.15 an hour, but that's several times the minimum wage of workers in Honduras or Nicaragua. The minimum wage in Mexico is under US$4 a day, half that of Belize. Belizean workers also have comparatively strong workplace protections, including a mandatory two weeks of paid vacation and participation in Belize's Social Security system, mostly funded by employer contributions of about 7.5 percent of wages, 16 days of sick leave annually, and a required two weeks' notice or pay in lieu of that notice should the employee be terminated after having been on the job at least a year. By American standards, the average wage of about US$10–20 a day for unskilled workers and an average salary of under US$100–150 a week for office and clerical workers may not seem high, but by the standards of Belize's poorer neighbors, these are princely sums. Businesses in highly competitive export industries may be at a disadvantage if they are located in Belize.

Volunteer Opportunities

Want to take a break from school, work, or other regular responsibilities? Would you like to help others less fortunate than you, or perhaps do something for the world by assisting in conservation activities?

Would you like to learn a new skill or spend time investigating the mysteries of the Maya world? Then you may want to consider volunteer opportunities in Belize. Note, however, that the Belize government requires even short-term volunteers in Belize to obtain work permits. In 2005, the volunteer work permit fee was increased to US$100.

There are basically three kinds of volunteer opportunities available:

Church and medical-related "mission" work: This typically involves a week to several weeks of volunteer work in a medical or dental clinic, building churches or homes or providing other assistance. Usually these mission groups are based outside of Belize, often at a church or school or as a part of a local medical society, and volunteers typically travel to Belize at the same time in a group. In most cases, volunteers pay for their own transportation to Belize, along with personal expenses in the country, but food and lodging are sometimes provided by the mission and paid for by donations. Because these medical and religious missions are so diverse and fragmented, it's not possible to provide a list of them. Your best bet is to contact your church, college, or local medical society and ask if they know of missions to Belize.

Organized volunteer programs: These organized programs are of two general types: In the first—which may be run either by a for-profit firm, such as a travel company, or by a not-for-profit charity or university—volunteers provide for their own transportation to and within Belize, pay a fee of perhaps US$10–25 a day for lodging and board, and may also pay a placement fee or "contribution," which can be several hundred dollars or more. Some programs of several weeks or months in length can cost the volunteer thousands of dollars. In the second type of program, volunteers do not pay a fee and may receive food and lodging in exchange for their volunteer work, but they usually have to pay transportation and incidental expenses out of pocket.

These volunteer programs generally revolve either around conservation, such as working with wildlife or reef preservation, or around archaeology, with volunteers assisting on a dig at a Maya site. A few programs offer volunteer opportunities in education, animal care, or social work. Some of these programs are Belize-based, such as those at the Belize Zoo or Programme for Belize. Others are based in the United States, United Kingdom, or elsewhere outside the country.

Advantages of these structured programs include the fact that they are available to all kinds of volunteers, and they can usually be arranged before arriving in Belize. A commitment of at least a couple of weeks is often required for these programs. This benefits both the organization, which has to train volunteers, and the volunteers themselves, who require time to adjust to the work and the Belize climate and environment.

Independent volunteering: In Belize, as in most countries, it is possible and usually easy to just go to a worthwhile organization and volunteer your services. Conservation organizations, churches, libraries, medical clinics, humane societies, and schools are among those that may welcome volunteers. The YWCA in Belize City, for instance, accepts volunteers to help teach sports and arts activities. And there are hundreds of churches and schools in Belize, many of which would welcome volunteers to help out with teaching, outreach, or other activities. Usually, you will not receive any lodging or food in return for your volunteer activities, but this might be available in a few cases. To arrange independent volunteer work, it is usually necessary to be in Belize and make personal contact with the organization you are seeking to help. It is rare that you will be able to arrange satisfactory volunteer work before you arrive. In fact, most of these volunteer opportunities in Belize are completely unstructured. It's up to you to dig out areas of need, and then go and volunteer your services.

> Conservation organizations, churches, libraries, medical clinics, humane societies, and schools are among those that may welcome volunteers.

VOLUNTEER ORGANIZATIONS

This information was accurate at press time, but keep in mind that things change quickly. Check with individual organizations directly for current information. Note that some of these organizations charge fees—which may be tax-deductible as contributions—for transportation, room, board, and placement. (See the *Contacts* section of the *Resources* chapter for contact information.)

Within Belize

For almost four decades, the Belize Audubon Society (BAS) has been considered the premier conservation organization in Belize, and it has done an immeasurable amount of good. BAS, which is entirely independent from the National Audubon Society, has 1,700 members. Through an agreement with the government of Belize, it manages eight parks and protected areas, including Cockscomb, Crooked Tree, Half

Moon Caye, and Tapir Mountain. While BAS does not have a highly organized volunteer program, those interested in volunteering can contact BAS to see if any help is needed in the office or in its education and field programs. The annual Christmas Bird Count, held in Belize City, Punta Gorda, Belmopan, and Gallon Jug, is a time when volunteer birders gather to do their thing.

The Belize Community Service Alliance, a small NGO sponsored and supported mostly by individuals and businesses in Illinois and Cayo, annually conducts several projects in Belize. It is associated with Radio Ritmo, a community radio station in Cayo. There is no intern program in place, but local and international volunteers, typically high school, college, and med school students, can help for a period of up to several weeks. Its best-known project is the "Village Tour," an annual event of several months' duration in which Alliance staff and volunteers visit many remote villages in Cayo, giving educational programs on basic nutrition, sanitation and waste disposal, disease control, environmental protection, and community-building. Other projects include a "Save Our Rivers" program, an effort to clean up waterways in Belize.

The Belize Zoo is one of the truly great conservation organizations in Central America, and its director, Sharon Matola, has done a tremendous amount to further ecoawareness and education in Belize, though her work has not always been appreciated by the country's powers-that-be. The adjoining Tropical Education Center offers a wide range of education and outreach programs. Motivated volunteers may be accepted to assist Belize Zoo and TEC programs.

Birds Without Borders is a research, education, and conservation organization coordinated by the Zoological Society of Milwaukee County (Wisconsin). It operates in Belize in association with the Belize Zoo and Tropical Education Center and with private landowners. The group was formed in 1996 to study migratory birds common to both Wisconsin and Belize (there are at least 114 of these common species). Occasional volunteer opportunities may be available.

The nonprofit Cornerstone Foundation is one of the best-known volunteer organizations in Belize, with various cultural, community service, and peace-related volunteer programs in Cayo District. Volunteers commit for a minimum of three weeks (three months in the longer-term programs). For longer-term programs, individuals pay US$300–400 a month for housing, US$600 for couples and families. There is a US$100 application fee, a weekly meal fee of around US$15,

The Belize Zoo offers a wide range of volunteer opportunities.

and some other fees. Those involved in three-week programs, such as the AIDS Education or Natural Healing programs, pay a fee of around US$550–650. At any one time, the foundation may have from one to 18 volunteers in Belize, plus local administrators and staff.

Founded in 1996, Green Reef is a private, nonprofit group based in San Pedro and devoted to protecting Belize's marine and coastal resources. Among its projects are establishing mooring buoys to protect the barrier reef, managing two cayes near Ambergris as bird sanctuaries, and monitoring jewfish populations in Belize. Green Reef doesn't have a volunteer coordinator but says it is interested in hearing from prospective volunteers, especially those with skills in Web design, photography, fund-raising, community involvement, and education. In the past, Peace Corps members have served as full-time volunteers, and the organization has also worked with Smith College and Kansas State University to bring in volunteers.

King's Children Home (KCH) is a nonprofit organization that assists children in Belize who have lost parents through death, abandonment, abuse, and/or neglect. KCH needs volunteers to help out, for any period of time, but preferably for 2–6-month periods or longer. Volunteers work with kids from 1–18 years of age. Activities may include tutoring, counseling, clerical duties, and preschooling.

Highly unusual Mount Carmel High School has an all-volunteer faculty. Volunteers, who must be four-year university graduates and "willing to teach in a Catholic environment," commit to teach for a period of up to two years, and in return, they receive room, board, and US$12.50/week in spending money. The minimum commitment is one school year, from mid-August until mid-June, and the typical length is two years with the summer off. Living arrangements are spartan but clean. Meals are taken together in the rectory.

Formed in 1997, Toledo Institute for Development and Environment (TIDE) focuses on conservation in Toledo District. The group helps manage the Port Honduras Marine Reserve and Paynes Creek National Park. To raise funds, it offers ecotours. Contact the organization to see what volunteer opportunities may be available.

Programme for Belize, a completely Belizean-run organization, manages the 260,000-acre Rio Bravo Conservation and Management area, the country's second-largest protected reserve, representing about 4 percent of Belize's land area. Programme for Belize accepts paying guests at its Rio Bravo and Hill Bank research stations, where visitors enjoy simple but pleasant accommodations and hearty local fare. Volunteer opportunities may occasionally be available in conservation or archaeology. La Milpa is one of about 60 Maya sites on the Rio Bravo lands. (Also see the associated University of Texas/Programme for Belize archaeological project in the *Outside Belize* section.)

Monkey Bay is a private wildlife sanctuary and environmental education center on 1,070 acres near the Belize Zoo. Links to other conservation organizations in Belize and Monkey Bay's own programs provide some volunteer opportunities in conservation and community service. Monkey Bay also offers homestay programs, as well as 12- to 21-day education and adventure programs for students (middle school to university). The education programs cost about US$75 a day.

Founded in 1999, SAGA Society is a nonprofit organization whose purpose is to assist homeless and suffering dogs, cats, and other animals on Ambergris Caye. Most of the stray dogs and cats on Ambergris, as elsewhere in Belize, are not neutered, and many are undernourished and suffer from a variety of diseases. The local approach to control has been strychnine poison. SAGA is trying to raise funds to build an animal shelter on the island and establish a subsidized neutering program. This small group has no organized volunteer program, but local volunteers are welcomed. More volunteers will be needed if and when a shelter is up and running.

Outside Belize

A variety of volunteer and religious mission opportunities are available through Belize Faith Missions, ranging from one- and two-week programs to longer-term pastor positions. Accommodations and food may be provided to volunteers.

Explorations in Travel places volunteers and interns at several sites in Belize, including Monkey Bay Wildlife Sanctuary. Commitment is usually for 2–3 weeks. Volunteers typically pay US$15 per day for meals and lodging, and there is a placement fee of US$975.

EcoLogic Development Fund works with local Maya organizations in protect their homelands from a government-sanctioned logging concession. EcoLogic is also working to create Maya alternatives to managing Sarstoon-Temash National Park that respect traditional land rights and safeguard areas of biodiversity.

Maya Research Organization at Blue Creek, an archaeological research station organized by Texas Christian University (TCU), is in rural Orange Walk District. It attracts about 30 students and paying volunteers to each of its four two-week programs, where they work with 15–30 professional staff. The day starts around 6 A.M., with breakfast at 6:30, and most of the workday (until 3:30 P.M.) involves strenuous activity at a Maya site. Your required contribution (likely tax-deductible) is US$1,250 for a two-week program (US$1,000 for each program if you participate in two or more programs), which includes lodging and food but not transportation to Belize or personal expenses. A few scholarships are available for students who intend to pursue archaeology as a career. Academic credit through TCU or another university may be available.

Plenty International places volunteers with medical, midwifery, marketing, and other skills in Toledo District and elsewhere. This grassroots organization, founded in Tennessee in 1974, places 8–10 volunteers a year, mostly in Belize. There is a minimum three-month commitment.

A nominal (US$30) placement fee is charged, and there are no stipends or other payments to volunteers, but volunteers may receive food and housing in some cases.

The University of Texas at Austin's Department of Anthropology has operated a field research station on Programme for Belize lands since 1992. Volunteers must commit for a minimum of one week, up to a maximum of 15 weeks. The field school program involves survey, excavation at several Maya sites, and laboratory experience working directly with excavated Maya artifacts. Field techniques, lectures on Maya culture, history, and instruction concerning artifact analysis are provided during each session. Program fees are US$620/week or US$1,880/month; after four weeks, the cost is US$300 for each additional week. Fees do not cover transport to Belize and personal expenses but do include meals and lodging. Students have the opportunity to earn university credits.

Getting More out of Your Experience

Keeping the following factors in mind will help prepare you for the experience of volunteering in Belize and will help your expectations stay realistic:

Don't expect to get free room and board or other compensation. In some cases, this may happen, but more commonly, you will have to pay your own way and may even have to pay a fee for the "privilege" of volunteering.

Expect to work hard. Some programs, such as archaeological digs, require hard manual labor. At least initially you also will have to acclimate your body to Belize's hot, humid subtropical climate.

You may have to put up with primitive living conditions. While some medical mission volunteers stay at nice hotels, many volunteers live local, staying in Belize-style housing (usually without air-conditioning or fans and perhaps without indoor plumbing). Conservation and archaeological volunteers may even basically camp out.

Volunteer organizations and their programs change constantly, so be sure you have the latest information on programs and costs. The most up-to-date information is usually on the Internet. Just go to a search engine such as Google and search using keywords such as "volunteer work Belize." Also check out specialized websites on working, going to school, and volunteering abroad, such as www.gapyear.com and www.transitionsabroad.com.

Although volunteer organizations usually do good work, keep in mind that for the staff and administrators, these programs may be their career. Some of the international volunteer organizations are relatively large businesses, and in at least a few cases, their good works appear to be subsidiary to maintaining and building the organization.

A work permit is required in Belize for short-term volunteer work. There is a small fee, now US$100. For information, contact the volunteer organization, the Immigration and Nationality Department, or the Labour Department.

Have realistic expectations of what you can accomplish in a short time. Belize has many problems, varying from underfunded schools to crime, drug, and gang problems to family disintegration and child-abuse issues to destruction of the rainforest and natural habitats, and none of these will be solved quickly.

The most typical volunteer in Belize is a college student or a young person who has recently finished college, but volunteers come in all ages and from all backgrounds.

While not really volunteer organizations, a number of specialized travel and education organizations, such as ElderHostel, offer trips and programs in Belize. Many of these are worth investigating.

Finance

Your dollar (or pound, yen, or euro) probably will stretch a little further in Belize than it does in your home country. Whether you're retired on a fixed income or just trying to make ends meet on your salary or investments, it's certainly possible to live on much less in Belize than in the United States or most other developed countries. A typical Belizean family gets along on only a few thousand dollars a year. With the judicious adoption of the Belizean way of life (relishing the simpler, natural things in life rather than expensive imports), you can enjoy a sea view, tasty tropical meals, and a maid to help around the house, all for less than you would pay for a small apartment in a big U.S. city. As you might expect, money, finance, banking, and taxes are handled a little differently in Belize. This chapter gives you the information you'll need to make sound financial decisions in Belize.

Cost of Living

When you ask the expat's inevitable first question about moving abroad—"How much does it cost?"—you'll often hear that there are two ways of looking at the cost of living in Belize: The country is either the most expensive place in Central America or the least expensive in the Caribbean. That's true enough, but there's another point to make about living costs in Belize: They vary tremendously, depending on what lifestyle you choose and where in the country you decide to live.

Like most places, Belize has not one but several costs of living. If you want to live in the North American style, the cost of living is likely higher than for a similar lifestyle in the United States or Canada. However, if you live closer to the Belizean style—choose a simple frame house built to catch the cooling breezes, eat beans and rice and chicken, drink local rum, and take the bus or ride a bike—you can live for less than in the United States, and even a modest income or Social Security check will stretch a long way. Between the two lifestyles, you can live well on a moderate income by enjoying some American-style "necessities," such as a car, along with Belizean luxuries, such as full-time domestic help, which usually runs only about US$10–15 a day in most areas of the country.

Costs also vary a great deal depending on where in Belize you end up. Real-estate and other living costs are usually highest in Belize City and on Ambergris Caye. Costs are lowest in rural areas and in smaller towns and villages.

In general, the cost of anything that is labor-intensive in Belize is likely to be less expensive than in the United States, Canada, or Western Europe, because wage levels and salaries in Belize are usually one-third or less of what they are in developed countries. Thus, domestic help, medical care, and all types of services often cost less in Belize. Keep in mind, though, that lower costs for labor may mean less efficiency. It may take two people in Belize to do the job of one well-trained person elsewhere. Materials that are produced in Belize using Belizean labor may also be relatively inexpensive, and that holds for fruits and vegetables grown locally, seafood, and other Belizean foodstuffs, along with things such as Belizean-made furniture. There are exceptions, however, sometimes because of high taxes and import restrictions and also because of natural inefficiencies in the small Belize marketplace. For example, it typically costs more to grow kidney or black beans in Belize than it does to import them from Guatemala, and beer is artificially expensive in Belize because imported cheap Mexican beer is prohibited and alcohol is taxed at a fairly high rate. Anything that is imported is likely to cost more in Belize than in its country of origin

Saving Money

The following tips may help you save some money here and there on purchases in Belize:

- Ask a trusted Belizean friend to buy for you—the "Belizean price" is almost always less than the "rich foreigner" price.
- If you are doing the buying yourself, buy in person rather than by computer or phone—Belizeans like to do business face-to-face.
- If you are a resident of Belize, ask at hotels, museums, and other attractions (but not restaurants or stores) for the rate for Belizean citizens and residents, which may be half of the nonresident price.
- Pay cash—credit cards may be surcharged, and any credit price is usually much higher than the cash price.
- Bargain if appropriate—ask politely if there is a "discount"—but prices are fixed in most stores and shops.
- Don't buy in haste—the longer you're in Belize, the better you'll understand the system, and the lower price you'll probably pay.

because of shipping costs and import duties. Thus, most manufactured goods, including home appliances, cars and trucks, clothing, sporting goods, and toys, cost more in Belize—often up to twice as much as in the country of origin.

Belize has no stock market or other formal investment infrastructure. Most people who wish to invest in Belize should look into real estate, especially beachfront property. (See the *Housing Considerations* chapter.)

FOOD

Belize City has modern supermarkets. The two best are Save U and the Northern Highway location of Brodies, both in the northern "suburbs." District towns, including San Ignacio and San Pedro, have smaller but still well-stocked groceries. Most towns have markets, sometimes only weekly, where fresh fruit and vegetables are sold at low prices. In coastal areas and on the cayes, fresh seafood is sold off the dock or at a local seafood co-op.

Many grocery items in Belize are imported from the United States, Mexico, or England and are more expensive than back home. Examples: 15-oz. box of Kellogg's Raisin Bran, US$5.13; 3-oz. box of Jell-O brand gelatin, US$.80; can of Campbell's Chicken Soup, US$1.75; single 12-oz. can of Budweiser beer, US$2.65; bottle of Gallo Turning Leaf Cabernet, US$12.50. But locally produced products are fairly inexpensive:

© Lan Sluder

grocery shopping, Hopkins-style

red beans, US$.40 a pound; eggs (only brown eggs are legal in Belize, because of import prohibitions against foreign white eggs), US$1.25 a dozen; T-bone steak, US$2.50 a pound; ground beef, US$1.50 a pound; liter of premium One Barrel local rum, US$9; corn, US$.10 an ear; pork chops, US$2 a pound; banana, US$.5; potatoes, US$.50 a pound; milk, US$4.25 a gallon.

Restaurant dining costs vary but generally are about the same as in a small city in the United States. At the top end, at the most expensive restaurants in Belize City and on Ambergris Caye, figure US$30–40 a person for a three-course dinner with drinks and tip. But at a restaurant catering to locals in Corozal Town, Caye Caulker, or San Ignacio, you can have a filling meal of stewed chicken with rice and beans for US$4–5, a spicy Mexican meal for US$3, or fresh local fish with salad and sides for US$6 or less. Good local beer (Belikin) is US$1.50–2.50 in most restaurants, and local rum drinks are seldom more than US$2 or US$3. Wine is expensive. A 10–15 percent tip in most restaurants is sufficient.

ENERGY AND TRANSPORTATION

Energy costs in Belize are two to 2-4 higher than in the United States or Canada. Electricity is around US$.21 per kilowatt hour, so using 1,000 kwh a month will cost you US$221. Some electricity is generated in Belize, and some is imported from Mexico.

Butane is widely used to heat water and for cooking. Prices vary, but a tank sufficient for about a month's typical use is around US$30.

Gasoline costs roughly twice as much in Belize as in the United States and Canada. In 2005, unleaded gas cost more than US$4 a gallon, and in some areas more than US$4.30. Some projections say that gas could rise to US$5 or more a gallon before long. Diesel is about one-third less than gasoline.

Most Belizeans don't own automobiles. They take the bus. There's frequent bus service on the main roads—Western, Northern, Southern, and Hummingbird Highways—and to some larger villages off these roads. Prices are low. Most trips cost US$5 or less. On average, the cost is about five or six U.S. cents a mile.

TYPICAL BUDGETS

Here are some budgets for different lifestyles in Belize. Of course, each individual situation is different, and your budget could vary significantly from these, but they can serve as a jumping-off point for calculating your expenses.

High-End Monthly Budget

This budget reflects the cost of living for an affluent expat couple who rent a two-bedroom condo on Ambergris Caye. Assumptions: The couple own a golf cart for transportation, own a small boat, and spend freely for entertainment and personal expenses. All costs are given in U.S. dollars.

Rent: $1,250
Electricity (1,000 kwh): $210
Telephone (including long distance): $150
Water: $100
Bottled water: $80
Butane: $50
Groceries: $400
DSL Internet: $100

Entertainment and dining out: $600
Cable TV: $25
Golf cart maintenance: $100
Boat expenses: $350
Health insurance: $400
Out-of-pocket medical/dental care: $150
Domestic travel: $200
Other travel expenses: $300
Clothing: $100
Household help: $400
Misc. personal expenses: $200
Total: $5,165

Middle-Class Monthly Budget

This budget reflects the cost of living for an expat couple with their own small home in Placencia. It assumes that the couple have paid for their US$150,000 house and therefore do not have a house payment. Also assumed: Their Ford Explorer is paid for and they choose to buy health insurance, which includes medevac coverage, from an international insurer. All costs are given in U.S. dollars.

Electricity (750 kwh): $158
Telephone (including long distance): $110
Butane: $35
Groceries: $250
Cable TV: $25
Internet: $50
Entertainment and dining out: $200
Property tax: $24
Auto insurance: $20
Health insurance: $400
Out-of-pocket medical expenses: $150
Home insurance: $150
Gasoline (40 gallons): $160
Auto maintenance: $100
Clothing: $75
Household help/caretaker (part-time): $250
Misc. personal expenses: $275
Total: $2,432

Bare-Bones Monthly Budget

This budget is for a single permanent resident in a rented house near San Ignacio or Corozal Town. Assumptions: The individual uses public transportation and takes advantage of the local public health care system. All costs are given in U.S. dollars.

Rent: $150
Transportation (bus and taxi): $40
Telephone: $40
Groceries: $100
Entertainment: $75
Butane: $25
Water, dirt (trash) pickup: $25
Electricity (400 kwh): $84
Local health care and medicine: $95
Cable TV: $20
Clothing: $20
Misc. personal expenses: $50
Total: $724

BALANCING YOUR BUDGET

Because every situation is different, it's impossible to provide hard and fast figures on what it costs to live in Belize. Remember that the typical Belizean family lives on US$6,000 or less annually. However, here are a few guidelines for a couple planning to live in Belize. For purposes of comparison, it is assumed that housing is rented.

To live in a large, modern, American-style house in a high-cost area such as Belize City or Ambergris Caye, with all the modern conveniences, such as air-conditioning and electrically powered appliances, a car (except on Ambergris Caye), and imported personal goods and food items, dining out and entertaining frequently, and taking occasional trips to the United States for medical care, the cost would be as much or more as to live in Florida or other retirement area of the States: US$3,000–5,000 or more per month. Depending on housing costs and other factors, it could be much higher.

To live in a nice but unpretentious small home in a town such as San Ignacio or Corozal, with some modern conveniences and a car, moderate spending on entertainment and dining out, with medical care provided locally or in Belize or Guatemala, the monthly cost is likely

Comparing Three Options for Staying in Belize

Here are how the three options for staying in Belize stack up in key areas. (All figures are in U.S. dollars)

	Tourist Card	Retired Residency	Regular Residency
Age	None	45+	None
Fee for Individual	$50/month*	$705	$1,000 ($250 for Caricom citizens)
Fee for Couple	$100/month*	$705	$2,000 ($500 for Caricom citizens)
Money required for deposit in Belize	None	$2,000 monthly	None (but must show financial stability)
Time in Belize before you can apply	N/A	None	one year
Period valid	30 days (renewable monthly for up to one year)	Three years— can be renewed	Lifetime
Time required for approval	Immediate	Three months	Usually 6–12 months
Duty-free import of household goods	No	Yes	Yes (up to $10,000)
Duty-free import of vehicle	No (as tourist you pay no import duty)	Yes (must be three years old or less)	No
Work for pay	Only with work permit ($1,500)	No	Yes
Must stay in Belize to maintain residency?	Yes (can leave and restart 30-day period)	Live in Belize two months per year	No

*Free for the first month, then renewals are US$25 for the first three months, then US$50 per month, per person for up to 12 months. Tourist cards are good for an initial 30-day entry and are free for citizens of the United States, Canada, the United Kingdom, Mexico, European Union countries, Caricom countries, and most British Commonwealth countries; citizens of most other countries must obtain a visa, and the visa application fee costs US$100–$2,000.

to be in the US$1,000–2,000 range. Many frugal expats in Belize live nicely for considerably less than this.

To live more in the local style, in a modest, Belizean-style frame or concrete home, with electricity and running water, but without air-conditioning or luxury appliances such as a dishwasher, using local transportation, eating Belizean-style food, and getting health care in Belize, the cost per month would be well under US$1,000.

The cost of living, like beauty, is often in the eye of the beholder. Some expats complain that living in Belize costs much more than they expected. On the other hand, some expats find the country to be relatively cheap and eminently livable. As one Cayo District resident says, "Living well in Belize does not mean living lavishly. It is a place to come and scale down and appreciate life for its own richness."

Banking

Belize has five commercial banks, not including offshore banks. Three are based in Belize—Alliance Bank, Belize Bank, and Atlantic Bank—and two others, First Caribbean Bank (formerly Barclays) and Scotia-Bank, are large multinational banks with branches in Belize. The local banks are small, about the size of a small-town local bank or savings and loan in the United States. Belize also has several credit unions and small mortgage lending institutions.

Banking hours are shorter in Belize, typically only until 1 or 2 P.M. most days, and in other cases, banks close for lunch. Many bank offices have modern conveniences, such as ATMs, but they may be out of order as often as they are working, and only two banks—Belize Bank and First Caribbean—accept ATM cards issued outside Belize.

Here are the basic facts about each bank in Belize (see the *Contacts* section of the *Resources* chapter for contact information):

Alliance Bank of Belize is the newest of the commercial banks in Belize. It has offices in Belize City, Big Creek, and San Pedro. It is associated with Glenn D. Godfrey, who also operates Provident Bank, an offshore bank.

Belize Bank traces its history to 1902, when it was founded as the Bank of British Honduras. It is owned by Carlisle Holdings Ltd., (NAS-DAQ: CLHL, London: CLH), a billion-dollar-plus (revenue) outsourc-ing company with cleaning and support operations in Britain and the

United States. Carlisle also held a majority interest in Belize Telecommunications Ltd., which it sold to a company based in St. Thomas in the U.S. Virgin Islands in late 2004. Carlisle is 75 percent owned by chairman Lord Michael Ashcroft, a British billionaire and Conservative party officer who holds dual citizenship in the United Kingdom and Belize. Belize Bank bills itself as the largest commercial bank in Belize, with a 46 percent share of deposits and 48 percent share of loans in Belize. It has 12 offices around the country: Corozal Town, the Corozal Free Zone, Orange Walk Town, International Airport, Belize City (two), Belmopan, San Ignacio, San Pedro, Dangriga, Big Creek, and Punta Gorda. Belize Bank has assets of more than US$250 million and had operating income of nearly US$25 million in fiscal 2003. It also has an international banking division.

Atlantic Bank was founded in 1971. It is majority owned by Sociedad Nacional de Inversiones, S.A., a Honduran company, along with some individual stockholders in Belize and Honduras. Atlantic Bank, with assets of around US$100 million, has nine offices in Belize: Corozal, the Corozal Free Zone, Belize City (two), International Airport, Caye

© Lan Sluder

Corozaleños wait in line to transact banking business at Belize Bank in Corozal Town.

Caulker, San Pedro, Placencia, and San Ignacio. Atlantic Bank's international banking operation is Atlantic International Bank.

First Caribbean International Bank (formerly Barclays) was formed in 2003 by the merger of the Caribbean operations of Barclays, the giant U.K.-based financial services firm, and Canadian Imperial Bank of Commerce (CIBC). Operations in 15 Caribbean countries, including Belize, are being rebranded as First Caribbean International Bank. First Caribbean has assets of around US$10 billion. In Belize, First Caribbean has five offices: Belmopan, Belize City (three), and Dangriga.

ScotiaBank, formerly Bank of Nova Scotia, is a large Canadian bank with operations in the Caribbean, Latin America, and Asia, with assets of more than US$300 billion. In Belize, it has offices in Corozal Town, Orange Walk Town, Belize City (two), and Dangriga.

OPENING AN ACCOUNT

Most expats find that banking is a little different in Belize. In most cases, you can't just sashay in to your local bank office and open an account. You will usually be asked for references, including a letter from your former bank. There is no standard format for this reference letter, but it should state something along these lines: "Mr. Jones is currently a customer of our bank and has maintained a satisfactory banking relationship here since 1985. His savings, time, and demand deposit accounts with us total about US$150,000." The letter should be on the institution's letterhead stationery and signed by an officer. Most banks also require passport identification.

Some commercial banks also require that you have official residency status of some sort before you can open a bank account (the offshore banks in Belize are just the opposite: You can't be a citizen or resident and bank there). In late 2004, the Central Bank of Belize issued a statement that it would enforce the rule that only Belizean citizens and official residents could have bank accounts in local banks. So far, enforcement has been spotty. Some bank offices still permit nonresidents to open accounts.

U.S.-Dollar Accounts

While U.S.-dollar accounts theoretically are available, they are not easy for the average person to open in a Belize bank, and nearly all accounts are Belize-dollar accounts. The Belize dollar is not a "hard currency" and, outside Belize, it is difficult, if not impossible, to convert it to other currencies. Devaluations of the Belize dollar are occasionally rumored. From time to time, the Belize Central Bank also runs short of U.S. dollars, and businesses in Belize have to scramble to find enough greenbacks to take care of their international business transactions. Therefore, most expats find it wise to limit their exposure to Belize currency. Nearly all expats and business owners maintain their principal banking relationship with a bank outside Belize, typically in the United States. Funds are then transferred as needed to a local bank in Belize by check, wire, or cash from an ATM or credit-card advance. Western Union has offices in Belize City and most towns and is frequently used by those wishing to wire U.S. currency funds to Belize.

> While U.S.-dollar accounts theoretically are available, they are not easy for the average person to open in a Belize bank, and nearly all accounts are Belize-dollar accounts.

If you do deposit money in a certificate of deposit or other savings instrument at a bank in Belize, you can, at current Belize dollar rates, expect to earn about 6 percent to 9 percent interest.

Loans

While bank personnel in Belize are usually very friendly—this is Belize, after all—you can't always say the same about bank policies, especially for loans. Loan interest rates are high. Even as the U.S. prime rate was under 5 percent, Belize banks were getting 14–18 percent or more on business loans, and even more on some personal loans. And the hidden fees and charges can add several percentage points to the loan interest. Modern consumer protection laws haven't all made it to Belize yet.

Most banks in Belize won't lend to those who are not Belize official residents or citizens. Expats who need loans should try to get them outside Belize, or, in the case of loans for buying property in Belize, try to arrange owner financing. About the best owner-financing deals available for property in Belize are 10-10-10: That is, 10 percent down, with the rest paid out over 10 years at 10 percent interest.

ATMs

Many banks in Belize have ATMs at many of their branches. Belize Bank, for instance, has ATMs at 10 of its 12 branches. However, as of press time, only Belize Bank and First Caribbean ATMs accept ATM cards issued outside of Belize. Belize Bank's ATMs are in most areas of Belize, except Caye Caulker and Placencia. They work on the CIR-RUS and PLUS networks. You get cash in Belize dollars. Thus, if you are living in Belize, you can tap your U.S. or other home bank account via an ATM in Belize.

Offshore Banks

In addition to commercial banks in Belize serving local customers, Belize has developed a small but growing community of offshore (or international, as they like to be called) banks. These offshore banks were authorized by the Banks and Financial Institutions Act of 1995, the introduction of the Offshore Banking Act of 1996, and the Money Laundering (Prevention) Act of 1996. By law, these banks cannot serve customers who are citizens or legal residents of Belize.

Several offshore Class-A banks are in operation in Belize. These banks are regulated by the Belize Central Bank, have physical offices in Belize, and offer various services, including international bank cards and demand, savings, and time deposit accounts. Accounts maintained with these banks are not subject to local taxes or exchange control restrictions. International banks tout their privacy for their customers, although if the Belize courts find that funds in the banks are proceeds of crime, the banks are required to release the identity of the account owner. Funds are transferred into and out of Belize in foreign currencies, with no conversion to Belize dollars taking place.

Here's information on the larger offshore banks in Belize (see the *Contacts* section of the *Resources* chapter for contact information):

Atlantic International Bank: Owned by Atlantic Bank, this bank offers demand deposit accounts with a minimum of US$1,000, personal savings accounts paying around 2 percent interest, time deposits with a minimum of US$20,000, credit cards, and investment/brokerage accounts. Other services include offshore trust services, such as establishing International Business Companies (IBCs).

Provident Bank and Trust: This bank, with an office in Belize City, is associated with Glenn D. Godfrey, a well-connected attorney and businessman in Belize, though a controversial one. (Allegedly, Godfrey has been linked to the Belize Social Security fiasco.) Established in 1998, Provident says it is the largest international (offshore) bank in Belize and claims that it controls 80 percent of the international banking business in Belize. Demand deposits may be opened with a minimum of US$1,000, savings accounts with US$5,000, and time deposits with a minimum of US$25,000. The bank also offers online banking, credit cards (interest rate of 1.5 percent per month on balances), and other services.

CURRENCY

The Belize dollar is pegged to the U.S. dollar at the rate of two Belize to one greenback, although moneychangers at border areas and elsewhere sometimes will give a little more than that, occasionally as much as 2.15 or 2.25 to 1, depending on the current demand for U.S. dollars. Technically, if you want to change money in Belize, you must do so at a bank or authorized *casa de cambio*, though freelance moneychangers are tolerated at border areas. If exchanging through a bank, you'll normally get a little less than 2 to 1, typically around 1.98 to 1. U.S. dollars are accepted everywhere in Belize, so if you have American money, there's no need to exchange anything; in stores, you may get change in Belize dollars. Canadian dollars and other currencies are rarely accepted in Belize, except at banks where the exchange rate may be poor. It's best to convert other currencies to U.S. dollars before you arrive in Belize. In mid-2005, the Belize government said it planned to get rid of the *casas de cambio*.

Paper-money Belize denominations are the BZ$100, BZ$50, BZ$20, BZ$10, BZ$5, and BZ$2 bills. Belize coins come in BZ$1 and 50, 25, 10, 5, and 1 Belizean cent units. The 25-cent piece is often called a shilling.

CREDIT CARDS

Credit cards—mainly Visa, MasterCard, and, in some places, American Express—are widely accepted in Belize except at small shops and restaurants. But sometimes if you pay with plastic, rather than cash, you'll be hit with a surcharge, usually 3 percent to 5 percent. Belizean banks can issue Visa and MasterCard cards to their customers.

INVESTING

Belize has no stock market or other formal investment infrastructure. Most people wishing to invest in Belize look at real estate, especially beachfront property. (See the *Housing Considerations* chapter for details.)

Taxes

Most expats and other foreign residents in Belize are subject to a variety of taxes. Tax matters are complex, and I am not offering tax advice. For full information, and for advice on your specific situation, seek the counsel of an accountant, tax attorney, or other competent tax adviser. Here are some of the most important taxes you may face in Belize:

CONSUMPTION TAXES

A national sales tax of 9 percent, plus an additional 2 percent "environmental tax"—calling it an environmental tax doesn't make it one—for a total of 11 percent, covers most goods and services. Basic foodstuffs, such as rice, beans, flour, bread, fresh meat, corn, and sugar are excluded, as are many medicines. The sales tax replaced the unpopular 15 percent VAT in 1999, but the sales tax is creeping back up to nearly the VAT level. The combined sales tax started at 8 percent in 1999, went to 9 percent in 2004, and in 2005 was increased to 11 percent.

A few luxury items, such as yachts, have a luxury sales tax of 14 percent.

A hotel tax of 9 percent is charged on hotel room rates. The rate increased from 7 percent to 9 percent in April 2005.

Excise taxes on tobacco and alcohol were doubled in 2005. For example, the excise tax on rum was doubled from US$15 to US$30 a gallon.

The government of Belize gets about a half of its revenue from import duties. This is one reason why many imported items, from automobiles to home appliances, are more expensive in Belize than in the United States or Canada. Import duties range from zero to about 80 percent. On average, they are about 20 percent. (See the sidebar *Belize Customs Duties on Imports* in the *Making the Move* chapter for examples of current import duties.)

REAL-ESTATE AND OTHER TAXES

Property taxes in Belize are low. Outside of town limits, the annual property tax has been about 1 percent of the assessed value of the land, with no tax on the house or other improvements. Within city limits, taxes vary from area to area, but are in the range of 3 percent to 8 percent of the land value (not the developed value). Tax bills even for luxury properties are seldom more than a few hundred dollars, and in the past, most expats have had tax bills of under US$100. However, in 2004–2005, the Belize government announced plans to increase property taxes. As of press time, the extent of these increases, and their actual application, was unclear. Overall, however, it is expected that property taxes in Belize will remain low by U.S. standards.

Belize has introduced a speculation tax of 5 percent of value on land holdings of 300 acres or more.

> Tax bills even for luxury properties are seldom more than a few hundred dollars, and in the past, most expats have had tax bills of under US$100.

Property taxes in Belize are due each year on April 1. You can pay your taxes at Lands and Survey offices in Belize City, Belmopan, Corozal Town, Orange Walk Town, Dangriga, Punta Gorda, and San Ignacio. In San Pedro, you pay your taxes in the town board offices. In most cases, you must pay with cash or money order, not personal check.

Land transfer taxes for noncitizens are a one-time charge of 15 percent of the sales price, consisting of a 5 percent stamp duty and 10 percent alien land holding tax. This alien transfer tax rate was doubled in mid-2005. Belizean citizens and Caricom nationals do not pay the 10 percent alien tax, but they do pay the 5 percent stamp duty. Typically, these transfer taxes are paid by the buyer, although the parties may agree to another arrangement.

At present, Belize has no capital gains or inheritance tax. A capital gains tax has been under consideration by the government.

BELIZE INCOME TAXES
Personal Income Tax

Belize has a progressive personal income tax, starting at 25 percent with a top personal rate of 45 percent. As workers who earn US$10,000 or less pay no income tax at all, the vast majority of Belizeans are not subject to income taxes. Of course, this leaves Belize tax workers with a lot of time to look at the returns of those who *do* owe taxes. If you have a sizable income in Belize, you can expect to be audited.

As an expat resident of Belize, you will be subject to Belize income tax only on income you earn in Belize, not on income, earned or unearned, from elsewhere.

Business Tax

In 1999, the graduated Belize corporate income tax was replaced with a gross revenues business tax. A business tax of .75 percent to 25 percent is

This hotel in Placencia bit the dust—always a risk in seasonal businesses.

levied on gross or top-line revenues. The business tax is credited toward the total corporate income tax due at the rate of 25 percent of profits. If the corporate income tax due is less than the business tax, the difference between the business tax and the corporate tax due is payable. Thus, a company that is losing money can still be liable for a sizable business tax. Business tax rates vary by industry and type of business. Here are some of the rates on gross business income, which were increased to these levels in 2005. Small businesses that gross less than BZ$75,000 (US$37,500) annually are exempt from these taxes:

Professions and trades: 6 percent of gross revenues
Media: .75 percent
Banks: 15 percent
Real-estate agents: 15 percent of commissions
Most retail and service firms: 1.75 percent
Casinos: 15 percent
Rental income: 1.75 percent–3 percent

Expat Profile: Why One Expat Couple Decided to Leave Belize

Eva and Dan Garber moved to Unitedville, a small village in Cayo District, in 2003. In early 2005, they packed up and moved back to Arkansas. Eva Garber just arrived back in the United States and explains why.

"We made it back just fine. We're staying with my parents for a few days while we get our house livable again. We flew into Houston and got a rental car and drove up here to Arkansas overnight. Tiring, but great. It still feels a little weird, like we're just on vacation. It'll take a while to get used to it.

OK, here's what everyone wanted to know: Our reasons for leaving Belize. It really is no big thing. No one threatened us or told us 'Go home, Gringo.' Part of it is economic. There is so much more that we can do in the States that we can't do in Belize—garage sales, cheap wholesale items that can be resold on eBay, stuff like that. Lots of ways to make a little extra money and just live better.

The new residency/extension fees also are a big issue. [Fees for renewal of tourist cards were increased by 400 percent in January 2005, from US$12.50 per month, per person, to US$25 per month for the first three months, then US$50 a month. Application fees for permanent residency also were increased.] We could come up with the money if we wanted to, but then we'd be stuck in Belize for a long time, with very limited resources, and no way to leave if our situation changed in some way.

Also, I have parents in their 60s, in not the best health. I worry about them a lot. I don't want to be so far away, in case something happens.

Of course, the recent events in Belize [the work stoppages and demonstrations of early 2005] are a huge factor, at least in pushing us to get out sooner. We chose Belize partly because it seemed so safe. Most other countries in Central America and the Caribbean are having or did recently have wars, gangs, large amounts of crimes against foreigners, political unrest and coups, and so on. When I was in high school, we had a lot of kids from El Salvador because they were having a civil war! Their parents were leaving for better jobs, but also because there were bodies in the street and stuff. Of course, we didn't want to get into something like that. Belize has a history and reputation of being peaceful and laid-back, which was a good thing.

I don't really think things will escalate, but I do think it is likely to get more serious and things could happen. We had to go into Belmopan a lot, where a lot of demonstrations were held, and it's a little freaky to be so close to everything. And we've got a little kid. It's different if it was our own country, but Belize wasn't yet 'ours.' I'm not willing to put myself in danger for Belize. I do wish the country the best. I hope everything turns out OK."

Social Security Taxes

As in the United States, employers and employees pay into the Social Security system. However, in Belize, employers pay the largest share of the taxes—more than two-thirds. Social Security taxes were increased in 2003. Unless you work for pay in Belize or are an employer, you won't be involved with Belize Social Security. For an employee with weekly earnings of BZ$300 (US$150), the employer pays BZ$16.05 (US$8.03) in Social Security and the employee pays BZ$9.55 (US$4.63). For lower-wage employees, the employer pays a proportionately higher percentage.

U.S. INCOME TAXES

American citizens living in Belize may face income taxes in the United States based on their total income, including income in Belize. The U.S. Internal Revenue Service has long arms. However, a U.S. citizen who lives in Belize for at least 330 days in the tax year and whose tax home is Belize (that is, your place of business or place of employment) may qualify for the Foreign Earned Income Exclusion for income up to US$80,000. You may owe U.S. income taxes on any income or business profit over US$80,000, plus self-employment taxes (Social Security and Medicare). Income from dividends, interest, and other so-called unearned income are not excluded from U.S. taxes. For details, get IRS Publication 54, *Tax Guide for U.S. Citizens and Resident Aliens Abroad.* The American tax system is incredibly complex; if in doubt, it's best to consult your tax adviser. That holds for citizens of other countries with highly evolved tax systems, too.

Communications

When it came to communications, Belize used to be a black hole. There were no television stations or daily newspapers, radio consisted of mostly Spanish-language stations from Mexico or Guatemala, and many villages had no telephones. The coconut telegraph—word of mouth—was the state-of-the-art communications option.

Today, Belize still has no daily newspaper, and the coconut telegraph is still remarkably effective at circulating the latest news and gossip, but almost everything else has changed. The country has two local television stations, and cable or satellite TV from the United States is beamed into even remote villages. Belize radio stations blare rap, reggae, punta, and other music day and night. Weekly tabloid newspapers compete for circulation with lurid headlines and crime news. Cell phones and pagers are everywhere. And Belize is wired: Most businesses and many individuals are hooked into the Internet, with broadband DSL or satellite access available. Cybercafés have opened in most towns and resort areas.

Whether all this is good for Belize—and how modern communications may be changing daily life for the worse—are subjects often under debate in Belize. But like it or not, visitors and residents alike have to admit this little country is in the middle of the global information revolution.

Telephone Service

Belize has one of the best telephone systems in the region, with a combination of fiber-optic cable and microwave, plus cell service in most of the country. There are about 60,000 cell phone subscribers, 32,000 landlines, and more than 10,000 Internet accounts in Belize. You can dial to or from even remote areas of Belize and usually get a clear, clean line. That's the good news. The bad news is that telephone service in Belize is expensive for both users and Belizean taxpayers who are footing the bill.

> Belize has one of the best telephone systems in the region, with a combination of fiber-optic cable and microwave, plus cell service in most of the country.

Belize Telecommunications Ltd. (BTL) is a company with a history dating to 1956, when a British firm, Cable and Wireless, set up the first telecommunications system in what was then British Honduras. After several changes, it became BTL in 1987. In 2001, majority ownership in BTL was purchased from the Belize government by Carlisle Holdings Ltd., a U.K. company under the control of Michael Ashcroft, a British lord and politician.

BTL retained a legal monopoly on all types of telecommunications services in Belize, including the Internet, until the end of 2002, when its license to operate all forms of telecommunications in Belize expired. It is no longer the monopoly it once was, since BTL now has some limited competition, but it's still the 800-pound gorilla of Belize telcom—and if you live in Belize, you can't escape its clutches.

Phoning Home

To call Belize from the United States or Canada, dial 011, then the Belize country code (501), then the seven-digit Belizean number. For example, to call anywhere in Belize from the United States, you'd dial 011-501-XXX-XXXX.

To call either the United States or Canada from Belize, dial 00 plus the country code (1), then the area code and local number. For example, to call New York City from Belize you dial: 00-1-212-XXX-XXXX.

Like a bad dream, BTL keeps coming back. Lord Ashcroft's Carlisle Holdings sold its interest in BTL back to the Belize government in 2004. Later that same year, the Belize government sold BTL to Innovative Communications Corporation (ICC), an American company based in the U.S. Virgin Islands. ICC added 5,000 landlines and claims to have brought on 30,000 new cell users. Now, in 2005, it appears that BTL is coming back to Belize in a convoluted and complex deal, one that will probably cost taxpayers a bundle. Lord Ashcroft reportedly has repurchased some BTL shares and some shares are expected to be sold to the public. As of press time, the Belize government and ICC are in U.S. Federal District Court in Miami, arguing over who actually controls the company.

In spring 2005, a new Belizean-owned wireless company, Speednet, began offering digital cell service in Belize, with an interconnect to BTL. The new competition for BTL could mean lower rates for Belizean cell phone users.

WIRELINES

Basic local landline service (called "wireline" service in Belize) is fairly inexpensive. Installation of a residential or business phone costs US$50. For those who are not citizens or official residents, there is a security deposit which is typically US$500. There's also a US$100 deposit to make calls around Belize and internationally. It may take a week or two to get your service installed—but it's not necessary, as it is in some other developing countries in the region, to bribe telephone installers to get your service. In a few cases, that might help move you up to the top of the list, but if you're patient, you'll get your phone installed without paying off anybody.

Basic monthly residential service is US$10, and the monthly business rate is US$25 a month. Usage rates and long distance are where BTL rakes in the dough. Local daytime calls are US$.5 per minute (half that rate at night), and long distance within Belize costs US$.10 a minute within a district and US$.20 per minute between districts.

International calls to the United States from Belize are US$.80 a minute (US$70 after 10 P.M. and on weekends). Calls to Canada, the Caribbean, and South America from Belize are around US$1.25 a minute during the day and US$.95 a minute after 10 P.M. and on weekends. Even at that economy rate, a one-hour call to friends or family in the United States will set you back US$42.

Public phones are common in towns and in Belize City—there are about 650 public pay phones around the country. All now work with prepaid phone cards that are widely sold in stores in denominations of US$5–25. Calls to police emergency (911 or 922) and directory assistance (113) are free and don't require a phone card. Remote bush villages usually have a community phone.

WIRELESS

Wireless service, both analog and digital, is available from BTL in all six districts of Belize. BTL and its small competitors are all putting the emphasis on building wireless networks in Belize. There are about twice as many wireless users as landline users in Belize.

BTL's Digicell service is on the GSM 1900 MHz technology; the old analog is at 800 MHz. GSM technology is used in about 70 percent of the world. Like cell phone rates in most countries, those in Belize are complicated and varied, but you can get basic Digicell service for US$25 a month, including 150 minutes of usage. Additional minutes average around US$.25 apiece. You will also have to buy the cell phone itself.

If you are visiting Belize and have a cell phone operating on the GSM 1900 system, as Cingular does, you can use your phone in Belize, but you'll need to have a new SIM card installed at the BTL office at the international airport. The charge is US$25. Otherwise, you can rent a cell from BTL, car-rental companies, and some stores for US$5 a day. You must also pay a usage charge by buying a prepaid phone card. Most calls within Belize are US$.25 per minute. In addition, there are long-distance charges to make or receive calls outside Belize. For example, U.S. calls cost about US$1.40 a minute outbound and US$2.25 inbound.

Cellular service is good around most of the country except remote bush areas. There's even digital service on Ambergris Caye and Caye Caulker. BTL has more than 30 cell towers.

A single telephone book of about 200 pages covers all of Belize. Published for BTL by Verizon, it comes out annually in February and is available from BTL. Usually, you can pick up a phone book at any BTL office for nothing or a minimal charge. BTL also maintains an online telephone directory at www.btl.net, where you can look up Belize phone numbers.

Note that BTL is serious about having customers pay their wireline and wireless bills on time. If you're even a day late paying, BTL will cut off your service.

VOICE OVER INTERNET PROTOCOL (VOIP) SERVICES

With Belize and international long-distance and cell phone rates so high, some Belizeans with personal computers are turning to Voice Over Internet Protocol services (VoIP). Several of the popular services, such as Yak, do not work in Belize at present. One that does is Vonage, and many businesses, especially hotels, and some individuals use VOiP. However, the Belize Public Utilities Commission still considers VOiP to be "illegal" in Belize. VOiP requires a broadband connection.

Email and Postal Service

INTERNET

Internet access in Belize has vastly improved in the past few years. BTL now offers DSL in most of the country for both PC and Mac computers. However, costs are higher than in the United States and most other countries. Rates range from US$50 a month for 128 kbps to US$150 for 512 kbps to US$250 for 1 mg bps. In addition, there is an installation charge of US$100 and a monthly modem rental fee of US$15 (or you can buy a modem for US$155.) DSL is available in the Belize City area, San Pedro, Caye Caulker, Belmopan, San Ignacio, Benque Viejo, and Placencia.

Dial-up accounts are also available from BLT. Connection speed is moderate, usually 28–52 kbps. Dial-up Internet service starts at around US$20 a month, which provides 10 hours of access. After that, access is US$2 an hour. BTL also offers prepaid Internet cards; a 312-minute card is US$25, or about US$.8 per minute.

Internet via digital cable is available in Belize City for around US$50 a month and may soon be available elsewhere. There also are a couple of wireless Internet providers in Chetumal, Mexico, and in the Corozal Free Zone, serving the Corozal area. Heavy Internet users in Belize often go with a satellite service, mainly Starband and sometimes DirecWay. Setup, installation, and activation fees vary but are in the US$800–1,000 range, with monthly fees of around US$60 for unlimited service.

Most businesses and nearly all hotels in Belize have Internet access. Internet access is also available at cybercafés in San Pedro, Caye Caulker, Placencia, San Ignacio, Punta Gorda, Belize City, Corozal Town, and elsewhere. BTL has also installed Internet kiosks for public access in several locations around the country.

POST OFFICES

The postal system in Belize is generally reliable and fairly efficient. You can't send wads of cash by mail, but otherwise, you can usually depend on letters and packages arriving safely. Airmail to and from Belize City to the United States or Canada typically takes about a week. However, service to outlying towns and villages is slow. Some villages have only weekly mail service. Mail between remote areas and the United States or Canada may take 2–3 weeks or longer. A first-class air letter from Belize to the United States or Canada costs BZ$.60 (US$.30) and BZ$.75 to Europe. Packages being sent by mail have to be wrapped in brown paper and tied with a string.

There is home mail delivery in Belize City and most towns and villages in Belize. In a few areas, such as San Pedro and around San Ignacio, you'll have to open a post office box. Post offices are usually open Monday–Friday 8 A.M.–4:30 P.M., but in smaller communities, hours may be shorter. Belize City has a Mail Boxes Etc. location.

Within Belize, some people use Novelo's or other bus lines, or the Belizean airlines, to deliver mail and packages. To send or pick up, go to the nearest bus terminal or airstrip.

EXPRESS AND COURIERS

DHL, UPS, and FedEx have service offices in Belize City and will deliver to most of the country. From the United States, you can usually get delivery within 24–48 hours, but you'll pay a pretty penny: Shipping a 15-pound box from the United States to Belize City via DHL costs US$277.

International airmail is usually a cheaper alternative to the express services, if you do not need next-day delivery. A 15-pound box sent from the United States to Belize via USPS air parcel post takes 4–10 days and costs under US$50.

Media

The media in Belize is free and often freewheeling, if not always fully professional. Reporters and editors sometimes butcher the Queen's English and fail to follow basic journalistic procedures, such as getting multiple sources. Most of Belize's media is accessible online. AmbergrisCaye.com offers www.belizenews.com, from which you can visit a dozen different media outlets in Belize.

NEWSPAPERS AND MAGAZINES

Belize has no daily newspaper, but it has a number of feisty weeklies and monthlies. The best of Belize's weekly newspapers are the *Reporter*, the *San Pedro Sun,* and the *Amandala*. (See the *Contacts* section of the *Resources* chapter for website information on all the publications discussed here.)

The *San Pedro Sun* is a chatty, informal, and sprightly weekly published by expats Ron and Tamara Sniffin. They are the third expat couple to operate the newspaper since it was established about 15 years ago by a couple from California. The *Sun* concentrates almost entirely on news about Ambergris Caye and claims the largest foreign circulation of any paper in Belize. Six-month mail subscriptions are US$20 in Belize and US$40 elsewhere. A competing weekly in San Pedro is *Ambergris Today*.

Amandala claims to have the largest circulation of any newspaper in Belize. It serves up independent political commentary and a healthy dose of sports. The *Reporter* is a feisty tabloid heavy on crime news and politics but frequently with insightful articles.

The *Belize Times* is the official organ of the People's United Party and the current Belize government. The *Guardian* is the organ of the opposition United Democratic Party.

Placencia Breeze is a monthly newsletter oriented to visitors to the peninsula, published by the local branch of the Belize Tourism Industry

Free Press

Belize's weekly tabloid newspapers are full of local color, even if the news is not always 100 percent accurate. In this country, news is heavy on crime and politics. But even the trials and tribulations of daily home life make headlines in little Belize.

Here's a selection of headlines from weekly newspapers in Belize City:

American Retiree, 51, Gives Up Life After Wife Leaves!
Unruly Teenagers Pack Up and Leave Home
Alligator Tries to Snack on New River Swimmer
Liar, Liar, Pants On Fire!
Bus-Riding Cop Guns Down Ex-Cop Turned Jacker
Mangoes + Minors = Murder
Castrate, Cut Penis Off, Hang, Whip, Torture Rapists and Child Molesters!
The Travails of a 15-Year-Old Girl and Her Nutty Neighbour
Villager Drank Poison Because He "Was a Failure"
Barrios, Bullets, Belize Bodies!

Association. There are several other weekly and monthly newspapers around the country.

Many people considering Belize for retirement or relocation hope to find classified ads for home rentals and sales, but few Belize newspapers have more than a handful of classifieds. The best classifieds are usually in *Amandala* and the *San Pedro Sun* (classifieds relate only to Ambergris Caye).

Two Internet-based magazines focus on Belize. *Belize First Magazine*, edited and published by yours truly, covers travel, life, and retirement in Belize. It maintains an archive of back issues going back more than 10 years. *Belize Magazine* is a new entry that is doing a good job covering both local and tourism-related stories.

TELEVISION

Two main television stations broadcast in Belize: Channel 5 and Channel 7. Channel 5, Belize's first licensed television broadcaster, formerly had the strongest local news and information programming—although

the small library in San Pedro

Channel 7 has improved, and many Belizeans now prefer it. Transcripts of the stations' evening news programs are available online. Channel 5, which began as a video production company, also maintains the world's largest video archives about Belize. Mexican and Guatemalan TV stations can also be picked up in Belize.

Cable TV, usually with 30 or more U.S. and some Mexican channels, is available in Belize City, most towns, and some villages. Rates are around US$20–25 a month for basic cable, including channels such as HBO that would be premium channels in the United States. In the past, some Belize cable operators pirated cable signals and put them on their systems without paying anything for them. However, with the passage in 2000 of a new Belize copyright law, this practice is changing.

RADIO

LOVE-FM, which programs mostly easy listening at 88.9, 95.1, and 98.1 Mhz, is the most popular radio station. You can (sometimes) listen to it online also. Other stations include WAVE-FM at 105.9 Mhz and KREM-FM at 96.5.

Stations in Guatemala, Honduras, Mexico, and elsewhere can be heard in various parts of the country. The government-run Broadcasting Corporation of Belize (BCB), long a fixture in Belize, no longer operates.

Satellite radio is now an option in Belize. Both XM Radio and Sirius can be picked up in Belize. However, reception in some areas may be poor, depending on the positioning of the satellites. Also, you have to have a U.S. mailing address to subscribe to these services.

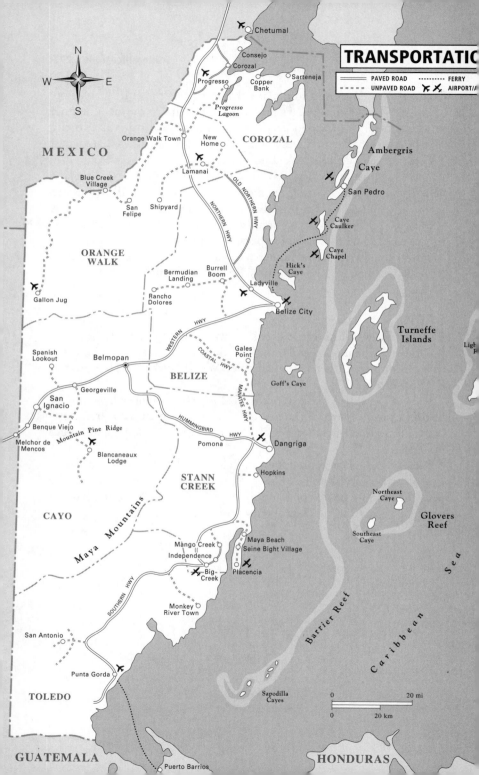

Travel and Transportation

Belize is less than three hours by air from major gateways in the United States. You can leave most major U.S. cities in the morning and be in Belize by the late afternoon. Once in Belize, you can get around very cheaply by bus, and driving is similar to that in the rural United States or Canada. Belize's main roads, once among the worst in Central America, have been vastly improved in recent years. Driving is on the right. Belize has no railroads. Under British colonial rule, bananas and timber were transported by rail—old railroad bridges still can be seen on the Hummingbird Highway—but these railroads were shut down before World War II.

By Air

FLYING TO BELIZE

At present, five international airlines fly to Belize: American, with daily nonstop flights from Miami and Dallas-Fort Worth; Continental, with daily nonstop flights from Houston and a weekly nonstop from Newark; US Air, with a daily nonstops (less frequently off-season) from Charlotte; Delta, with a weekly nonstop from Atlanta; and TACA, with flights from Houston and Miami. There is no direct scheduled service from Canada or Europe. Flying time nonstop from the Houston, Miami, and Dallas-Fort Worth main gateways is a little more than two hours, and it's slightly longer from other gateways. Limited regional service is available from Flores and Guatemala City, Guatemala, on Tikal Jets; and from Honduras, on Atlantic Air.

Travelers often complain about the high cost of air travel to Belize. From most U.S. cities, you can expect to pay US$400–700 round-trip. My advice: Find a good travel agent specializing in Belize (see the *Contacts* section of the *Resources* chapter). Sign up for fare deal notifications by email from the airlines flying to Belize. Keep checking online reservation sites, such as Expedia and Travelocity, along with the airline sites. Fares change constantly. Several airlines offer special Internet-only fare sales to Belize, but these usually have a narrow window of opportunity.

Another idea is to fly into Cancún, Mexico, on a cheap scheduled or charter flight and take the bus to Belize from there. From the Cancún airport, there are buses to the central bus terminal in Ciudad, Cancún. You can also take a bus to Playa del Carmen and bus from there to Chetumal. ADO is the main bus line to Chetumal from Cancún and Playa. Deluxe and first-class buses have reserved seats, air-conditioning, free videos, and clean bathrooms. Some have attendants who provide drinks. Rates vary with the value of the peso, bus class, and other factors, but most are under US$20 from either Playa or Cancún to Chetumal. It takes about 5–6 hours from Cancún and 4.5 hours from Playa del Carmen to Chetumal, depending on the stops, traffic, and type of bus.

At the Chetumal main bus station, you switch to a Belize-bound bus, usually Novelo's or Northern Transport. About a dozen buses a day go from Chetumal to Belize City, starting at around 4 A.M. and running to 6:30 P.M. (Note: Early morning buses from Chetumal to Belize depart from the Nuevo Mercado (New Market) station in Chetumal and do not stop at the main terminal; you will have to take a short taxi ride between the two terminals.) The trip to Belize City takes 3–4 hours and costs about US$4.50 for regular buses and US$6 for express. The Belize buses stop at the border. You get off to clear Mexican immigration. Then you reboard the bus, cross the Rio Hondo, and go through Belize immigration and customs. The whole process usually takes about 30 minutes. If you just want to go from the border to Corozal Town, where you can take a water taxi or flight to San Pedro, the cost by bus is US$1.50. Belize does not observe daylight saving time, and Mexico does. Keep track of the time change when crossing the border.

DOMESTIC AIR

Tropic Air and Maya Island Air are the two domestic air carriers in Belize, and they are about equal in service, price, and reliability. Each offers service to Belize City (international and municipal), San Pedro, Caye Caulker, Corozal Town, Dangriga, Placencia, and Punta Gorda, with limited service to a few other destinations. They also fly to Flores, Guatemala. You can book flights on these carriers by phone or via the airlines' websites, or your hotel in Belize can do it for you.

Which is the better airline? It's a toss-up. Both have good safety records and very similar prices. For most people, the decision comes down to which airline has the more convenient flight. Domestic flights from the municipal airport, about a mile from the center of Belize City, are about 15 percent to 45 percent cheaper than from the international

the new Maya Island Air terminal building at the Placencia airstrip

airport. For example, a flight to San Pedro on Ambergris Caye costs approximately US$95 round-trip from international, US$52 from municipal; from international to Placencia, US$140 round-trip; from municipal, US$118. There are usually no savings on round-trip over two one-way fares, and, except for occasional off-season specials, fares are about the same year-round, with no advance purchase or other discounts. Sometimes you can get a 10 percent discount by paying cash rather than by credit card.

The airlines fly only during daylight hours except at peak times, when they have permission to continue flying into San Pedro until all waiting passengers are taken care of.

Are air reservations necessary? Except at peak high-season travel periods, you can probably get on a convenient flight without reservations. Even with reservations, it's often first-come, first-served on busy days. Still, having a reservation gives you a little extra edge at any time of year, and it's essential to do so for holiday periods, such as Easter and Christmas.

By Bus

Travel by bus in Belize is inexpensive. You can travel the whole length of the country from the Mexican border in the north to Punta Gorda in the far south for about US$20, or go from Belize City to the Guatemalan border in the west for US$3. It's also a good way to meet local people and get a real feel for the country.

Bus travel in Belize falls somewhere between the chicken-bus experience in rural Guatemala and the deluxe coaches with comfortable reserved seats and videos in Mexico. Buses are usually recycled American school buses or old Greyhound diesel pushers. On the Northern and Western Highway routes, a few buses are modern coaches offering "premier" express service at slightly higher rates. There is no bus service from point to point within Belize City; you either have to take a taxi, walk, or go on a regular bus route out of the city.

The country has a franchised bus system, with the government granting rights for certain companies to operate on specific routes. After a period of consolidation, Novelo's and its subsidiaries, Northern Transport and Southern Transport, now comprise the only major bus company in Belize, although there are smaller regional and local bus companies.

Getting Around Belize

Belize is a small country, less than 200 miles long from top to bottom and 75 miles wide at its widest point, but getting from one place to another takes longer than you'd expect from looking at a map. Here are some mileages and typical driving times. Your time and even mileage may vary, depending on your point of departure, the weather, and the traffic.

Mexican border to Punta Gorda: 290 miles, 7.5 hours

Belize City to Guatemalan border at Benque Viejo: 82 miles, 2 hours

Corozal Town to Belize City: 96 miles, 2.25 hours

Orange Walk Town to Belize City: 57 miles, 1.25 hours

Belize City to Dangriga (via Coastal Road): 85 miles, 2.5 hours

Belize City to Placencia (via Hummingbird): 156 miles, 3.75 hours

Belize City to Mountain Pine Ridge entrance gate: 82 miles, 2.25 hours

Dangriga to Punta Gorda: 100 miles, 2.5 hours

Hopkins to Placencia: 43 miles, 1.25 hours

San Ignacio to Placencia: 122 miles, 3.5 hours

Novelo's has a new terminal in the Collet Canal area of Belize City. In 2004, financially pressed Novelo's filed for reorganization. Although it is still operating, changes could be ahead.

You can make reservations by calling the bus companies, although most people don't make reservations. If boarding at a terminal, you pay for your ticket at the window and get a reserved seat. If boarding elsewhere, you pay the driver's assistant.

Shuttle Vans

If you are going to Cayo, you may want to use a shuttle bus, as there is no air service to San Ignacio. Several companies operate shuttle vans from the international airport to San Ignacio for about US$30 per person. One shuttle service is provided by the Aguada Hotel in Santa Elena, Cayo. Others are offered by Mayawalk Tours in San Ignacio and by the Cahal Pech Village hotel. You should make reservations. A Guatemalan company, Linea Dorado, also known as Mundo Maya, offers daily shuttle service between Chetumal and Flores, with pickups in Belize City at the Marine Terminal. The price is around US$20 from Belize City to Flores.

By Car

DRIVING TO BELIZE

A few adventurous folk drive through Mexico to Belize. The trip from Brownsville, Texas, is about 1,225 miles and usually takes 3–4 days. Total nonstop driving time is around 28 hours. The fastest route from Brownsville/Matamoros is via Veracruz, Tampico, and Villahermosa. The toll roads are expensive, but you can travel at 70 mph on them, much faster than on the regular roads.

Driving through Mexican towns and cities can be confusing, because roads are poorly signed. In general, avoid going through the town centers *(Centro),* as you can easily get lost and the hotels are more expensive than in the suburbs.

To enter Mexico (and later, Belize) by car, you need your original vehicle title, and if your vehicle is not paid for, a notarized letter of permission from the lien holder. Besides paying the new Mexico tourist entry fee of 160 pesos, which allows entry for up to six months, you have to provide a credit card in lieu of posting a cash bond to guarantee that you will bring the car out of Mexico. As a resident of the United States or Canada, you can bring in such items as binoculars, laptop computer, TV, camping equipment and fishing equipment.

If you are transporting goods of US$1,000 or more and are going through Mexico to Belize, you should use the services of a customs broker at the U.S.–Mexico border to get transmigratory status. There are fees involved in acquiring this status and many say it can also require bribing Mexican federal officers along the way. Most people suggest entering Mexico as a tourist rather than going the transmigratory route.

Mexican auto insurance is required; it costs around US$50 for five days. Insurance for a month or two is not much more than for a few days. Sanborn's (www.sanbornsinsurance.com) is a good source of information on travel in Mexico and Mexican auto insurance.

You should exchange enough U.S. dollars to pesos to get you through Mexico, as U.S. dollars are not widely accepted or are accepted at a low rate of exchange.

On arrival at the Mexico-Belize border, you need your original vehicle title (no photocopies), or, if you do not own it free and clear, a notarized statement from the lien holder that you have permission to take the car out of the United States. You also have to buy Belizean auto insurance (there are brokers at the border). Three months of insurance should cost about US$50–80 or more, depending on the coverage you require. Crossing the border, you may have to have your car sprayed to kill hitchhiking bugs—the fee is around US$5.

If you plan to stay in Belize and keep your vehicle there, and you are not duty-exempt as a participant in the Qualified Retired Persons program, you have to pay import duty. See the *Making the Move* chapter for details. The import duty can range from 10 percent to almost 80 percent of the vehicle value, depending on the type of vehicle and number of cylinders. If you are just visiting, you should not have to pay the import tax, but the car is entered on your passport so you cannot sell it in Belize. There are customs brokers at the border to assist you with your paperwork. They're worth the small fee—perhaps US$25–50—they typically charge. Avoid border crossings on Mondays, the busiest day.

Expats can get by without a car in Belize. Golf carts and bikes are the preferred method of transportation on Ambergris Caye and other islands, and on the mainland, bus service is cheap and frequent. Belize does not have an AAA or other auto club, so your club membership will do you no good in Belize.

DRIVING IN BELIZE

The roads in Belize are seeing an improvement—more roads are now paved, and even the gravel or limestone byways seem to be scraped more frequently. A few roads, such as the Southern and Hummingbird Highways and resurfaced sections of the Western Highway, are very good indeed, among the best in all of Central America and the equal of any rural road in the United States or Canada.

Signage, too, is improving and has become better than in most of Mexico or the rest of Central America. Most critical turns and junctions are marked. Many roads have mile markers—although roadwork on the Southern Highway and elsewhere means many markers are missing. Around Belize City, San Ignacio,

> The roads in Belize are seeing an improvement—more roads are now paved, and even the gravel or limestone byways seem to be scraped more frequently.

and elsewhere, new signage helps visitors navigate to key destinations, such as the international airport or the Mountain Pine Ridge.

Main Roads

Northern Highway: This 85-mile route is a very good, two-lane, black-topped road from Belize City to Corozal Town, and then a few miles to the border with Mexico at Chetumal. The only thing that will slow you down are a few "sleeping policemen" in villages, along with slow-moving trucks when the sugar-cane harvest happens in late winter through late spring, and a tollbooth at the bridge over New River (BZ$.75 or US$.38). There is now a bypass around Orange Walk Town. Your first glimpse of the azure waters of Corozal Bay is a highlight of this route.

Overall Road Condition: Very Good
Paved Section: 100 percent
Gas Availability: Excellent—there are many gas stations, including a few new ones that are open 24 hours.

Old Northern Highway: If you want to see Altun Ha ruins, you'll have to drive at least part of this 41-mile arc to the east of the New Northern Highway. Under the British, this highway was paved, and at last, the Belize government is patching the remaining blacktop. The section south of Maskall village is better than the section north. Most sections are narrow, and some are dirt. The two-mile access road to Altun Ha is not paved.

Overall Road Condition: Fair
Paved Section: 70 percent
Gas Availability: None.

Western Highway: This 78-mile road takes you from Belize City quickly past Hattieville, the Belize Zoo, the capital of Belmopan, the "twin towns" of San Ignacio and Santa Elena, and then on the Benque Viejo road to the Guatemalan border. Just past San Ignacio, you hit "cottage country," where a number of excellent lodges offer cold beer and soft beds under quiet Central American skies. The Western Highway is still in pretty good condition, and some sections have been resurfaced. More *topes* (speed bumps) are popping up as the road passes villages.

Overall Road Condition: Very Good to Excellent
Paved Section: 100 percent
Gas Availability: Good.

Hummingbird Highway: This 56-mile highway stretches from the Western Highway at Belmopan to Dangriga. The Hummingbird dips and swoops through some of the most beautiful territory in Belize. This was once a terrible road. Now it is in very good condition, with only a couple of bridges that are still one lane. Take a break at the Blue Hole, where a swim in the truly blue water is refreshing (a guard will watch your car, don't worry) or at Five Blues Lakes National Park. Technically, the road is called the Hummingbird for only about 33 miles, from the Western Highway to the village of Middlesex, and then it is known as the Stann Creek Valley Road. The section into Dangriga Town is fully paved.

Overall Road Condition: Excellent

Paved Section: 100 percent

Gas Availability: Poor—best to gas up at Belmopan or near Dangriga.

Coastal Highway: This 36-mile gravel road, connecting Democracia near Mile 30 of Western Highway with the Stann Creek Valley Road near Melinda, is also known as the Manatee Highway, or the "Shortcut." It does save time on trips to Dangriga or Placencia from Belize City. However, the road is washboarded in places and dusty in dry weather. During heavy rains, bridges occasionally wash out. It is far less scenic than the Hummingbird.

Overall Road Condition: Fair

Paved Section: None

Gas Availability: Poor—gas up in Dangriga or on the Western Highway.

Southern Highway: The Southern Highway, long known as the worst major road in Belize, is now the best road in Belize. It is all paved except for a nine-mile section near Big Falls. The scenery, save for views of the Maya Mountains at about the halfway point, is unexceptional.

Overall Road Condition: Good to Excellent

Paved Section: 91 percent

Gas Availability: Fair—best to gas up in Dangriga or near Punta Gorda; in a pinch, there's gas in Independence and on the Placencia Peninsula.

Belize City: The roads and streets of Belize City confuse many visitors. Many streets are not signed, and some are little more than narrow, one-way alleys. Streets abruptly terminate at Haulover Creek, and you have to find a bridge to get from one side to the other. Taxis, bicycles, and pedestrians dart in and out of traffic. However, things are getting better. New roundabouts on the Northern Highway have improved traffic flow, and new signage has popped up on main routes. Most streets are paved. Belize City is so up-to-date these days, it even has a rush hour and traffic jams.

a modern Texaco service station, where gas is about US$4.25 a gallon

Overall Road Condition: Fair to Excellent
Paved Section: 95 percent
Gas Availability: Excellent—modern gas stations have everything that U.S. stations do, including convenience stores, except that you don't have to pump your own gas.

Other Important Roads
Road to Consejo: This level, eight-mile stretch takes you from Corozal Town to the Chetumal Bay, where there is a Belize customs station.
Overall Road Condition: Fair
Paved Section: None
Gas Availability: None.
Road to Shipstern: Once you're past the paved section near Orange Walk Town, this road just goes on and on, over rough, washboarded limestone. It's about 40 miles to Sarteneja Village and Shipstern, but it will seem like twice that. A redeeming feature of this road is Progresso Lagoon, the quintessential tropical lagoon. If you want to go to Cerros instead of Shipstern, you start the same way, but about 12.5 miles from Orange Walk Town and 6.5 miles past the village of San Estevan, you go straight instead of turning right; this takes you to Progresso, Copper Bank, and Cerros. The road can be tricky after heavy rains. From Corozal Town, take the new hand-pulled ferry across the New River, saving yourself several hours of driving time.

Overall Road Condition: Fair to Poor
Paved Section: 15 percent
Gas Availability: Fair.

Road to Chan Chich and Gallon Jug: From Orange Walk Town, it's about a three-hour, 68-mile drive to Chan Chich, the stupendous Barry Bowen lodge. Along the way, on a stretch that varies from poor rubble road to excellent paved road at Gallon Jug, you'll pass a number of villages, some farms, the Mennonite settlement of Blue Creek (where you can also spend time as a hardworking, paying volunteer at a major Maya archaeological site), and plenty of jungle. As you cross the Programme for Belize preserve and Bowen land (you'll have to stop at two guardhouses), you'll almost certainly see a variety of wildlife, including Belize's two species of deer and oscellated turkey. At San Felipe Village, about 23 miles from Orange Walk Town, you can turn on a dirt road to the Lamanai ruins and Lamanai Outpost Lodge, about 13 miles from San Felipe. This road is now passable year-round.

Overall Road Condition: Mostly Fair to Poor, with some Good to Very Good sections
Paved Section: 15 percent
Gas Availability: Fair (gas up at the Linda Vista "shopping center" at Blue Creek, run by Mennonites; closed Sunday).

Burrell Boom: You have two choices to get to Burrell Boom, Bermudian Landing, and the Baboon (Black Howler Monkey) Sanctuary. Either turn off the New Northern Highway at about Mile 13, or turn off the Western Highway at Mile 15.5. The road to the Boom also functions as a shortcut if you're going between points on the Northern and Western Highways, eliminating the need to drive through Belize City. The road from the Western Highway past the prison is now beautifully paved.

Overall Road Condition: Good to Excellent
Paved Section: 100 percent
Gas Availability: Fair.

Road to Spanish Lookout Area: This part of Cayo will remind you a bit of the Midwest, with spiffy Mennonite farms. The roads are mostly gravel and better maintained than average.

Overall Road Condition: Fair to Good
Paved Section: 10 percent
Gas Availability: Fair to Good.

Mountain Pine Ridge Road to Caracol: By the route from Georgeville, it is about 46 miles from the Western Highway to the ruins of Caracol. From San Ignacio, the trip is a few miles longer—this route connects with the Mountain Pine Ridge Road near the village of San Antonio. The road to Caracol has been improved and a few sections paved. It's a three-hour rough ride to Caracol, even with recent improvements.

Overall Road Condition: Fair to Good

Paved Section: 10 percent

Gas Availability: None.

Road to Placencia: This 25-mile, mostly dirt and gravel road runs from the Southern Highway to the tip of the Placencia Peninsula, passing Maya Beach and Seine Bight. In wet weather, this road can be dicey. To placate real-estate developers, who want more seafront land to sell, a section of the road along the sea has been moved closer to the lagoon. Small sections near Placencia and Seine Bight Villages are paved. The paving set for spring 2005 has now been postponed. Again.

Overall Road Condition: Fair to Poor

Paved Section: 3 percent

Gas Availability: Fair (one station in Placencia Village and one at Riverdale).

Road to Maya Villages in Toledo: A series of connected roads take you from the Southern Highway near Punta Gorda to the Maya villages of San Antonio, Santa Cruz, and Pueblo Viejo, or, in the other direction, to San Pedro Columbia Village, Lubaantun ruins, and San Miguel Village, and then back to the Southern Highway near the Nim Li Punit ruins. This area was badly hit by Hurricane Iris.

Overall Road Condition: Fair to Poor

Paved Section: None

Gas Availability: Poor (gas up at the junction to the road to San Antonio).

Ambergris Caye: You can't rent a car on the island, although residents seem to be stocking up on pickups and cars, crowding out golf carts, bikes, and pedestrians on the caye's sandy roads. Sections of Coconut Drive, one at the airstrip and the other at Island Supermarket, are paved with cobblestones. You can rent a golf cart and putt south to near the tip of the island, and north (if the rental company allows its carts to go over the river on the hand-pulled ferry) to around Belizean Shores. After rains, these cart paths are rough and muddy, and away from the water the mosquitoes will swarm you if you slow down.

Overall Road Condition: Fair to Poor

Gallons and Inches

As with the English language, refugees from the United States will not have to learn a new measurement system in Belize. No kilometers here. The metric system, regardless of its merits, hasn't made much of an inroad in Belize. Distance is measured in miles, feet, yards, and inches. Road signs say 55 mph. Liquids are measured in quarts and ounces, not liters, and you buy gasoline by the U.S. gallon. And speaking of inroads, you drive on the right in Belize, despite its British heritage. Electrical currents and outlets in Belize are the same as in the United States and Canada, as well.

Paved Section: 2 percent

Gas Availability: Fair (boat gas is available, but most golf carts run on batteries).

Practical Driving Tips

The best general road map to Belize is from ITMB. A fifth edition was released in 2001. The color, 1:350,000-scale map retails for US$8.95. Even more useful for most travelers is the mile-by-mile *Driver's Guide to Beautiful Belize*, published annually by the famous Emory King. Although the maps are rough, this 8.5- by 11-inch guide is reliable and easy to use.

Belize has Texaco, Shell, and Esso service stations, with a total of around 50 stations in the country. Unleaded gas is widely available now in Belize, but it costs more than US$4 a gallon. Leaded is a few cents less, and diesel about a third less (though in some areas, such as Punta Gorda, it is more expensive). Skilled mechanics are few and far between, but you can get a tire changed almost anywhere. Someone will come out and pump gas for you, and there's no need to tip. Belizean gas stations accept Belize or U.S. dollars, and sometimes credit cards.

Like the United States, Belize has been loathe to accept the metric system. Distances are given in miles, and gas is sold by the U.S. gallon. However, some Japanese-made cars rented and sold in Belize have speed and distance shown in kilometers only, a source of confusion on Belize's mile-denominated roads.

Car insurance in Belize is relatively inexpensive, rarely more than US$300 a year. F&G and Regent are two well-known insurance companies based in Belize City.

Rules of the Road

Driving laws in Belize are similar to those in the United States. One difference is making a left turn across traffic. If you are turning left, the practice in Belize is to pull to the right and wait for all traffic, front and back, to pass.

You occasionally see a speed limit sign in Belize, but there is little, if any, traffic law enforcement. Belize drivers, to be charitable, are not always the best in the world.

Speed-breaker bumps are used to slow traffic coming into residential areas. In many cases, you'll get no warning about the bumps, but expect them as you enter any town or village.

Unlike in some other countries in the region, where shaking down gringos in rental cars is a small industry, in Belize you will not be pulled over for phony traffic offenses, and if you are stopped at a checkpoint, which often happens, no one will promote a bribe. Just answer the questions, if any, show your license or passport and visitor entry card, and you'll be on your way with a friendly smile and wave from the police.

© Lan Sluder

Golf carts are the favored form of transportation on the cayes.

Traffic accidents are now the number one cause of death in Belize. Belize drivers are often not well trained, and driving after drinking is unfortunately common. Watch carefully when passing stopped buses—kids may suddenly dart around the bus to cross the road. Outside of settled areas, you may drive for an hour or more and never see another car. Be prepared: Bring water, a flashlight, and other basic supplies, and maybe a cell phone, just in case. In a poor country such as Belize, anyone driving a car is, ipso facto, wealthy. Don't leave valuables in your car, locked or unlocked. In Belize City, it's best to park in a secured lot or at least a well-lit area. Do not pick up hitchhikers.

Driving at night in developing countries is seldom a good idea, but in Belize, night driving is easier than elsewhere because there are so few people on the roads after dark. Jaguars and snakes, yes; people, no. Still, it's hard to see potholes and speed bumps after dark.

Best Vehicles for Belize

Do you really need four-wheel drive in Belize? On the main thoroughfares such as the Western and Northern Highways, no. In the dry season, even backroads are generally passable without four-wheel drive, if you have sufficient road clearance. But four-wheel drive is good insurance, just in case you hit a stretch of soft muck or sand. On long trips in Belize, there are usually a couple of occasions when four-wheel power comes in handy. After a period of heavy rains, some backroads become quagmires.

Many expats think that a tough, Japanese-made compact truck with four-wheel drive and diesel power is the best option for Belize. An example would be a Toyota Hi-Lux. Pickup trucks enjoy the lowest duty fees (10 percent), diesel is cheaper than gas, and Toyotas have a reputation for dependability and ruggedness.

Car Dealers

Ford, Jeep, Suzuki, Mitsubishi, Toyota, Land Rover, and other American, Japanese, and European vehicles are sold at new-car dealerships in Belize City. Because of import taxes and limited competition among dealers, the cost to buy a new or used car in Belize is usually considerably higher than in the United States.

Used cars are available for sale in Belize City at car dealerships and elsewhere around the country from private individuals and garages. Some expats say they've successfully bought used cars in Belize. However, few vehicles are advertised for sale in the weekly newspapers, so finding the vehicle you want may take some time.

You can ship a vehicle from the United States (generally from Miami) by sea freight for about US$800–1,000, not including duty and any other import or landing fees.

Car Rentals

The focus of car rental in Belize is the international airport, where about 10 rental agencies have booths. Just walk out the main airport exits from the lobby and cross the street, and the car-rental offices are

Dog Flea Caye and Pull Trouser Swamp

Many place-names in Belize tell a story. Exactly what story, I'm not sure, but the names make fascinating conjecture. Pull out a map and check out some of these fascinating places:

Go-to-Hell Camp

Pull Trouser Swamp

Never Delay

Dog Flea Caye

Meditation

More Tomorrow

Condemned Point

Good Living Camp

Double Head Cabbage

Bound to Shine

Pork and Doughboy Point

Hen and Chicken Cayes

Black Man Eddy

Cowboy Camp

Baking Pot

Wee Wee Caye

a few yards away at the far side of the airport parking lot. Among recommended auto-rental firms in Belize City are Budget, Crystal, Hertz, and Thrifty. The operator of the Budget franchise in Belize, JMA Motors, also owns the Land Rover, Suzuki, and Mitsubishi new-car dealerships, so Budget vehicles tend to be well-maintained and have fewer miles on them than most. I've found Budget to be, overall, the best auto-rental company in Belize.

Getting a Driver's License

If you have an international driver's license (available from AAA or CAA offices and some other automobile clubs) or driver's license from the United States or most other countries, you can drive in Belize for up to 90 days without getting a Belizean license. Some expats have been told by government officials that they can drive for up to one year on their home licenses. To get a Belize license, you go to the Ministry of Works office in Belmopan, Belize City, or other main location and pick up an application form. You'll need a statement from a Belizean doctor that states you are in good health and able to drive. You also need front- and side-view photos of your face. If you have a driver's license from the United States or some other countries, you have to take only the Belize written test, not the road test. The fee is BZ$60 (US$30). Usually, after taking the test, you come back in about a week and pick up your license.

But this being Belize, it doesn't always work that way. What actually happens may depend on how the government workers are feeling on the day you go in. Also, some Belizeans reportedly pay a small fee and get their licenses without having to take any kind of test. Some have a license even though they don't know how to drive.

Taxis

Taxis are available in Belize City, all towns, and some villages. The cost from the international airport to Belize City is US$20 (total, not per person). Within Belize City, most fares are under US$4. Rates elsewhere vary, but prices are usually higher than they should be. Tipping taxi drivers is not customary.

By Boat

WATER TAXIS

If you are going to San Pedro or Caye Caulker, you have the option of taking a water taxi. The Caye Caulker Water Taxi Association runs fast, open boats from the Marine Terminal in Belize City to both islands roughly every 1.5 hours. *Thunderbolt* and other boats also offer service from the Swing Bridge area. From Belize City to San Pedro takes about 75 minutes and costs US$15 per person one-way; to Caulker, it is about 45 minutes and costs US$10 per person. Between Caulker and San Pedro (a little more than 30 minutes), the cost is also US$10 one-way. To get to the water taxi terminals in Belize City from the international airport is a US$20 cab ride. There is also once-daily water taxi service between Corozal Town and San Pedro (US$22.50) and a couple of water taxis daily between Punta Gorda and Puerto Barrios, Guatemala (US$12.50). There is a weekly boat between Placencia and Puerto Cortes, Honduras (US$50), and, at times, also a twice-weekly boat between Dangriga and Puerto Cortes. Elsewhere, such as from Dangriga to Tobacco Caye, you can arrange a boat (US$17.50), but service is not scheduled. Boats to remote cayes and the atolls have to be arranged individually and are expensive, often US$100–200 or more one-way.

CRUISE SHIPS

Belize has become a major destination for cruise ships. In 2004, more than 800,000 cruise passengers visited Belize, almost four times as many as other international visitors coming to Belize for vacations. At present, as the harbor is shallow, the ships dock off Belize City and passengers are tendered in small boats to the Tourist Village in the Fort George area. A US$50 million cruise ship terminal is being built by Carnival Cruise Lines, scheduled for completion in 2006. If you arrive by private boat, you can process your entry paperwork at Belize City, San Pedro, Big Creek, Dangriga, and Punta Gorda.

PORTS

Besides being the major passenger port in Belize, Belize City is also a cargo port. It is set up to handle containerized cargo. Eight or nine shipping lines move freight from Belize to other parts of Central and North America, Europe, and Japan. As of press time, negotiations were under way by the government to privatize the port. The second-largest port in Belize is at Commerce Bight, near Dangriga, which is set up to handle exports of bananas and citrus. Belize's other deep-water port is at Big Creek near Placencia.

Housing Considerations

O f the many appealing things about Belize, probably none is more important to prospective retirees, relocatees, prospective second-home buyers, and others than the relatively low cost of housing here. To be sure, in a few prime areas you can spend hundreds of thousands of dollars on a North American–style luxury home, but you can also buy raw land at prices not seen in the United States since the 1970s; and, in some areas, find a simple but pleasant rental house near the sea for less than US$200 a month.

Add to that the ease of purchase or rental—there are few restrictions on the purchase or use of real estate by foreigners, and legal documents are in English and follow English common-law traditions—and it's even more apparent why Belize can be a terrific alternative to other areas.

If you are interested in buying or renting property in Belize, how do you go about finding properties for sale or rent? Except for occasional ads in weekly newspapers, few properties are advertised for sale. Real-estate agencies do maintain listing brochures, and you can contact them to request a copy. Many real-estate brokers use the Internet as their primary way of presenting listings and of getting prospective buyers. (See the *Contacts* section of the *Resources* chapter for real-estate websites in Belize.)

Even using the Internet, however, you'll miss three-fourths of available properties. To find out what's really for sale, you'll have to spend time on the ground in Belize. Most properties are for sale by owner rather than being listed with a broker. In many cases, you will see no sign or other indication that a property is for sale. Just start asking around, and before long, you'll have more deals being offered you than you can even begin to consider. This goes double for rentals.

Renting

Even if you plan to buy or build a home, you'd be well advised to rent for a while in Belize before you make the purchase plunge. The longer you're in Belize, the better you'll understand the system and the less you'll pay for real estate.

FINDING A RENTAL

Houses for rent are usually not advertised in newspapers, except in San Pedro, and brokers handle only the most expensive rentals. It's difficult, if not impossible, to find a rental before you arrive. About the only way to find a house or apartment to rent is to spend some time in the area where you wish to live. Here are some tips on finding rentals:

• Drive around and look for vacant homes.

• Ask other foreign residents for leads or tips.

• Talk to real-estate agents in the area—they may not handle rentals, but they'll be informed about what's available, especially at the upper end.

• Put the word out in the local community that you are looking for a place to rent.

• Inquire at local hotels and condo developments. Often, especially off-season, hotels offer monthly or longer-term rentals of some of their units.

THE BELIZEAN HOUSE

There's no one typical Belizean house. House types vary depending on the area of the country and, to some degree, on the ethnic and economic background of the occupant.

In Maya areas, such as rural Toledo District, many people still live in traditional thatch and wattle huts with bare dirt floors. In Belize City, there are still some colonial-era homes made of wood with zinc or tin roofs, although here and in most coastal areas, newer homes are of concrete block or poured, reinforced concrete to provide better hurricane protection. In rural villages in the west and north, many Belizeans' houses are simple wood-frame buildings with wood shutters, similar in style to those on Caribbean islands, and set up on pilings for protection from insects and animals. In Belmopan, you'll find small concrete houses set in rows in the local equivalent of subdivisions. On Ambergris Caye and in affluent areas around Belize City, there are large and expensive concrete buildings with tile roofs, not unlike what you'd find in parts of Florida or California.

Rental houses, especially less expensive ones, come with few, if any, furnishings or fixtures. You're most likely to get just a bare shell without appliances.

RENTAL COSTS

Rent levels in Belize vary widely, being highest on Ambergris Caye and in Belize City. In upscale areas of Belize City, you can expect to pay around US$.80–1.50 per square foot per month, or about US$800–1,500 a month for a 1,000-square-foot, two-bedroom apartment. On Ambergris Caye, a one-bedroom apartment goes for US$350–900 per month, and a two-bedroom for US$650–1,500. Upscale houses on the sea can rent for US$2,000 or more per month.

> In rural areas and low-cost towns, such as Corozal, you can find a small house in a safe area for under US$250 a month and sometimes for half that amount.

Elsewhere, rentals are much lower. In rural areas and low-cost towns, such as Corozal, you can find a small house in a safe area for under US$250 a month and sometimes for half that amount. I know of expats in Corozal who rent for US$100–200 a month or less. While their homes are not fancy, they are comfortable, typically of concrete block construction with a couple of small bedrooms, bath, a living room, and a kitchen with stove and refrigerator.

In all areas, North American–style housing with air-conditioning, modern appliances, and security will be many times more expensive than a traditional Belize rental, usually a simple concrete or wood house, with only basic amenities and probably no appliances except for a butane stove and a small fridge.

SHORT-TERM RENTALS

If you're coming to Belize on a scouting expedition of a few weeks to a few months, consider a short-term rental. Staying in a house or apartment, rather than in a hotel, can help you decide if Belize is really for you. Unfortunately, there are not a lot of short-term vacation rentals in Belize. Most of them are concentrated on Ambergris Caye, but there are a few in other areas, including Placencia and Corozal. In most areas, you can find a hotel or condotel with housekeeping facilities at weekly or monthly rates. On Ambergris Caye, for example, condotels and suite places such as Banana Beach and Royal Palms offer monthly rentals for US$800–1,400, depending on the size of the unit and whether or not utilities are included.

Buying

RESTRICTIONS

Belize imposes few restrictions on ownership of land by nonnationals. Unlike Mexico, which prohibits direct ownership of land by foreigners on or near the coast, foreigners can buy and hold beachfront real estate in Belize in exactly the same way as Belizeans.

Formerly, an alien landholder's license was needed for purchases of 10 acres or more (or more than half an acre within a town or city). However, such a license is no longer needed. The only limitations on ownership by foreign nationals are these: Government approval is required, from the Ministry of Natural Resources, before the purchase of any island, regardless of size. In a few coastal and caye areas, such as Caye Caulker, there are rules limiting purchases by nonlocals, and approval by the local village council or board must be obtained in advance.

REAL-ESTATE AGENTS

In Belize, anyone can be a real-estate broker. No license is needed— no schooling, no bonding, no continuing education. All you need is enough money to print business cards, and presto, you're a broker. Selling real estate is a popular first job for expats in Belize, and some do it on the side without a work permit. Quite a few hoteliers, dive shop

Real-Estate Sampler

Here's a sampling of what you can expect to get for your money in Belize in 2005.

Under US$15,000
- Five to 10 acres of farmland in Cayo or other rural area
- Small seaview (not seafront) lot in Corozal District

Under US$25,000
- Canal/lagoon lot in Placencia
- Seaview lot on Ambergris Caye
- Small, Belizean-style, two-bedroom home in village or rural area
- 20-acre farm with small basic dwelling in rural area

Under $50,000
- Small beachfront lot on North Ambergris Caye
- Beachfront lot in Placencia, Hopkins, or Corozal
- Pleasant small concrete home in Belmopan, Corozal, or Cayo
- Mennonite "prefab" small house on canal/lagoon lot in Placencia (including lot)

Under US$100,000
- 50-acre farm with small dwelling and outbuildings in northern Belize, Cayo, or Toledo
- Modern, 1,000-square-foot home on waterfront in Corozal or Hopkins area
- One-bedroom condo on Ambergris Caye or Caye Caulker
- Small offshore island

Under $250,000
- Two-bedroom condo on water on Ambergris Caye
- Deluxe, 2,000-square-foot home on nice lot in San Ignacio, Placencia, or Corozal
- 150-acre farm with nice home, outbuildings, and equipment in rural area

Under $500,000
- Luxury 5,000-square-foot home on small estate in Cayo
- Luxury 3,000-square-foot home on the beach on Ambergris Caye
- 1,000-acre farm with home, outbuildings, and equipment in rural area

operators, and taxi drivers peddle real estate to tourists as well. One of the best-known real-estate agents in Placencia, until he left to sail his boat around the Caribbean, was also the proprietor and barkeep of one of the most popular bars on the peninsula. Not surprisingly, the quality of agents varies. Some are professional and honest. A few are out for a fast buck. Some are just not very knowledgeable.

Real-estate commissions in Belize are similar to those in the United States. Agents typically charge the seller 6 percent or 7 percent commission on residential property and around 10 percent on raw land. Rates are negotiable. Because many properties are in remote areas, brokers often charge prospective buyers expenses for travel and transportation incurred in connection with showing properties.

Real-Estate Agents

Some leading real-estate agents in Belize offered these words of wisdom for those thinking of buying property:

"Plan a trip to Belize, allowing sufficient time to see a variety of properties (10 days minimum is advisable). Make appointments with agents in several areas. Be honest about how much money you have to spend. Remember that most agents don't work on weekends, nor do they show property at night. Showings generally take more time than you imagine, and schedules are often subject to weather conditions. Don't wait till the last minute to look. Make a choice, make an offer, [and] hire a Belizean attorney to check [the] title and do the transfer for you. If what you seek is "remote," remember that the moment you arrived in Belize, you achieved remote. Locations that are truly at the back of beyond may seem romantic at first, but after a few weeks of true isolation, most buyers wish they had a few neighbors."
—*Diane Campbell, San Pedro*

"It seems like every week I see a new real-estate company hanging a shingle out in Belize. As there is no board of realty to oversee or vet these individuals, there is absolutely no assurance that any training or professional code of conduct is abided by. Consequently, my best advice would be for the potential investor to contact local business associations, such as the American Chamber of Commerce, for a competent firm to deal with. I think it is [also worthwhile] to mention again that anyone seriously thinking about purchasing property in Belize [should] make sure that they see copies of the seller's documentation of ownership and plan of survey. A true plan of survey will have a box showing the plan has been authenticated by the mapping section in Belmopan, as well as a registry and entry number."
—*John Burks, Regent Realty, Belize City*

"Be very cautious before investing in any offshore developments or planned communities in the atolls—be it Lighthouse or Turneffe. In most cases, the additional logistical expenses relating to construction and transportation more than offset any savings in land acquisition costs in comparison to prime property on Ambergris, Caye Caulker, or Placencia. If your real-estate broker cannot provide you with at least a couple of Belizean attorney personal references, then get another broker to represent you."
—*Chris Berlin, Sunrise Realty, San Pedro*

"We came here nine years ago and wish it had been 30 years ago. The longer a person waits, the more difficult it is going to be to come here. Bite the bullet and come, so you can enjoy the good life."
—*Howard Oldham, Tropic Real Estate, Cayo*

REAL-ESTATE PRICES

Property prices vary greatly in Belize from one area to another. They are generally highest in Belize City, on Ambergris Caye, and in Placencia, and lowest in remote rural areas. In large tracts, raw land is available in Belize for less than US$100–200 an acre, but for this price, access may be poor and surveying costs may exceed the cost of the land itself. Good agricultural land might range US$250–2,000 an acre, depending on quality and access. Home prices range from less than US$15,000 for a simple, Belizean-style home in a small village to US$500,000 or more for a luxury home on the beach in San Pedro. Finished, newer homes typically sell for US$40–100 per square foot, though, of course, the location of the lot or land is also a major factor.

The condominium type of ownership is new to Belize, and most condos are on Ambergris Caye. There are a few condos in Placencia and on Caye Caulker. Prices start at around US$100,000 for a one-bedroom unit and typically go to about US$300,000 or US$400,000 for a high-quality large unit. Belize has a few time-shares, also mostly on Ambergris Caye. These are rarely a good investment. One or two time-share properties in San Pedro have aggressive and unpleasant time-share touts. Don't encourage them.

Property in Belize has appreciated in the past two decades, but by exactly how much is difficult to say. Real-estate agents say that some

beach house on North Ambergris Caye

beachfront property in Placencia and elsewhere that was selling for less than US$200 a front foot in the early 1980s is now going for US$2,000 or more a foot. The best beachfront land on Ambergris Caye is now close to US$3,500 a front foot. Real-estate agents naturally talk up the appreciation potential, but keep in mind that the Belize economy is closely tied to the economy in the United States. Should America's economic machine go into another tailspin, expect to see little, if any, growth in real-estate values in Belize.

Even with appreciation, real-estate prices in Belize are still inexpensive by the standards of the United States and most of Western Europe. Waterfront lot prices on the Eastern seaboard of the United States or in Florida are rarely less than US$200,000, and in places such as Hilton Head, S.C., or Fort Lauderdale, Fla., can easily reach US$1 million or more; whereas beachfront building lots on Belize's Caribbean are still available for US$50,000–100,000.

Islands for Sale

The days of buying an island for a song are gone, but a few of Belize's many Caribbean islands are on the market. Here is a sample of islands for sale in 2005.

Hollywood Island: Approximately one acre, this island is one mile west of San Pedro, Ambergris Caye. US$350,000

Moho Caye, Belize District: Part of the other Moho Caye, this island about .5 mile from Belize City is also for sale. A 31-slip marina, lodge, and six acres of land are included. US$2,750,000

Moho Caye, Stann Creek: This 12-acre island, 12 miles off Placencia, has almost 3,000 feet of shoreline. US$1,900,000, with $500,000 down and financing over 10 years.

Monarch Caye: The six-acre island, formerly known as Hatchet Caye, comes with a three-level luxury home, furnished guesthouse, staff quarters, marina with two boats, a generator, satellite TV and Internet, and a 5,000-gallon water storage tank. US$1,900,000 (reduced from US$3,500,000)

Savannah Caye: This 25-acre island is 10 miles west of San Pedro in Ambergris Caye. US$750,000

Serenade Island: This six-acre island, 24 miles southeast of Placencia Village, has three cabins, a restaurant/bar, and quarters for workers. US$2,500,000

Tranquility Island: Formerly called Hulse Caye, this 20-acre island is in the Tobacco Range just 10 minutes by boat from Dangriga. US$295,000

A HOT NEW REAL-ESTATE MARKET

With an improving economy in the United States in 2005, baby boomers beginning to retire, and a cheap U.S. dollar luring buyers from Great Britain, Europe, and elsewhere, Belize is seeing an increase in foreign interest in real estate, especially for beachfront land.

More than one real-estate agent claimed that the market in 2005 was the hottest seen in years. "The entire Belize estate market has been hot for the last several months—I talk to agents and owners on a regular basis and this is the best real-estate market that I have ever seen in 18 years," says Ron Forrester, an agent who primarily sells in the Hopkins area. Other agents point out that even in the normally sleepy areas in the Corozal District, big tracts of waterfront land were being snapped up by investors.

More conservative observers, however, noted that real-estate agents and landowners often are inclined to hype properties in the hopes of stampeding lookers into becoming buyers. Also, they suggested that the political problems in Belize in 2005 could have an impact on real-estate sales, with would-be buyers shying away from a country that was seeing strikes, utility outages, and even some rioting and looting in Belize City.

PRECAUTIONS AND PITFALLS

Many of the same rules of thumb that apply when looking for a home, land, or apartment in the United States or Canada apply in Belize as well. But Belize also has its own special situations.

Be prepared to get out and hunt. You're not going to get a deal if you go only to a real-estate agent. Most properties in Belize aren't listed with brokers. You'll need to go out and look for available properties. Just start asking around, and you'll soon have plenty of choices. In Belize, money talks, and if you have the cash, some people who have never considered selling may decide it's time to cash in.

Understand that the Belize real-estate market is small and inefficient. Someone emailed me to ask why a piece of property near Placencia was still on the market three years after he had first seen it advertised. Was there something wrong with the property? No, I told him, nothing is wrong with the property. It's just Belize. The real-estate marketplace in Belize is even more inefficient than elsewhere. The pool of financially capable real-estate buyers in Belize is small, leaving many sellers dependent on foreign buyers.

There is little real estate classified advertising, and most properties are sold or rented by word of mouth. No formal multiple listing services exist, and many properties are for sale by owner. Thus, it's not easy to find out exactly what is on the market or what the prices are. There are few qualified real-estate agents, appraisers, and surveyors. Mortgage financing is not easily available for foreign buyers, further reducing the size of the buying pool and requiring cash sales or owner financing.

All this means that prices for similar properties can be all over the board. Also, the time to sell a property may be measured in years, rather than months. This is something to think about as you buy real estate, which you may someday want to sell.

Negotiate hard. If you're a good horse trader, you'll likely get a better deal in Belize than someone who isn't. Keep in mind that in most parts of Belize, there is far more available real estate than buyers with cold cash, so don't jump at the first deal that comes your way. Remember, too, that in real estate, you almost always make your money when you buy, not when you sell.

The more you know, the better price you'll get. A common saying among expats in Belize is that the second house you buy or rent is twice as large as the first and costs half as much. Spend as much time in Belize as you can before you put any money in real estate.

Consult an attorney. In Belize, it's important to have your own attorney in a real-estate transaction. The fee you'll pay, perhaps 2 percent of the land value, is good insurance against a bad title or other problem.

Caveat emptor. "Buyer beware" applies as much in Belize as anywhere else. Real-estate agents in Belize aren't licensed. That beachfront lot that looks wonderful in the dry season may be under two feet of water in the rainy season, and there are no laws in Belize that enable you to get your money back if the real-estate agent didn't provide full disclosure. In addition, as soon as the word gets out that you're in the market for a place to live, everybody and his brother will tell you about this little piece of property owned by a cousin of theirs. It may be a great deal, but look before you leap.

Avoid "rich gringo" deals. In Belize, there are sometimes two prices: one price for locals, and another for foreigners. The difference may only be a

> In Belize, it's important to have your own attorney in a real-estate transaction. The fee you'll pay, perhaps 2 percent of the land value, is good insurance against a bad title or other problem.

few dollars, but sometimes the Belizean price may be half or less of the "rich foreigner" price. From the expat's point of view, this is unfair. From the Belizean point of view, this is perfectly kosher and reflects the reality that Americans (or Canadians or Europeans) make far more money for the same work as Belizeans and can well afford to pay more. One way around this problem is to get a trusted Belizean friend to find out the "local price" for you. Another is to spend enough time in the country to get a feel for the difference between the Belizean price and the non-Belizean price, so that you can at least bargain with your eyes open.

FEES AND COSTS OF PURCHASE

Besides the cost of the property, you are likely to incur charges associated with the purchase that total 12 percent to 15 percent of the purchase price. These include the following:

1. Land title transfer fee, sometimes called a stamp tax: Belizean citizens pay a 5 percent transfer tax. Noncitizens pay a 15 percent transfer tax (the rate was increased from 10 percent in mid-2005). The only exception for noncitizens is for nationals of Caricom countries; they also pay the 5 percent Belizean rate.

2. Attorney's fee: For around 2 percent of the purchase price, an attorney will draw up transfer documents and search the title.

3. Property taxes: Property taxes vary but have traditionally been about 1 percent of the value of the undeveloped land, payable annually on April 1. In Belize, property taxes outside cities are based on land value, rather than the developed value of the property, to encourage development. Property taxes on homes and other developed land are low, even in cities. For example, the property tax on a nice four-bedroom, North American–style home is likely in the range of US$100–200. In 2005, the hard-pressed Belize government was looking for ways to overcome its budget deficit, and raising property taxes is one way that is being considered. Preliminary indications are that property taxes in some areas will go up as much as 400 percent, although by U.S. standards they remain quite low. Stay tuned. There is a 5 percent speculation tax on land of 300 acres or more, payable annually based on the value of the land.

Information on property taxes, including the specific amount owed on a particular parcel, can be obtained from the Ministry of Natural Resources in Belmopan. It is best to call or visit in person.

4. Miscellaneous costs: There are nominal registration and stamp fees.

Beachfront Land Costs

Many dream of living on a Caribbean beach—here's the reality of what you'll pay for beachfront lots in Belize today. These are typical selling prices per front foot on the beach. If the lot has 75 feet of beach frontage, multiply that by the per-front foot cost in U.S. dollars. The overall size and depth of the lot affects the total price, but a 200-foot-deep lot may be only a little more expensive than a 100- or 150-foot-deep lot. It's the frontage on the water that matters most. The top end of the price ranges is for better-quality lots on higher ground. Large tracts with extensive beachfront would be less than the prices shown here.

Corozal Town Area:
US$300–850
Cerros/Sarteneja Peninsula:
US$150–700
Ambergris Caye:
US$1,500–3,500
Placencia Peninsula:
US$1,450–2,000
Hopkins/Sitttee Point Area:
US$750–1,500
Toledo District:
US$300–900

a luxury beach house on North Ambergris Caye

© Lan Sluder

REGISTRATION AND TITLE

There are three different real property title systems in Belize: The first is the Registered Land Act system, in which application for transfer is made and a new Land Certificate is issued to the buyer. Belize is gradually moving to this system throughout the country, but at present, it is not available everywhere. Under this system, an application is made for title transfer and a new Certificate of Title is issued to the grantee. Any existing "charges" will be shown on the Land Register for that parcel of land. The owner holds a Certificate of Title, and this, together with the relevant Land Register entries, is the proof of ownership.

The second is the Conveyance system, which involves the transfer of land by conveyance and registration. This is the system used in much of the United States. In order to assure that the seller actually owns the land, a title search must be made in the Lands Unit in Belmopan to unearth the chain of title and to uncover any encumbrances, such as uncanceled mortgages. This search is usually done by an attorney. Unfortunately, it is sometimes difficult or impossible to trace old conveyances with any degree of certainty, because of the condition of the index books.

The third is the Torrens system, which involves a First Certificate of Title, followed by Transfer Certificates of Title. Unlike the Torrens system used in parts of the United States and elsewhere, the Belize system is not backed up by a fund that guarantees title. Under this system, the uncanceled charges or encumbrances and the transfers from the title are shown on the relevant Certificate, so no further search is normally needed before the new Transfer Certificate of Title is issued, after the application for transfer.

Which system you use depends on where your property is. You won't have a choice. If, for example, your property is in an area of Belize where the Registered Land Act system is in place, such as around Belmopan or in a planned subdivision, your property will be registered under that system. Land in Belize is being put into this system area by area, until eventually, the entire country will be included in it.

Title insurance is available in Belize, though most Belizeans buying property don't use it. Regent Insurance and other insurance companies offer title insurance. Typically, title insurance costs around 1 percent of the purchase price.

VALUE OF A LAWYER

In Belize, attorneys remain trusted advisers. They're usually well-connected, well-paid pillars of the community who wield real power. Fees are not all that different from what you would pay in a small city in the United States. A roster of attorneys in Belize (see the *Contacts* section of the *Resources* chapter) reveals the surnames of prominent families with histories in Belize going well back into colonial times, along with those of today's political leaders, including Barrow, Young, Shoman, Musa, Courtenay, and Godfrey. In any real-estate transaction, you should have your own Belizean attorney.

FINANCING

It is difficult for a nonresident to get a mortgage loan from a bank in Belize for buying or building, so you should be prepared to pay cash or get financing through a loan from a non-Belizean financial institution on your assets back home.

Acreage and building lots in Belize are often purchased on terms under an Agreement for Sale or Contract for Deed, whereby the seller keeps the title to the property until it has been paid for in full. Terms vary but can range from 10 percent down with 10 years to pay at 10 percent simple interest per annum—about the best deal you can hope for—to 50 percent down and three years to pay at 12 percent to 14 percent.

Residential property may also have owner financing, although commonly, the lowest price will be for all-cash deals. A few owners of condos and homes in San Pedro and elsewhere offer financing, typically with around 20 percent down.

For citizens and official permanent residents of Belize only, the Development Finance Corporation (DFC), a financial institution owned by the government of Belize, formerly made loans of US$2,500–50,000 or more for building or buying housing. Terms were for up to 25 years at interest rates of 8.5 percent to 13 percent. The DFC also developed housing subdivisions near Belmopan on Ambergris Caye, on the Northern Highway in Belize District, and in Corozal Town. These subdivisions offer new homes, such as a small, three-bedroom, concrete house near Belmopan for US$35,000 and a three-bedroom, two-bath home of 925 square feet at Ladyville for about US$47,000. Financing is at 12 percent for up to 25 years. Belizeans did not seem to care much for most of these subdivisions, and many homes were never sold. In 2004, the DFC ran out of financial string. As of press time, plans were being made to liquidate or perhaps reorganize the DFC. Its future is unclear.

FORECLOSURE AUCTIONS

From time to time, there are real-estate foreclosure auctions in Belize. They sell property put up as security for bank or other financial institution loans. Usually these are advertised in the weekly newspapers in Belize City. Foreigners can participate in these auctions. There may be no particular problems in buying at a foreclosure auction, other than those ordinarily associated with auctions—such as the fact that among the savvy bidders there may be local people who know more than you do about the property and its value. However, sometimes the owners of the property will still be in possession at the time of the auction. If so, you may face a real problem getting the owners out. Before putting up your money, you may want to consult with an attorney conversant with real-estate property law.

FREE LAND?

You may have heard about a program of homesteading or otherwise getting free land in Belize. Yes, there is such a program in place, but there are big catches: First, you must be a Belizean citizen or have lived in the country as an official resident for at least three years. Second, land is available only in certain areas. Mainly, it is small tracts or building lots. This is not the homesteading of hundreds of acres of prime farmland that you read about in your American history book. Third, you have to lease the land from the government, clear it, and actually construct a home or at least begin to make improvements. At that point, for a small amount (usually several hundred dollars), you can buy the property from the government and receive a title. Given all the time and red tape involved, and the low cost of land in Belize, it's hardly worth it to get a small piece of land worth a few hundred to a few thousand dollars. Frankly, if the only reason you moved to Belize is to take advantage of such a scheme, it's unlikely you'll have the financial resources to make it in Belize long enough to qualify for the program.

However, I have talked with expats who have benefited indirectly from this program. They bought land from Belizeans who had obtained the property through the government program. For whatever reason, the Belizeans decided they didn't want the property but needed quick cash, so they sold the property to foreign buyers at low prices.

Building

As a rule, you will get more for your housing dollar in Belize by building, rather than buying, a completed home. You'll also often get a lot more home. If you can put up with construction hassles—which are many—you can build a house with details such as built-in furniture, exotic tropical hardwood floors and ceilings, and custom-made mahogany cabinets that would be found only in the most upscale homes in the United States.

Construction Costs

The following are selected figures on the cost of materials and labor in Belize, as of early 2005. Figures are in U.S. dollars and vary around the country, being generally highest in San Pedro and elsewhere on the cayes.

Concrete block	$.50
Bag of cement	$7
Rebar (40 feet)	$12.50
Treated pine lumber	$.80 per board foot
30-inch corrugated roofing	$1.50 per running foot
Skilled laborer	
(block man, carpenter)	$20–25 per day (eight hours)
Laborer	$15 per day

Concrete construction runs $30–40 per square foot for standard-quality construction if you act as your own general contractor (not including septic, landscaping, and other finish costs); $40–60 per square foot for standard-quality construction from a builder); and $50–120 for higher-quality construction or on the cayes.

BUILDING COSTS

Construction costs vary, depending on such factors as the cost of transportation of materials to the building site, the terrain, and the quality of work. In Belize, construction costs are higher on the coast and cayes because of the need to use hurricane-resistant construction. In the case of the cayes, it also costs extra to transport building materials out to the islands by boat. Building costs are higher in Southern than in Northern Belize. Inexpensive building materials are more readily available in Northern Belize, since they can be imported from Chetumal, Mexico.

Labor in Belize is much less expensive than in the United States, with carpenters and masons typically getting around US$20–30 a day or less. But while labor may be cheap, jobs usually take longer in Belize. Workers may be skilled at construction techniques common in Belize but may lack knowledge about building in the American style. Outside of urban areas, it is difficult to find qualified craftspeople, such as electricians and plumbers. Building materials vary but are mostly no cheaper than in the United States, except for locally produced items, such as tropical hardwoods, which run about US$1,000 for 1,000 board feet. Treated pine (two-by-fours and similar) cost about US$.80

a board foot in 2005. Locally produced plywood is roughly half the U.S. cost (though plywood prices vary over time because of fluctuating demand). Cement is more expensive than in the United States—a 50-lb. bag typically costs around US$7–$8—as are most bathroom and kitchen fixtures that have to be imported. Concrete blocks are around US$.50 apiece. Flooring materials, such as salt tiles from Guatemala and Mexico, are moderately priced and of high quality.

Overall, building costs in Belize range around US$30–125 a square foot, not including the cost of land. At the bottom end, that would be a simple Belizean-style block house or frame construction; and at the top, it would be high-quality concrete construction with hardwood floors and trim and many custom details, such as handmade doors and windows. Most commonly, you'd expect to pay about US$50–60 a square foot, so a 1,500-square-foot home would cost US$75,000–90,000 to build. That's about half the typical cost for construction in the United States—or less.

Costs can vary tremendously from builder to builder. One resident of San Pedro said he got quotes for the construction of a five-bedroom reinforced concrete home that varied from US$60 to US$130 a square foot. Regardless of where or how you build, you need to be on-site to manage and oversee the construction, or pay someone you trust very well to do that for you. Expect that the process will take roughly twice as long as you expect—8–10 months to build a house is not uncommon.

© Lan Sluder

Building supplies being offloaded from a boat on North Ambergris Caye—the cost of transporting materials adds substantially to the cost of building on the cayes.

Especially in rural areas or on the coast, a lot of the cost of building is underground—foundations, pilings, cisterns, septic tanks. You may need two or more septic tanks for a large house. Cisterns for your drinking water cost roughly US$1 a gallon to construct.

Of course, if you have a nose for saving money, you can build for much less than that. I know one fellow who built a small house on a lagoon north of Corozal for about US$4,000. He collected building materials, such as old planks and boards that were floating in the lagoon, scrounged others from old houses, and did most of the actual construction work himself.

The charity organization Habitat for Humanity has constructed a number of affordable homes in Belize. Habitat says the cost of a two-bedroom, one-bath, 528-square-foot concrete block house with a septic tank is about US$11,000, and a 720-square-foot, three-bedroom house is US$15,000. That's a little less than US$21 a square foot.

In areas at risk of hurricanes and tropical storms, you'll have to put in deep pilings and raise the first floor above ground level to avoid water damage. Reinforced concrete is the preferred construction. Pilings on the cayes and coast may have to go 10–15 feet or farther underground. Generally, builders recommend that 50 percent of the piling be underground. Hurricane straps and rafter ties are inexpensive protection against having the roof blown away.

Most insurance companies in Belize will no longer cover traditional thatch construction, and many will not cover wood frame construction if the house is on the coast or cayes. Insurance, if available at all, will vary with the construction: wood-frame construction in coastal or island areas will incur annual premiums of up to 4 percent of value, whereas steel construction will see premiums of around 1.25 percent of value, and reinforced concrete about 1 percent or less.

In the past, the only building codes in Belize have been those imposed by local municipalities. Many rural areas had no codes at all. However, Belize is developing a national building code calling for nationwide standards of construction. It's unclear when the code will be imposed and enforced nationally. In 2003, Belize Electric Ltd. (the national power company) began requiring that new electrical work would have to be performed only by a licensed electrician, although this is not always enforced. In some areas, especially on the coast and on the cayes, environmental impact assessments are required before development can begin.

Building contractors are not licensed in Belize. You'll usually need to monitor their work carefully, and be sure to hold back a portion of their payment to assure completion of the work to your standards.

Pilferage is a serious and constant problem at building sites in Belize. You will have to provide security at your site if you don't want to lose all your tools and building supplies.

UNUSUAL CONSTRUCTION TECHNIQUES

Belize is home to several interesting experiments in hurricane-resistant construction. Xanadu resort on Ambergris Caye claims to be the world's first "monolithic dome resort." Owner Ivan Sheinbaum showed me a new unit that was under construction. The building process is costly, but the result is a masonry dome with foam insulation that, according to Ivan, a Canadian originally from South Africa, is fireproof and can withstand winds of up to 300 mph. The domes are covered with thatch *palapa* roofs to give them more of a local look.

Calico Jack's beach hotel on the Placencia Peninsula uses "Uro-Block" construction developed by Chester Williams of Seattle. His website says that a patent has been issued in Belize and is pending in the United States. UroBlock uses industrial urethane foam for in-fill in what the developer says is essentially post-and-beam construction. A two-part urethane is combined with a 1.5-inch concrete veneer. The oversized concrete blocks can be made on-site by unskilled laborers. Structures built of UroBlock can stand up to severe coastal weather conditions, according to the inventor. Calico Jack's did survive Hurricane Iris in October 2001.

TRAILERS AND MANUFACTURED HOMES

Trailer trash? Not in Belize. You won't find many mobile homes, trailers, or "manufactured homes" (except from the Mennonites—see the *Mennonite Prefab* section). There are several reasons for this: For one, trailers aren't known for durability or safety in hurricanes. For another, the cost of shipping prefab units to Belize is high. Also, mobile homes and trailers don't stand up well to the hot, humid semitropical climate—rusting, abandoned RVs you see in the bush are proof of that. Perhaps most important, import duties make bringing in trailers an unattractive option compared with building locally.

However, some expats do decide to import prefab buildings. The first owner of the Nautical Inn beach resort in Seine Bight on the Placencia

Peninsula brought in prefab hexagonal buildings from North Carolina and had them set up on the beach by local laborers.

Mennonite Prefab

An inexpensive alternative to building from scratch in Belize is to have a prefabricated Mennonite house set up on your lot. Mennonite builders in Spanish Lookout build and sell small frame buildings, which they will deliver and install on pilings on your site. This is an inexpensive and quick way to get a home up in Belize, and even some resorts, such as the Green Parrot on the Placencia Peninsula, use these buildings.

They are typically made of local hardwoods and come with mahogany or glass louvered windows. You can get them as unfinished shells or complete, right down to electrical wiring, ceiling fans, and plumbing. There is usually a choice of roofing materials: zinc, tin, or asphalt shingles. The cabins are set up on 6- by 6-inch posts eight feet apart and about three feet off the ground. These houses are probably not going to last 100 years, but they're a cheap way to get a home up quickly.

You can buy them from standardized plans or custom order. You may want to upgrade the specs—for example, using two-by-fours for stud walls, rather than the smaller boards typically used. Costs vary, but here are some typical prices, including set-up on your lot: 20 feet by 24 feet (480 sq. ft.) for US$6,500–8,000; 20 feet by 30 feet (600 sq. ft.) for US$8,000–10,000; and 20 feet by 40 feet (800 sq. ft.) for US$12,000–16,000.

© Ian Sluder

Prefabricated Mennonite wood houses are an inexpensive way to build a home quickly.

Household Expenses

You'll get some good—and some bad—surprises when you open your household bills in Belize. On the positive side, you won't be getting a bill for fuel oil or gas to heat your home. Very few houses in Belize even have a furnace or heater, since winter temperatures rarely fall even into the 50s. If a cold front comes through, just put a blanket on the bed or pull on a cotton sweater. Also, cable television bills generally are lower in Belize than you're used to back home. Typical monthly rates are US$15–20.

However, electricity (it's usually called "current" in Belize) is much pricier than in the United States or Canada. Figure about US$.21 per kilowatt-hour, which is almost three times the average in the United States. In 2005, there was talk of a further rate hike of 10 percent to 15 percent. High electric rates are why most Belizeans don't have air-conditioning, or if they do have air-conditioning, it's only in the bedrooms. Belize Electricity Ltd. is the sole provider in Belize. About 40 percent of the electricity used in Belize is purchased from Mexico. As of press time, Belize was embroiled in a controversy regarding construction of the Chalillo Dam in Cayo. This dam is supposed to help Belize become energy-independent, but at the cost of wildlife habitat. If you're off the grid, as many still are in remote rural areas, either you do without power or run a diesel generator. Wind, hydro, and solar energy are making some headway in Belize, though initial set-up costs are high.

Water and sewerage bills vary around the country, but a typical monthly cost per household is about US$10–15. "Pipe water," as it's known in Belize, is costlier on Ambergris Caye. If you live in a rural area, you'll probably have your own water system, either a well or a cistern to collect rainwater, and a septic tank for wastes. Thus, your only expenses will be the initial cost of the systems, plus any electricity you use. Most households in Belize run stoves and, often hot-water showers, on butane. (Butane is sold in Belize instead of propane.) Rates vary according to energy prices, but on average, a small household may use US$25–35 worth of butane a month. Trucks deliver butane tanks to your home, or at least to the road in front of your home.

Aside from your telephone bills (see the *Communications* chapter), the only other utility expense you may face is garbage pickup. Belizeans refer to it as "dirt." Your dirt bill will probably not run more than US$10, and pickup is free in some areas.

© Lan Sluder

Resources

Contacts

Consulates and Embassies

Because of the Belizean government's budget problems, some embassies and consulates abroad are expected to close in 2005. Most of the honorary consulates are run by private individuals, from their individual homes or offices. In countries where there is no Belize embassy, the interests of Belize usually are represented by the British High Commission.

UNITED STATES
Embassy of Belize
2535 Massachusetts Ave. NW
Washington, D.C. 20008
tel.: 202/332-9636
fax: 202/332-6888
www.embassyofbelize.org

Consulate General of Belize
5825 Sunset Blvd., Ste. 206
Hollywood, CA 90028
tel.: 323/469-7343
fax: 213/469-7346
belizeconsul@earthlink.net

Permanent Mission of Belize to the United Nations in New York
885 2nd Ave.
1 Dag Hammarskjold Plaza, 20th Fl.
New York, NY 10017
tel.: 212/593-0999
fax: 212/593-0932

Honorary Consulates
California
Consulate of Belize
American Zoetrope
916 Kearny St.
San Francisco, CA 94133
fax: 415/788-7500
shanno_lail@ffnotes.com

Florida
Consulate of Belize
4173 S. Le Jeune Rd.
Coconut Grove, FL 33146
tel./fax: 305/666-1121
bzconsulmi@mindspring.com

Illinois
Consulate of Belize
201 North Church St., Rm. 200
Belleville, IL 62223
tel.: 618/234-4410
fax: 618/234-8634
verduem@smtp.bacnet.edu

Consulate of Belize
c/o Ezetech Manufacturing Inc.
1200 Howard Dr.
West Chicago, IL 60185
tel.: 630/293-0010
fax: 630/293-0463
eztecmfg@aol.com

Louisiana
Consulate of Belize
c/o Westbank Optical Inc.

419 Lapalco Blvd.
Gretna, LA 70056
tel.: 504/392-3655
fax: 504/392-3809
jsbenard@hotmail.com

Michigan
Consulate of Belize
24984 Glen Orchard Dr.
Farmington Hills, MI
   48336-1732
fax: 810/477-8768
lennox-p@prodigy.net

Ohio
Consulate of Belize
410 Corporate Center Dr.
Vandalia, OH 45377
bradlw@mgmainnett.com

Puerto Rico
Consulate of Belize
567 Ramon Gandia St.
Hato Rey
Puerto Rico 00918
tel.: 787/280-6600

Texas
Consulate of Belize
7101 Breen
Houston, TX 77086
tel.: 281/999-4484

CANADA
Consulate of Belize in Quebec
1800 McGill College, Ste. 2480
Montreal, Quebec H3A 3J6
tel.: 514/288-1687
fax: 514/288-4998
dbellemare@cmmtl.com

Consulate of Belize in Vancouver
2321 Trafalgar St.
Vancouver, British Columbia
   V6K 3T1
tel.: 604/730-1224
dwsmiling@hotmail.com

Consulate of Belize in Ontario
c/o McMillan Binch
Ste. 3800, South Tower
Royal Bank Plaza
Toronto, Ontario M5J 2JP
tel.: 416/865-7000
fax: 416/864-7048

UNITED KINGDOM
Belize High Commission
22 Harcourt House
19 Cavendish Sq.
London W1G 0PL
tel.: 44 020/7499 9728
fax: 44 020/7491 4139
bzhc-lon@btconnect.com

CENTRAL AMERICA
Consulate of Belize in Costa Rica
Apartado Postal 11 121-1000
San José
tel.: 506/253-5598
fax: 506/233-6394
gprisma@sol.racsa.co.cr

Embassy of Belize in Guatemala
Edificio El Reformador
8th Fl., Ste. 803
Avenida Reforma 1–50
Zone 9
Guatemala City
tel.: 502/334-5531
www.belize-guatemala.gov.bz

Embassy of Belize in El Salvador
Calle El Bosque Norte
Col. La Lima IV
San Salvador
tel.: 503/248-1423
fax: 503/273 6744

Consulate of Belize in Panama
P.O. Box 0819–12297
El Dorado
tel.: 507/236-4132

MEXICO

Embassy of Belize in Mexico
215 Calle Bernardo de Galvez
Col. Lomas de Chapultepec
11000
Mexico, D.F.
tel.: 52 55/20-1274
fax: 52 55/20-6089
embelize@prodigy.net.mx

EUROPE

**Embassy of Belize and Mission
of Belize to the European
Communities**
Boulevard Brand Whitlock 136
Brussels 1200
Belgium
tel.: 32 2/732-6204
fax: 32 2/732-6246
embel.bru@pophost.eunet.be

**Permanent Mission of Belize to
the UNESCO in France**
1 Rue Miollis
Rm. M339
Paris 75015
tel.: 33 1/45 68 32 11

fax: 33 1/47 20 18 74
dl.belize@unesco.org

ASIA

**Embassy of Belize in Tokyo,
Japan**
No. 38 Kowa Building
4-12-24-907
Nishi-Azabu Minato-ku
106 00 31
Tokyo
tel.: 81 3/3400 9106
fax: 81 3/3400 9262
belize@mxd.mesh.ne.jp

**Embassy of Belize in Taipei,
Taiwan**
11F, No. 9, Ln. 62
Tien Mu West Rd.
Shih Lin
Taipei
tel.: 886 2/287 60894
fax: 886 2/287 60896
embelroc@ms41.hinet.net
www.embassyofbelize.org.tw

FOREIGN EMBASSIES
IN BELIZE

United States

**Embassy of the United States of
America**
29 Gabourel Ln. (P.O. Box 286)
Belize City
tel.: 501/227-7161
fax: 501/223-0802
embbelize@state.gov
www.belize.usembassy.gov
Visitors to Belize and U.S.

citizens resident in Belize can register electronically with the Embassy of the United States in Belize by visiting www .travelregistration.state.gov /ibrs.

Canada
Canadian Embassy/Belize Representative
80 Princess Margaret Dr.
(P.O. Box 610)
Belize City
tel.: 501/223-1060
fax: 501/223-0060
cdncon.bze@btl.net
www.guatemala.gc.ca
The Canadian Embassy in Guatemala represents Canada's interests in Belize.

United Kingdom
British High Commission
P.O. Box 91
Belmopan City
tel.: 501/822-2146
fax: 501/822-2761
brithicom@btl.net

European Union
Delegation of the European Commission to Belize
Blake Building, 3rd Fl.
Hutson and Eyre Sts.
P.O. Box 907
Belize City
tel.: 501/223-2070
fax: 501/223-2785
eudelblz@delblz.cec.eu.int

In addition, as of 2005, the following countries maintained embassies or consulates in Belize. All are in Belize City, except the embassies of El Salvador and Venezuela, which are in Belmopan City:

Costa Rica
Cuba
El Salvador
Guatemala
Honduras
Mexico
Republic of China (Taiwan)
Venezuela

Making the Move

GENERAL RESOURCES
www.ambergriscaye.com
Impressive site with massive amount of material about Ambergris Caye. Good links to other sites, including most hotels, dive shops, real-estate firms, and other businesses on the island. Active message board at www.ambergriscaye .com/cgi-bin/ultimatebb.cgi.

www.travelbelize.org
Official site of the Belize Tourist Board, with tons of information on hotels and sightseeing,

plus links to the Qualified Retired Persons site and Belize tourism statistics.

www.toucantrail.com
New in 2005, this Belize Tourist Board site focuses on small hotels with rooms for less than US$60 per night.

www.belize.gov.bz
Official site of the government of Belize—but not always up-to-date, unfortunately.

www.belizenet.com
Well-done site on Belize travel and other information by folks who provide Web design services in Belize. Associated with an active message board, Belize Forums, at www.belizeforum .com/cgi-bin/ultimatebb.cgi.

www.belize.com
Somewhat commercial but useful site with a variety of articles and ads on Belize, developed by Manolo Romero.

www.belizex.com
Travel and other information on Cayo District.

www.belizenorth.com
Terrific resource for anyone considering moving to the Corozal Town area. Lots of nitty-gritty information on daily life by

people who live in Belize. Developed by American expat Rick Zahniser.

www.localgringos.com
Excellent source of information on expat life in Northern Belize, developed by American expat Margaret Briggs.

www.belizeans.com
Oriented to native Belizeans living outside Belize. Good local message board.

www.belizefirst.com
Online magazine about Belize (Lan Sluder, editor and publisher) with dozens of articles on travel, life, and retirement in Belize.

www.belizezoo.org
Information about the best little zoo in the Americas.

www.belizeretirement.org
Basic information on the Qualified Retired Persons incentive program provided by the Belize Tourist Board.

www.corozal.com
Pretty good information about Corozal District, provided by students of Corozal Community College. A sister site, www.corozal.bz, has business listings and information.

www.hopkinsbelize.com
Information on Hopkins Village.

www.southernbelize.com
Information about Toledo District.

www.placencia.com
Valuable tourist and general
information on the Placencia
Peninsula.

www.destinationsbelize.com
All kinds of news and information about Placencia.

VISAS AND IMMIGRATION
Belize Immigration Department
Belmopan
tel.: 501/822-2423
fax: 501/822-2662

Belize Tourism Board
New Central Bank Building
Gabourel Ln., Level 2
(P.O. Box 325)
Belize City
tel.: 501/223-1913 or
    800/624-0686
fax: 501/223-1943
info@travelbelize.org
www.travelbelize.org

MOVING WITH PETS
**Belize Agricultural Health
Authority (BAHA)**
Permit Unit
Belmopan Showgrounds
Belmopan City
tel.: 501/822-0197

fax: 501/822-3084
baha@btl.net

Dr. Michael Deshield
Animal Medical Centre
Castle and Lancaster Sts.
Belize City
tel.: 501/224-5230
deshield@btl.net

SHIPPING OPTIONS
Elbert Flowers
Cayo Adventure Tours
Santa Elena, Cayo
tel.: 501/824-3426
cattours@btl.net

Hyde Shipping
10025 N.W. 116th Way, Ste. 2
Medley, FL 33178
tel.: 305/913-4933
fax: 305/913-4900

Speed Cargo
9950 N.W. 17th St.
Miami, FL 33172
tel.: 305/463-4800

Tropical Shipping
9505 N.W. 108th Ave.
Miami, FL 33178
tel.: 305/805-7400 or
    888/578-5851
www.tropical.com

Yucatan Express
www.yucatanexpress.com

Storage
Caye Mini Storage
tel.: 501/226-3420
lorne@grumpyandhappy.com

CUSTOMS BROKERS
George Bradley
117 Albert St.
Belize City
tel.: 501/227-0702
fax: 501/227-0727

Steve Kuylen
Corozal Town
tel.: 501/422-3624 or
    501/610-4213

Calbert Reynolds
Belize City
tel.: 501/227-0381

Billy Valdes
160 N. Front St. (P.O. Box 4)
Belize City
tel.: 501/227-7436

BELIZE GOVERNMENT MINISTRIES
The names, organization, office addresses, and functions of Belize government ministries change frequently, as do their phone numbers and, of course, the ministers themselves. The current lineup may (or may not) be available on the Belize government website, www.belize.gov.bz.

Prime Minister
New Administration Building
Belmopan City
tel.: 501/822-0399
fax: 501/822-0898

Ministry of Agriculture, Fisheries, and Cooperatives
Belmopan City
tel.: 501/822-2241
fax: 501/822-2409

Ministry of the Attorney General
Belmopan City
tel.: 501/822-2504
fax: 501/822-3390

Ministry of Education, Youth, and Sports
Belmopan City
tel.: 501/822-2380
fax: 501/822-3342

Ministry of Finance
New Administration Building
Belmopan City
tel.: 501/822-2218
fax: 501/822-2195

Ministry of Foreign Affairs
Belmopan City
tel.: 501/822-2167
fax: 501/822-2854

Ministry of Health, Energy, and Communications
Belmopan City
tel.: 501/822-2325
fax: 501/822-2924

Ministry of Home Affairs and Investment
Belmopan City
tel.: 501/822-2832
fax: 501/822-2837

Ministry of Housing
Belmopan City
tel.: 501/822-2680
fax: 501/822-3337

Ministry of Human Development
Belmopan City
tel.: 501/822-2161
fax: 501/822-3365

Ministry of Local Government, Labour, and Rural Development
Belmopan City
tel.: 501/822-2161
fax: 501/822-3365

Ministry of Natural Resources and Environment
Belmopan City
tel.: 501/822-2249
fax: 501/822-2333

Ministry of National Development
Belmopan City
tel.: 501/822-2526
fax: 501/822-3673

Ministry of Public Service, Works, and Transport
Belmopan City
tel.: 501/822-2136
fax: 501/822-3282

Ministry of Tourism and Culture
Belmopan City
tel.: 501/822-3393
fax: 501/822-3815

WEATHER

The Belize government National Meteorological Service site (www.hydromet.gov.bz) usually has the best information and forecasts. Other occasionally helpful sites include the following—but remember that data shown for Belize is usually for Belmopan or Belize City and may not apply for the rest of the country, especially the cayes:

www.weather.com
www.intellicast.com
www.usatoday.com/weather
/forecast/wglobe.htm

Language and Education

GENERAL RESOURCES
National Kriol Council of Belize
www.belizekriol.bz

Teachers for a Better Belize
www.twc.org

PRIMARY SCHOOLS
Belize Elementary School
Princess Margaret Dr.
Belize City
tel.: 501/223-5765

Island Academy
Coconut Dr.
San Pedro, Ambergris Caye
tel./fax: 501/226-3642
www.ambergriscaye.com/academy

SECONDARY SCHOOLS
**Corozal Community College
(High School)**
San Andres (P.O. Box 63)
Corozal Town
tel.: 501/422-2541
www.corozal.com/ccc/default
  .html

Mount Carmel High School
Benque Viejo Del Carmen
tel.: 501/823-2331

Saint Catherine Academy
6 Hutson St.
Belize City
tel.: 501/223-4908

fax: 501/223-0057
administration@sca.edu.bz
www.sca.edu.bz/index.html

St. John's High School
P.O. Box 548
Belize City
tel.: 501/223-3731
fax: 501/223-2752
www.sjc.edu.bz/high_school
  /index.html

**Toledo Community College
(High School)**
West Campus, Punta Gorda
tel.: 501/702-2101

JUNIOR COLLEGES
Corozal Junior College
San Andres
Corozal Town
tel.: 501/422-3806
www.corozal.com/cjc

St. John's Junior College
P.O. Box 548
Belize City
tel.: 501/223-3731
fax: 501/223-2752
contactsjcjc@yahoo.com
www.sjc.edu.bz/junio_college
  /index.html

COLLEGES AND UNIVERSITIES

Galen University
Mile 62 1/2, Western Highway
(P.O. Box 177)
San Ignacio, Cayo
tel.: 501/824-3226
fax: 501/824-3723
galen@btl.net
www.galen.edu.bz

University of Belize
University Dr. (P.O. Box 579)
Belize City
tel.: 501/223-0256
fax: 501/233-0255
www.ub.edu.bz

Offshore Medical Schools

Central America Health Sciences University Belize Medical College
P.O. Box 989
Belize City
tel.: 501/225-4288
fax: 501/225-4289

Central America Health Sciences University Belize Medical College
U.S. Information Office
P.O. Box 55996
Washington, D.C. 20040
tel.: 877/523-9687
admissions@cahsu.edu
www.cahsu.edu

Medical University of the Americas
P.O. Box 127
San Pedro, Ambergris Caye
tel.: 501/226-3744
fax: 501/226-3835
muabelize@btl.net
www.mua.edu.bz

St. Luke's University School of Medicine
P.O. Box 557
Belmopan, Cayo
tel.: 877/545-8537
admissions@stluke.edu.bz
www.stluke.edu.bz

A fourth medical school, planned to provide specialties and techniques not now available in Belize, will reportedly begin operations in 2005-2006, probably in the Corozal Town area. For information, contact Romeo Shayne Pavlic at tel. 501/601-3534 or 501/422-3000.

Health

GENERAL HEALTH
Centers for Disease Control and Prevention(CDC)
tel.: 877/394-8747
www.cdc.gov
This U.S. Department of Health and Human Services division offers expert advice on health and immunization issues for travelers to Belize and elsewhere in the world.

World Health Organization (WHO)
www.who.int/en
The WHO website has specific information in six languages on health risks and health information in Belize and elsewhere in the world.

EMERGENCIES
To reach the police, call tel. 911 countrywide.

In Belize City only:
Fire, Ambulance, and Police: tel. 90
Crimestoppers Hotline: tel. 922

PUBLIC HOSPITALS
Belmopan Hospital
Belmopan City
tel.: 501/822-2264

Corozal Hospital
Corozal Town
tel.: 501/422-2076

Karl Heusner Memorial Hospital
Belize City
tel.: 501/223-1548

Northern Regional Hospital
Orange Walk
tel.: 501/322-2072

Punta Gorda Hospital
Punta Gorda
tel.: 501/722-2026

San Ignacio Hospital
San Ignacio
tel.: 501/824-2066

Southern Regional Hospital
Dangriga
tel.: 501/522-2078

PRIVATE HOSPITALS
Belize Medical Associates
5791 St. Thomas St. (P.O. Box 1008)
Kings Park
Belize City
tel.: 501/223-0302
fax: 501/223-3827
bzemedasso@btl.net
www.belizemedical.com

La Loma Luz Medical Center
Santa Elena, Cayo
tel.: 501/824-2087
fax: 501/824-2674

Universal Health Services
Blue Marlin and Chancellor
    Aves. (P.O. Box 2403)
West Landivar
Belize City
tel.: 501/223-7870
fax: 501/600/8628
admin@universalhealthbelize
    .com
www.universalhealthbelize.com

DENTAL WORK
Dr. Osbert Usher
16 Magazine Rd.
Belize City
tel.: 501/227-3415

HEALTH INSURANCE

Insurance Brokers in Belize
Belize Insurance Center Ltd.
212 N. Front St.
Belize City
tel.: 501/227-7310, 501/227-
    77311, or 501/227-4541
fax: 501/227-4803
info@belizeinsurance.com
www.belizeinsurance.com

F&G Insurance
6 Fort St. (P.O. Box 438)
Belize City
tel.: 501/227-7493
fax: 501/227-8617

fandg@btl.net
www.fandginsurance.com

International Insurance Brokers
Capitol Life/Global Insurance Net
7700 N. Kendall Dr., Ste. 505
Miami, FL 33156
tel.: 305/274-0284 or
    800/975-7363 (U.S.)
info@globalinsurancenet.com
www.globalinsurancenet.com

Insurance Consultants International
308 Epps St.
Tomball, TX 77375
tel.: 281/516-3633 or
    800/575-2674
fax: 603/843-6662
www.globalhealtinsurance.com

MediBroker
www.medibroker.com

International Health Insurance
Amedex
7001 S.W. 97th Ave.
Miami, FL 33173
tel.: 305/275-1400
amedex@amedex.com
www.amedex.com

British Fidelity Assurance
tel.: 501/422-2038
fax: 501/422-3835
bfaltd@blt.net.bs
www.britishfidelity.com

PHARMACIES

Brodies
Northern Highway (and other
    locations)
Belize City
tel.: 501/223-5587

Community Drug Stores
Farmers Market (and other
    locations)
Belize City
tel.: 501/224-5587

The Pharmacy
24 West St.
San Ignacio
tel.: 501/824-2510

PERSONAL SAFETY

AAA Security Services Corp.
tel.: 501/223-4900

KBH Security Systems
tel.: 501/227-2263
www.kbh-security.com

Employment

PERMITS

**Immigration and Nationality
Department**
tel.: 501/822-2611

Labour Department
Belmopan
tel.: 501/822-2633
fax: 501/822-1275

PROFESSIONAL RESOURCES

Attorney General's Ministry
www.belizelaw.org/lawadmin

**Institute of Chartered Accoun-
tants of the Caribbean**
www.icac.org.jm

TRADE AND INVESTMENT

**Belize Trade and Investment
Development Service (Beltraide)**
14 Orchid Garden St.

Belmopan City, Cayo
tel.: 501/822-2832
fax: 501/822-2837
www.belizeinvest.org

Ministry of Finance (Revenue)
New Administration Building,
    2nd Fl.
Belmopan City
tel.: 501/822-2218
fax: 501/822-2195
finrevenue@mof.gov.bz

VOLUNTEER ORGANIZATIONS

Within Belize

Belize Audubon Society
12 Fort St. (P.O. Box 1001)
Belize City
tel.: 501/223-5004
www.belizeaudubon.org

Belize Community Service Alliance
c/o Mr. Luis Garcia
Hudson St.
San Ignacio, Cayo
tel.: 501/824-3985 (Belize) or
    217/528-2183 (U.S.)
www.belizealliance.org

Belize Zoo and Tropical Education Center
P.O. Box 1787
Belize City
tel.: 501/220-8003
tec@btl.net
www.belizezoo.org

**Birds Without Borders
(Aves Sin Fronteras)**
10005 W. Blue Mound Rd.
Milwaukee, WI 53226
tel.: 414/258-2333
www.zoosociety.org

Cornerstone Foundation
90 Burns Ave.
San Ignacio, Cayo
tel.: 501/824-2373
peace@btl.net
www.peacecorner.org

Green Reef
100 Coconut Dr.
San Pedro, Ambergris Caye
tel.: 501/226-3254
greenreef@btl.net
www.greenreefbelize.com

King's Children Home
38/40 Unity Blvd.
(P.O. Box 144)
Belmopan
tel.: 501/822-2021

Monkey Bay Wildlife Sanctuary
P.O. Box 187
Belmopan
tel.: 501/820-3032
mbay@btl.net
www.monkeybaybelize.org

Mount Carmel High School
Benque Viejo del Carmen, Cayo
mchs@btl.net
www.mchsbenque.org
When emailing for informa-
    tion, put the name of school
    principal Tim Robinson in the
    subject line.

Programme for Belize
1 Eyre St. (P.O. Box 749)
Belize City
tel.: 501/227-5616
pfbel@btl.net
www.pfbelize.org

SAGA Society
Coconut Dr.
San Pedro, Ambergris Caye
tel.: 501/226-3266
saga@btl.net
www.ambergriscaye.com
    /sagasociety

Toledo Institute for Development and Environment (TIDE)
P.O. Box 150
Punta Gorda Town, Toledo
tel.: 501/722-2274
tidetours@btl.net
www.belizeecotours.org

Outside Belize
Belize Faith Missions
c/o Conner's Bookkeeping
5790 Riverside Ave.
Riverside, CA 92506
www.belizefaithmissions.org

EcoLogic Development Fund
P.O. Box 383405
Cambridge, MA 02238
tel.: 617/441-6300
www.ecologic.org

Explorations in Travel Inc.
2458 River Rd.
Guilford, VT 05301

tel.: 802/257-0152
www.volunteertravel.com

Maya Research Program at Blue Creek
Box 298760
Texas Christian University
Fort Worth, TX 76129
tel.: 817/257-5943
www.mayaresearchprogram.org

Plenty International
www.plenty.org

University of Texas/ Programme for Belize Archaeological Project
Mesoamerican Archaeological
    Research Laboratory
The University of Texas
Austin, TX 78712
tel.: 512/232-7049
www.uts.cc.utexas.edu/~marl
    /program_details.html

Finance

DOMESTIC BANKS
Alliance Bank of Belize
106 Princess Margaret Dr.
Belize City
tel.: 501/223-678
fax: 501/223-6785
www.alliancebank.bz

Atlantic Bank
Atlantic Building
Freetown Rd.
Belize City

tel.: 501/223-4123
fax: 501/223-3907
www.atlabank.com

Belize Bank
60 Market Sq.
Belize City
tel.: 501/227-7132
fax: 501/227-2712
www.belizebank.com

First Caribbean
International Bank
Albert St.
Belize City
tel.: 501/227-7129
fax: 501/227-8572
www.firstcaribbean.com

ScotiaBank
Albert St.
Belize City
tel.: 501/227-7027
fax: 501/227-7416
www.scotiabank.com

OFFSHORE BANKS
Atlantic International Bank
Cleghorn St. and Freetown Rd.
Belize City
tel.: 501/223-0681
fax: 510/223-3528
services@atlanticibl.com
www.atlanticibl.com

Provident Bank and Trust
35 Barrack Rd.
Belize City
tel.: 501/223-5698
fax: 501/223-0368
services@providentbank.bz
www.providentbelize.com

Communications

INTERNET SERVICE PROVIDERS
Belize Telecommunications Ltd.
St. Thomas St. (P.O. Box 603)
Belize City
tel.: 501/227-7085 or
    800/225-5285 (Belize)
fax: 501/223-1800
www.btl.net

PHONE COMPANIES
Belize Telecommunications Ltd.
St. Thomas St. (P.O. Box 603)
Belize City
tel.: 501/227-7085 or
    800/225-5285 (Belize)
fax: 501/223-1800
www.btl.net

Speednet Communications Ltd.
Belize City
tel. 501/223-1919

VOICE OVER INTERNET PROTOCOL (VOIP)
Vonage
www.vonage.com

EXPRESS AND COURIER SERVICES
DHL
C./K.C. Dunn and Associates
    (service contractor)
38 New Rd.
Belize City
www.dhl.com

Federal Express
1 Mapp St. (service contractor)
Belize City
www.fedex.com

United Parcel Service
Belize Global Travel Service
   (UPS representative)
41 Albert St.
Belize City
www.ups.com

MEDIA

Newspapers
Amandala
www.amandala.com.bz

Ambergris Today
www.ambergristoday.com

The Belize Times
www.belizetimes.com

The Guardian
www.guardian.bz

Placencia Breeze
www.placenciabreeze.com

San Pedro Sun
www.sanpedrosun.net

Magazines
Belize First Magazine
www.belizefirst.com

Belize Magazine
www.belizemagazine.com

Television and Radio
Channel 5
www.channel5belize.com

Channel 7
www.7newsbelize.com

LOVE-FM
www.lovefm.com

Travel and Transportation

INTERNATIONAL AIRLINES
From the United States:

American
tel.: 800/433-7300
www.aa.com
Service to Belize from Dallas-
   Fort Worth and Miami.

Continental
tel.: 800/523-3273
www.continental.com

Service to Belize from Houston
   and Newark.

Delta
tel.: 800/221-1212
www.delta.com
Service to Belize from Atlanta.

TACA
tel.: 800/400-8222
www.taca.com

Service to Belize from Houston and other cities via the airline's hub in San Salvador.

US Airways
tel.: 800/622-1015
www.usairways.com
Service to Belize from Charlotte.

From other parts of Central America:

Atlantic Air
www.atlanticairlines.com.ni
Service to Belize from Honduras.

Tikal Jets
tel.: 502 2361 0042 (Guatemala)
www.tikaljets.com
Service to Belize from Guatemala City and Flores.

BELIZEAN AIRLINES
Maya Island Air
www.mayaairways.com
tel.: 501/223-1140
Service throughout Belize and to Flores, Guatemala.

Tropic Air
www.tropicair.com
tel.: 800/422-3435
Service throughout Belize and to Flores, Guatemala.

AIRPORTS IN BELIZE
Philip S. W. Goldson
International Airport
Ladyville (Belize City)

Airport code: BZE
tel.: 501/225-2014
Belize's only international airport, nine miles north of Belize City.

Municipal Airport
Belize City
Airport code: TZA
tel. 501/224-5349
Small airstrip in Belize City for domestic flights—ask to be taken to the "small airport."

Other airports/airstrips in Belize with scheduled service:

Caye Caulker
Corozal Town
Dangriga
Placencia
Punta Gorda
San Pedro
Savannah (Big Creek)

BUS COMPANIES
ADO
tel.: 525/133-2424 (Mexico)
info@adogl.com.mx
www.adogl.com.mex

Novelo's Bus Line
West Collett Canal
(P.O. Box 2031)
Belize City
tel.: 501/227-2025

Housing Considerations

GOVERNMENT AGENCIES
Ministry of Natural Resources and the Environment
Market Sq.
Belmopan City
tel.: 501/822-2226
fax: 501-822-2333
www.mnrei.gov.bz/contact
_us.asp

TITLE INSURANCE
Regent Insurance
Belize City
tel.: 501/227-3744

MENNONITE HOUSES
Linda Vista Lumberyard
Rte. 40 W.
Spanish Lookout, Cayo
tel.: 501/823-8052

Midwest Lumber
Spanish Lookout, Cayo
tel.: 501/823-8000

Plett's
Rte. 40 W.
Spanish Lookout, Cayo
tel.: 501/823-0447

REAL-ESTATE AGENTS

Northern Cayes
Diane Campbell
San Pedro, Ambergris Caye
tel.: 501/226-5203
diane@dianecampbell.net

Caye Caulker Rentals
tel.: 501/226-0029
www.cayecaulkerrentals.com

Paradise Found Belize Ltd.
Galleria
San Pedro, Ambergris Caye
lenny777@sbcglobal.net
www.paradisefoundbelize.com

Pelican Properties
San Pedro, Ambergris Caye
tel.: 501/226-3234
fax: 501/226-3434
info@pelicanbelize.com
www.pelicanpropertiesbelize.com

Southwind Properties
P.O. Box 1
San Pedro, Ambergris Caye
tel.: 501-226-2005
fax: 501/226-2331
southwind@btl.net
www.belize-real-estate.net

Sunrise Realty
1 Barrier Reef Dr. (P.O. Box 236)
San Pedro, Ambergris Caye
tel.: 501/226-3737
fax: 501/226-3379
info@sunrisebelize.com
www.sunrisebelize.com

Triton Properties
Barrier Reef Dr.
San Pedro, Ambergris Caye

tel.: 501/226-3783
fax: 501/226-3549
triton@btl.net
www.triton-properties.com

Northern Belize
Alpha and Omega International Realty and Consultants
Corozal Town
tel.: 501/207-8887
broker@alphaomegabelizereal-
  estate.com

Belize North Real Estate Ltd.
P.O. Box 226, Corozal Town
tel.: 501/422-0284
fax: 501/422-2710
czl@belizenorthrealestate.bz
www.belizenorthrealestate.bz

Consejo Shores Ltd.
Bill Wildman
P.O. Box 35
Corozal Town
tel.: 501/423-1005
fax: 501/423-1006
wildman@direcway.com
www.consejoshores.com

EZBelize Real Estate
4 Progress St. (P.O. Box 175)
Orange Walk Town
tel.: 501/322-0503
info@ezbzrealestate.com
www.ezbzrealestate.com

Charlotte Zahniser
(home-finder service)
tel.: 501/422-0135
har@belizenorth.com

Western Belize/Cayo District
Belize Realty Services
29 Burns Ave.
San Ignacio, Cayo
tel.: 501/801-0195
www.belize-real-estate-services
  .com

Cayo Connection
Western Hwy.
Santa Elena, Cayo
tel.: 501/824-4943
rallen@btl.net
www.cayoconnection.com

Tropic Real Estate
P.O. Box 453
Belmopan, Cayo
tel.: 501/824-3475
fax: 501/824-3649
tropic@realestatebelize.com
www.realestatebelize.com

Southern Belize
Bayshore Limited
100 Embarcadero Rd.
Maya Beach, Placencia Peninsula
tel.: 501/523-8019
jwildman@lincsat.com
www.bayshorebelize.com

British American Cattle Company (U.S.)
4600 Spicewood Springs Rd., Ste. 102
Austin, TX 78759
tel.: 512/346-7381
fax: 512/346-7395
baccbelize@cs.com
www.bacc.com

Southern Belize Real Estate Company
Na' Taat Paal Jungle Camp Mile 1
San Felipe Rd.
Toledo
info@southernbelizerealestate
    .com
www.southernbelizerealestate
    .com

Yearwood Properties
General Delivery
Placencia
tel./fax: 501/523-3462
brian@belizebeachfront.com
www.belizebeachfront.com

Belize City

Belize Land Properties Ltd.
9 3rd St.
King's Park, Belize City
tel./fax: 501/223-4807
info@belizelandproperties.com
www.belizelandproperties.com

Belize Real Estate
160 N. Front St. (P.O. Box 354)
Belize City
tel.: 501/227-2065

fax: 501/223-1023
bzreal@btl.net
This agency comprises W. Ford Young Real Estate in Belize City and Langdon Supply in Ambergris Caye.

Deloitte Property Management Ltd.
40A Central American Blvd.
Belize City
tel.: 501/227-3020
fax: 501/227-5792
properties@deloittebelize.com
www.deloittebelize.com

Emerald Futures Real Estate
13 Cork St., No. 3
(P.O. Box 1442)
Belize City
tel.: 501/223-6559
fax: 501/223-6559
realgem@btl.net
www.emeraldfutures.com

Realty Management of Belize Ltd.
24 Daly St.
Belize City
tel.: 501/223-3523
fax: 501/223-3375
s.allen@realtymanagementofbelize
    .com
www.realtymanagementofbelize
    .com

Regent Realty
81 N. Front St.
Belize City

tel.: 501/227-3744
fax: 501/227-2022
regent@btl.net
www.regentrealtybelize.com

RE/MAX Central Belize
2A S. Park St.
Belize City
tel.: 501/223-7667
info@remax-centralbelize.com
www.remax-centralbelize.com

ARCHITECTS
Guerra Consulting Architects
88 N. Front St.
Belize City
tel.: 501/223-0190

Gutierrez and Associates
4264 Central American Blvd.
Belize City
tel.: 501/227-5803
gutarch@hotmail.com

Strukture Architects
122 Eve St.
Belize City
tel.: 501/223-0617
www.strukturearchitects.com

BUILDING SUPPLIES/ MATERIALS DEALERS
Belize Aggregates
Mile 4 1/2, Northern Hwy.
Belize City

Benny's Homecenter
3 Regent St.
Belize City

tel.: 501/227-3347
www.bennysonline.com
Other Benny's locations can be
found at 54 Freetown Road
and at Mile 3 of the Northern
Highway.

Brothers Habet Ltd.
Mile 4, Western Hwy.
tel.: 501/222-4964

Caribbean Depot
San Pablo, Ambergris Caye
tel.: 501/226-2619

Linda Vista Lumber Yard
Spanish Lookout, Cayo
tel.: 501/823-0257

Midwest Lumber Mill
Center Rd.
Spanish Lookout
tel.: 501/823-0308

Midwest Steel and Agro Supplies
Center Rd.
Spanish Lookout
tel.: 501/823-0131

Professional Building Supplies
Placencia
tel.: 501/523-3238

Ricks Block and Tile Factory
7 Progress St.
Orange Walk Town
tel.: 501/322-2421

ATTORNEYS

The following attorneys may be able to assist you with real-estate or other transactions in Belize. When selecting an attorney in Belize, ask for references and check them out as you would anywhere else. Most attorneys have their offices in Belize City, although they will usually handle work in other parts of the country.

Denys A. Barrow
Barrow and Co.
23 Regent St.
Belize City
tel.: 501/227-0810
fax: 501/227-8460
barrowco@btl.net

Michel Chebat
Shoman and Chebat
53 Barrack Rd.
(P.O. Box 2491)
Belize City
tel.: 501/223-4160
fax: 501/223-4222
attorney@btl.net

Eamon H. Courtenay
W. H. Courtenay and Co.
1876 Hutson St.
Belize City
tel.: 501/224-4248
fax: 501/223-9962
whc_co@hotmail.com

Nicolas V. Dujon
Dujon and Dujon
4 Eve St.
Belize City
tel.: 501/224-5926
fax: 501/223-5869
dujondujon@btl.net

Tania M. Moody
Barrow and Williams
99 Albert St. (P.O. Box 617)
Belize City
tel.: 501/227-5280
fax: 501/227-5278
attorneys@barrowandwilliams
.com

Antoinette Moore
83 Commerce St.
Dangriga
tel.: 501/522-2457
moorelaw@btl.net

Margaret Musa-Nunez
Musa and Balderamos
91 N. Front St. (P.O. Box 571)
Belize City
tel.: 501/223-2940
fax: 501/223-1149
mandb@btl.net

Rodwell Williams
Barrow and Williams
99 Albert St. (P.O. Box 617)
Belize City
tel.: 501/227-5280
fax: 501/227-5278
attorneys@barrowandwilliams
.com

Glossary

Here are some words and phrases in common use in Belize. Like the country itself, they derive from a number of different cultures and languages. English is the official language of Belize and spoken—or at least understood—by the vast majority of the population, but Spanish, Creole, Garifuna, Low German, Mandarin Chinese, and Mopan, Kekchi, and Yucatec Maya are also spoken by sizable numbers of Belizeans.

achiote: also called annatto, a spice from a tropical shrub (*Bixaceae Bixa orellana* L.) used in cooking in Mexico, the Philippines, and Belize

alligator: crocodile (there are no true alligators in Belize, only crocodiles)

ants bear: anteater or tamandua

atoll: ring-shaped coral island surrounding a lagoon (Belize has three of the four in the Western Hemisphere: Turneffe, Glovers, and Lighthouse; the other is off Mexico)

baboon: black howler monkey

baktun: a Maya measure of time representing 144,000 days

bank: riverside logging camp; often used as a place name, as in Banana Bank

bashment: party (Creole)

Belice: Belize (Spanish)

blue note: BZ$100 bill

boil up: fish boiled with yams, cassava, plantains, or other vegetables

British Honduras: the former name of Belize

brukdown: traditional Creole music played with the jawbone of an ass and other instruments

burger: any kind of meat on a bun; if you want a hamburger, order a "beef burger"

bush: any area not cultivated; jungle

bush doctor: natural healer, herbal doctor, snake doctor

bush dog: tayra; a small, doglike mammal

buss brains: stress

bwai: boy (Creole)

caye: key or island (pronounced "key"); *cayo* in Spanish

Cayo, or *El Cayo:* the town of San Ignacio; also the district of Cayo

ceiba: a large flowering tree with an umbrella-shaped crown, also known as a "kapok tree"; holy to the Maya

cenote: collapsed cave exposing an underground river

cho-cho: a kind of squash

chupacabra: literally, "goat sucker" (Spanish); in Mexican folklore, a two-legged creature three or four feet tall that kills farm animals, sometimes believed to be seen in Belize

cohune: a type of palm; the town and district of Corozal are named for this palm

cook: mistress

Corker: another name for Caye Caulker

chancie: to try and take advantage of you (Creole)

cheecha, or *chicha:* homemade liquor (Spanish)

Chinee: person of Chinese or other Asian descent; not usually derogatory

Coro: short for Corozal, either the town or the district

cowfoot soup: a soup with a cow's hoof, spices, potatoes, onions, and other vegetables

cow's milk: real milk, as opposed to powdered milk

Creole, or Kriol: a person of African or partly African descent; also the language

directly: "I heard you, and I'll get to it eventually"

dirt: trash (a "dirt bin" is a box for trash or garbage)

dollah: Belize dollar, as in "Gimme five dollah"

dollah chicken: inexpensive fried chicken from a restaurant, regardless of the actual cost

dry season: usually February to April or May

ducunu: kernel corn boiled in coconut milk with onion and bell pepper, usually served in a corn husk, sometimes with chicken or other meat

dugu: a Garifuna religious ceremony involving communication with deceased ancestors

escabeche: a spicy soup with chicken, onions, and vinegar (Spanish)

evening: a greeting, used anytime after noon but before dark

fish coil: insecticide coil to ward off mosquitoes (named after the fish on the label of a popular brand)

football, or *futball:* soccer

fu we: for us, our (Creole); as in, *"Dis da fu we chickin"* ("This is our chicken"), the widely promoted slogan of Caribbean Chicken, a chicken producer in Belize

fry jack: fried bread served at breakfast (there is no past tense in Creole, thus "fry jacks" or "fry chicken," not "fried chicken"; and "stew chicken," not "stewed chicken")

fu tru: really, honest, for true (Creole)

garnaches: crisp tortillas topped with cabbage, cheese, and salsa (Spanish)

gibnut: paca, a kind of rodent sometimes eaten in Belize

GOB: Government of Belize

grind mean: ground meat

gringo: person of U.S., Canadian, or European descent; not usually considered disparaging

gyal: girl (Creole)

Hattieville: the main Belize prison near Hattieville, a village established after Hurricane Hattie in 1961

hudut or hoodut: fish simmered in coconut milk, a Garifuna dish

Ideal: a Popsicle (named after a local brand-name iced Popsicle)

jack: to stop or hijack; as in "jack a car"

johnnycakes, or *journeycakes:* flat biscuits served at breakfast

juk: literally, "stick" (Creole), but also a reference to sexual intercourse; thought to be the origin of the word "jukebox"

kinep: (also known as a Spanish Lime or *mamoncillo*) a tree native to South America that bears clusters of tart fruit resembling large grapes.

lampin: loafing, slacking off" as in *"Stop deh lampin"* (Creole)

lee: little (Creole); as in *"lee gyal* ("little girl")

lighter: a small sailing dinghy built in Belize, with shallow draft

madda rass: literally, "mother's ass"; but also foolishness (Creole), as in "Stop yu madda rass"

maumee: (also known as *mamey* or *sapota*) a tree native to Central America whose sweet fruit is used to make preserves or sherbert

mawning: a greeting used anytime after midnight until noon

Mennos: Mennonites

Mestizo: person of mixed European and Maya heritage, often speaking Spanish as a first language

milpa: the traditional Maya organic agriculture system, specifically, a small planting of corn and other crops, burned annually

molly apple: Malay apple, a pear-shaped fruit

mountain cow: tapir, the national animal of Belize

night: hello, a greeting said after dark until around midnight

panades: meat pies usually made from tortillas; from the Spanish *empanadas*

pear: smooth-skinned avocado

pibil: barbecue cooked in the ground, a well-known Maya dish

pickni or pickney: child (Creole)

pipe water: tap water

pitch: field for playing cricket (the British game is still played in some areas of Belize)

punta: music invented by Garifuna musicians, based on traditional drum rhythms

quash: coatimundi

QRP: Qualified Retired Person; a retiree under the government's incentive program to attract foreign retirees

PG: Punta Gorda, the largest town in Toledo District

PUP: People's United Party, currently the political party in power

rasta: a follower of the Rastafarian creed

rainy season: generally June–November (but it varies in different parts of the country)

recado: blend of *achiote* and other spices pressed into a cake and used in many Belizean dishes; comes in both red and black versions

ridge: the predominant type of tree in an area; as in "pine ridge"

right now: "I'll probably get to it eventually"

right there!: shouted out, indicating you want the bus to stop so you can get off

roots Belizean: native Belizean, usually of the lower economic class

rum-popo: eggnog with rum

salbutes: tacos fried in oil (Spanish)

sere: Garifuna soup with fish and coconut milk

shilling: a Belizean quarter, worth just under US$.13

shilling water: water in a bag, as opposed to more expensive bottled water

Spanish: common expression for a person of Mexican, Guatemalan, or of other Latino descent

squash: a concentrate of orange or other fruit, used as a base for drinks

stamp tax: a government tax, especially on the sale of real estate; a tax of 5 percent to 10 percent of value

sweet: candy; most shops have shilling sweet and five-cent sweet

tea: afternoon meal

teef: thief (noun); to steal (verb)

tigre: jaguar (Spanish)

tommygoff: fer-de-lance snake

tope: speed bump (Spanish), "sleeping policeman"

UDP: United Democratic Party, currently the main opposition party

vex: upset, irritated

yerri so: gossip (Creole)

want to buy: called out in a store if the clerk isn't around

warrie: peccary

wowlas: boa constrictors

ziricote: tropical hardwood with a black, gray, and cream color, found mainly in Belize and neighboring countries

Suggested Reading

Archaeology

Coe, Michael D. *The Maya.* Thames and Hudson: 1993, 224 pp. First published in 1966, this is the best general introduction to the subject.

Ferguson, William M., and R. E. W. Adams, *Mesoamerica's Ancient Cities: Aerial Views of Precolumbian Ruins in Mexico, Guatemala, Belize, and Honduras.* University Press of Colorado: rev. ed. 2000, 272 pp.

Foster, Byron (Ed.). *Warlords and Maize Men: A Guide to the Maya Sites of Belize.* Cubola Productions: Belize, 1992, 82 pp. The first popular guide focused entirely on Maya sites in Belize, edited by the late Dr. Foster. Maps, color photos.

Guderjan, Thomas H. *Ancient Maya Traders of Ambergris Caye.* Cubola Productions: Belize, 1993, 40 pp.

Henderson, John S. *The World of the Ancient Maya.* Cornell University Press: 1981, 271 pp.

Kelly, Joyce. *An Archaeological Guide to Northern Central America: Belize, Guatemala, Honduras, and El Salvador.* University of Oklahoma Press: rev. ed. 1996, 352 pp. Includes coverage of many smaller sites. Photographs by Jerry Kelly.

Thompson, J. Eric S. *The Maya of Belize: Historical Chapters since Columbus.* Cubola Productions: Belize, 1972, 36 pp.

Boating

British Admiralty Nautical Charts. Nautical charts for the coast of Belize.

Calder, Nigel. *The Cruising Guide to the Northwest Caribbean.* International Marine/McGraw-Hill: 2nd ed. 1991, 262 pp. Navigational and anchorage information on the Caribbean coast of Mexico, Belize, Guatemala, and Honduras.

Rauscher, Freya. *Cruising Guide to Belize and Mexico's Caribbean Coast.* Windmill Hill Books: 2nd ed. 2004, 304 pp. with 119 charts and 133 photos. Comprehensive cruising guide, the best available for this region. Includes general charts of Belize's coast and Mexico's Caribbean coast.

Cookbooks

Belize Hospital Auxiliary Cook-book. Angelus Press: 82 pp.

Brown de Langan, Trady (Ed.), *Mmmm... A Taste of Belizean Cooking.* Angeles Press: c. 2003, 112 pp.

Burns, E. L. *What's Cooking in the Belizean Kitchen.* Angelus Press: 74 pp.

Los Angeles Belizean Educational Network (LABEN). *Belizeous Cuisine: Delicious Belizean Recipes.* LABEN: 2nd ed. 1998, 102 pp.

Nord, Alice, Myrna Martinez, and Kaaren Shrine. *Cooking Belize.* Self-published: c. 1995, 126 pp.

Fiction, Drama, and Poetry

Auxillou, Ray. *Blue Hole.* Self-published: 479 pp. A collection of tales about mercenaries, drug runners, and adventure. Other books in the same vein by Auxillou include *Belize Secret Service* and *The Belize Vortex.*

Edgell, Zee. *Beka Lamb.* Heinemann: 1982, 192 pp. Classic novel about ordinary life in British Honduras.

—*In Times Like These.* Heinemann: 1991, 320 pp. An English-educated Belizean returns home in this novel.

Ellis, Zoila. *On Heroes, Lizards, and Passion: Seven Belizean Short Stories.* Cubola Productions: Belize, 1994, 130 pp. "White Christmas an' Pink Jungle" is one of seven deliciously Belizean stories from a distinguished Belizean/Garifuna writer.

Esquivel, Cathy. *Under the Shade.* Angelus Press: 192 pp. Tales of the drug trade.

Hernandez, Felicia. *Those Ridiculous Years.* 1996, 64 pp. Self-published short stories about Garifuna life.

Lindo, Louis. *Tales of the Belizean Woods.* Cubola Productions: 1995, 82 pp. Short stories set in "backabush" Belize.

McKay, Claudia. *Twist of Lime: A Lynn Evans Mystery.* New Victoria Publishers: 1997, 188 pp. Mystery featuring a lesbian newspaper reporter on a Maya dig in Belize.

Miller, Carlos Ledson. *Belize, A Novel.* Xlibris Corp.: 1999, 402 pp. Fast-paced saga of father and sons through four decades, beginning with Hurricane Hattie in 1961.

Ruiz Puga, David Nicolas. *Old Benque.* Cubola Productions:

Belize, 160 pp. Short stories in Spanish.

Stray, P. J. *The Danger on Lighthouse Reef.* Silver Burdett Press: 1997, 144 pp. Children's mystery story.

Theroux, Paul. *The Mosquito Coast.* Houghton-Mifflin: 1982, 374 pp. An obsessed American drags his family to Central America. Actually set in Honduras, not Belize, but the movie of the same name was filmed in Belize.

Westlake, Donald. *High Adventure.* Mysterious Press: 1985, 326 pp. Dope, dummies, and deliverance in Belize, by the popular adventure writer.

Young, Colville. *Pataki Full.* Cubola Productions: Belize, 1991, 120 pp. Collection of short stories by a noted Belizean writer and scholar.

Guidebooks

Carlstroem, Carolyn M. *Lonely Planet Belize.* Lonely Planet Publications: 2002, 240 pp. Not the best guide LP has ever done.

Eltringham, Peter. *The Rough Guide to Belize.* Rough Guides: 3rd ed. 2004, 384 pp. Thoroughly researched guide by knowledgeable writer who has lived in Belize and Guatemala.

Gelula, Melissa, and Mark Sullivan (Eds.). *Fodor's Central America.* Random House: 2003, 312 pp. Coauthored by Lan Sluder.

Glassman, Paul. *Belize Guide.* Open Road Publishing: 12th ed. forthcoming in 2005, 312 pp. This author was one of the first travel writers to publish a guide to Belize.

Greenspan, Eliot *Frommer's Belize.* Frommer's: 2004, 352 pp. New entry in the Belize guide sweepstakes.

Hennessy, Huw (Ed.). *Belize Insight Guide.* Insight Guides: 2nd ed. 2003, 339 pp. Unmatched photos and good general background on the country, weak on travel details.

King, Emory. *Driver's Guide to Beautiful Belize.* Tropical Books: 2005, 56 pp. Mile-by-mile guide to most roads in Belize, with good maps. Updated annually.

Lougheed, Vivien. *Adventure Guide to Belize.* Hunter Publishing: 5th ed. 2003, 400 pp. Enthusiastic and detailed guide.

Mahler, Richard. *Adventures in Nature: Belize.* John Muir Publications: 1997, 360 pp. Reliable source of ecotravel information. Now out of print, but can be found used online.

Mallan, Chicki, and Joshua Berman. *Moon Handbooks Belize.* Avalon Travel Publishing: 6th ed. 2005, 328 pp. Favorite of many Belize travelers, with good maps and solid information.

Meyer, Franz O. *Lonely Planet Diving and Snorkeling Belize.* Lonely Planet Publications: 2nd. ed. 1998, 124 pp. Best diving and snorkeling guide to Belize.

Sluder, Lan. *San Pedro Cool: The Guide to Ambergris Caye.* Equator: 2002, 128 pp. The first guide to Ambergris Caye.

— *Belize Book of Lists 2000.* Equator: 1999, 112 pp. Lists the five or 10 best picks in each category—jungle lodges, seaside resort hotels, beaches, etc.

—*Belize First Guide to Mainland Belize.* Equator: 2000, 288 pp. Focuses on the mainland of Belize.

—*All the Best in Belize.* Equator: Forthcoming in 2005, 288 pp. Covers the entire country.

Sluder, Lan, and Gregory Benchwick. *Fodor's Belize and Guatemala 2005.* Fodor's Travel Publications/Random House: 2004, 220 pp. Belize section by Lan Sluder.

History and Culture

Barry, Tom, with Dylan Vernon. *Inside Belize.* Resource Center Press: 2nd. ed. 1995, 181 pp. Useful overview of history, politics, media, education, economy, and the environment.

Bolland, O. Nigel. *Colonialism and Resistance in Belize: Essays in Historical Sociology.* Cubola Productions: 2004, 239 pp.

Cayetano, E. Roy. *The People's Garifuna Dictionary.* Angelus Press: 82 pp. A work-in-progress dictionary of the Garifuna language.

Cayetano, Sebastian. *Garifuna History, Language and Culture of Belize, Central America and the Caribbean.* Angelus Press: 170 pp.

—*Heart Drum.* Cubola Productions: 1991, 60 pp. A look at *dagu* and other aspects of Garifuna life.

Heusner, Karla. *Food for Thought: Chronicles of Belize.* Cubola Press: 2004, 206 pp. A collection of newspaper columns on Belize life, culture, and politics.

King, Emory. *Diary of St.*

George's Caye. Tropical Books: 1994, 32 pp.

—*The Great Story of Belize, Volume 1.* Tropical Books: 1999, 53 pp. The first in a planned four-volume set, this volume covers the history of Belize from 1511, when the first Europeans arrived, until 1798, when the Baymen won the battle of St. George's Caye.

—*The Great Story of Belize, Volume 2.* Tropical Books: 1999, 87 pp. Volume 2 tells the history of Belize from 1800 to 1850, the period that shaped Belize's history for generations to come.

—*The Little World of Danny Vasquez.* Tropical Books: 1989, 116 pp. Tales of Old San Pedro.

—*1798: The Road to Glory.* Tropical Books: 1991, 348 pp. Fictionalized and somewhat glorified account of the Battle of St. George's Caye.

Koop, Gerhard S. *Pioneer Years in Belize.* Angelus Press: 1991, 144 pp. History of the Mennonites in Mexico and Belize.

Leslie, Robert (Ed.). *A History of Belize: Nation in the Making.* Cubola Productions: Rev. ed. 1995, 125 pp. First published in 1983, this history of Belize was written for Belize schoolchildren.

Maya Atlas: The Struggle to Preserve Maya Land in Southern Belize. Compiled by the Maya People of Southern Belize: Toledo Maya Cultural Council, 1997.

Merrill, Tim. *Guyana and Belize Country Studies.* Federal Research Division, Library of Congress: 2nd. ed. 1993, 408 pp. Part of the Area Handbook series sponsored by the U.S. Army; nevertheless, the historical, cultural, and economic information is first-rate.

Shoman, Assad. *Thirteen Chapters of a History of Belize.* Angelus Press: 1994, 297 pp. Somewhat left-wing interpretation of Belize history.

Sutherland, Anne. *The Making of Belize: Globalization in the Margins.* Bergin & Garvey: 1998, 202 pp. An American university professor with long family ties to Belize looks at "postmodern" Belize.

—*Caye Caulker: Economic Success in a Belizean Fishing Village.* Westview Press: 1986, 153 pp.

Waddell, D. A. G. *British Honduras: A Historical and Contemporary Survey.* Greenwood Press: orig. 1961, reprinted 1981, 151 pp. An academic history.

Young, Colville. *Creole Proverbs of Belize.* Cubola Productions: Belize, 1980, 44 pp.

Living in Belize

Conroy, Richard Timothy. *Our Man in Belize.* St. Martin's Press: 1997, 324 pp. Fascinating, readable memoir of life in former British Honduras in the late 1950s and early '60s.

Gray, Bill, and Claire Gray (pseudonyms). *Belize Retirement Guide.* Preview Publishing: 4th ed. 1999, 140 pp. Guide to "living in a tropical paradise for $450."

King, Emory. *"Hey, Dad, This Is Belize."* Tropical Books: 4th printing 1985, 114 pp. Collection of vignettes about Belize and Belizeans. Originally appeared in the *Belize Times* and other publications.

—*How to Visit, Invest, or Retire in Belize.* Tropical Books: 1989, 32 pp. Early booklet on the subject, still being sold at about US$1 a page.

—*"I Spent It All in Belize."* Tropical Books: 1986, 194 pp. More sketches of Belizean life.

Maps and Atlases

Atlas of Belize. Cubola Productions: 20th ed. 1995, 32 pp. with 11 maps and 80 photographs. Prepared for use in schools.

Belize Traveller's Map. ITMB: 2001. This map, at a 1:350,000 scale, is the best general map of Belize available.

British Ordnance Survey, Topographical Map of Belize. 1991. Two sheets, with helpful maps of Belize City and towns on reverse. 1:250,000 scale.

British Ordnance Survey, Area Topographical Maps. Various dates, 1970s–1990s. The country is divided into 44 sections, each mapped on a 1:50,000 scale.

Map of Belize. Macmillan. Wall map with laminated coating.

Natural History

Ames, Oakes, and Donovan Stewart Correll. *Orchids of Guatemala and Belize.* Dover Publications: 1985, 779 pp. with 204 black-and-white illustrations. Re-publication of Chicago Natural History Museum 1953 field guide and 1965 supplement. Exhaustive, covering 527 species.

Arvigo, Rosita, and Michael Balick. *Rainforest Remedies: One Hundred Healing Herbs of Belize.* HarperSanFrancisco: 2001, 240 pp. Guide to traditional Maya/Belizean herbal remedies.

Arvigo, Rosita, with Nadine Epstein and Marilyn Yaquinto. *Sastun: My Apprenticeship with a Maya Healer.* HarperSan-Francisco: 1994, 190 pp. Story of Dr. Arvigo's time with Don Elijio Panti.

Beletsky, Les. *The Ecotravellers' Wildlife Guide: Belize and Northern Guatemala.* Interlink Press: 2004, 477 pp. Lavishly color-illustrated guide to the most commonly spotted mammals, birds, amphibians, reptiles, fish, and corals. Oriented to the amateur.

Campbell, Jonathan A. *Amphibians and Reptiles of Northern Guatemala, the Yucatán, and Belize.* University of Okla-homa Press: 1998, 380 pp. with 176 color photographs. The best guide to herpetofauna of the region.

Edwards, Ernest Preston; illustrated by E. M. Butler, *A Field Guide to the Birds of Mexico and Adjacent Areas: Belize, Guatemala, and El Salvador.* University of Texas Press: 1998, 288 pp. This is used by many local guides in Belize.

Emmons, Katherine. *Cockscomb Basin Wildlife Sanctuary: Its History, Flora, and Fauna for Visitors, Teachers, and Scientists.* Community Conservation Consultants: 1996, 334 pp. Definitive on the subject.

Greenfield, David W., and Jamie E. Thomerson. *Fishes of the Continental Waters of Belize.* University Press of Florida: 1997, 311 pp. Comprehensive guide with black-and-white illustrations.

Horwich, Robert H. *A Belizean Rain Forest.* 1990, 420 pp. A look at the Community Baboon Sanctuary and the northern forests of Belize.

Jones, H. Lee, and Dana Gardner. *Birds of Belize.* University of Texas Press: 2004, 484 pp. The only comprehensive Belize-specific birding guide.

Lee, Julian. *A Field Guide to the*

Amphibians and Reptiles of the Maya World: The Lowlands of Mexico, Northern Guatemala, and Belize. Cornell University Press: 2000, 488 pp.

Matola, Sharon. *Birds of Belize: A Field Handbook.* Belize Zoo: 1995, 28 pp.

—*Hoodwink the Owl.* Macmillan Press: 1988, 32 pp. Children's ecostory by the founder of the Belize Zoo.

Meyer, John R., and Carol Farneti Foster. *A Guide to the Frogs and Toads of Belize.* Krieger Publishing: 1996, 80 pp.

Miller, Carolyn M., and Bruce W. Miller *Exploring the Tropical Forest at Chan Chich Lodge Belize.* Wildlife Conservation Society: 2nd. ed. 1994, 51 pp.

Peterson, Roger Tory. *A Field Guide to Mexican Birds: Mexico, Guatemala, Belize, El Salvador.* Peterson Field Guides/Houghton-Mifflin: 1999, 300 pp. The birder's pal, though it lacks Spanish names of birds.

Rabinowitz, Alan. *Jaguar.* Arbor House: 1986, 368 pp. Story of efforts to establish the Cockscomb preserve.

Snakes of Belize: Belize Audubon Society: 55 pp.

Woods, R. L., S. T. Reid, and A. M. Reid. *The Field Guide to Ambergris Caye.* 1988, 176 pp. Self-published, near-exhaustive study of the island and surrounding sea.

Travel Literature

Canby, Peter. *Heart of the Sky: Travels Among the Maya.* HarperCollins: 1992, 368 pp.

Chaplin, Gordon. *The Fever Coast Log.* Simon & Schuster: 1992, 229 pp. A couple sets sail aboard the *Lord Jim* to travel the Caribbean coast. You know it's all going to end badly.

Davis, Richard Harding. *Three Gringos in Venezuela and Central America.* Reprinted by Freedonia Books: 2002, 300

pp. Early travelogue begins in British Honduras.

Huxley, Aldous. *Beyond the Mexique Bay.* Greenwood Press: 1975, 295 pp. First published in 1934, this book by the author of *Brave New World* holds the record for the most quoted comment on British Honduras: "If the world had any ends, British Honduras would surely be one of them."

Parker, Franklin (Ed.). *Travels in Central America 1821–1840.*

University of Florida Press: 1970, 340 pp.

Pride, Nigel. *A Butterfly Sings to Pacaya.* Constable: 1978, 367 pp. A 1970s trip through Mexico, Belize, and Guatemala.

Roberts, Orlando W. *Voyages and Excursions on the East Coast and in the Interior of Central America.* University of Florida Press: orig. 1827, reprint 1965, 9 pp.

Straughan, Robert P. *Adventure in Belize.* A. S. Barnes & Co.: 1975, 215 pp. Explorations in Belize, described by the owner of a pet store and tropical fish store.

Stephens, John L. *Incidents of Travel in Central America, Chiapas, and Yucatán.* Reprinted by Dover Publications: 1969, 474 pp. The great classic of early Central American travel books.

Wright, Ronald. *Time Among the Maya: Travels in Belize, Guatemala, and Mexico.* Henry Holt: reprint 1991, 451 pp. A modern classic.

Index

U.S. ~ Metric Conversion

1 inch	=	2.54 centimeters (cm)
1 foot	=	.304 meters (m)
1 yard	=	0.914 meters
1 mile	=	1.6093 kilometers (km)
1 km	=	.6214 miles
1 fathom	=	1.8288 m
1 chain	=	20.1168 m
1 furlong	=	201.168 m
1 acre	=	.4047 hectares
1 sq km	=	100 hectares
1 sq mile	=	2.59 square km
1 ounce	=	28.35 grams
1 pound	=	.4536 kilograms
1 short ton	=	.90718 metric ton
1 short ton	=	2000 pounds
1 long ton	=	1.016 metric tons
1 long ton	=	2240 pounds
1 metric ton	=	1000 kilograms
1 quart	=	.94635 liters
1 US gallon	=	3.7854 liters
1 Imperial gallon	=	4.5459 liters
1 nautical mile	=	1.852 km

To compute Celsius temperatures, subtract 32 from Fahrenheit and divide by 1.8. To go the other way, multiply Celsius by 1.8 and add 32.

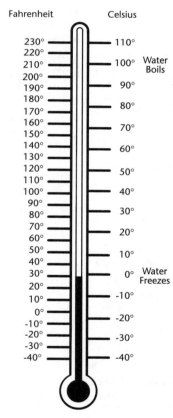

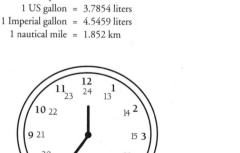

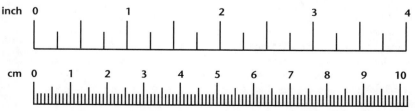

Living Abroad in Belize
Avalon Travel Publishing
1400 65th Street, Suite 250
Emeryville, CA 94608, USA
www.livingabroadin.com

Editor and Series Manager:
  Erin Raber
Design: Jacob Goolkasian, Justin Marler,
  Amber Pirker
Copy Editor: Mia Lipman
Graphics and Production
  Coordinator: Domini Dragoone
Map Editor: Kevin Anglin
Cartographers: Kat Kalamaras,
  Amy Tam
Proofreader: Karen Gaynor Bleske
Indexer: Judy Hunt

ISBN-10: 1-56691-919-3
ISBN-13: 978-1-56691-919-7
ISSN: 1555-9114

Printing History
1st edition—November 2005
5 4 3 2 1

Avalon Travel Publishing
is an Imprint of
Avalon Publishing Group, Inc.

Front cover photo:
  © Andrew Leanne Walker/
  Lonely Planet Images

Printed in the United States by Worzalla

Keeping Current

Although we strive to produce the most up-to-date book that we possibly can,
change is unavoidable. Between the time this book goes to print and the time
you read it, the cost of goods and services may have increased, and a handful of
the businesses noted in these pages will undoubtedly move, alter their prices,
or close their doors forever. Exchange rates fluctuate—sometimes dramatically—on a daily basis. Federal and local legal requirements and restrictions are
also subject to change, so be sure to check with the appropriate authorities before making the move. If you see anything in this book that needs updating, clar-
ification, or correction, please drop us a line. Send your comments via email to
atpfeedback@avalonpub.com, or write to the address above.